TENN-TOM COUNTRY

Map 1. The Tenn-Tom country of
Mississippi and Alabama

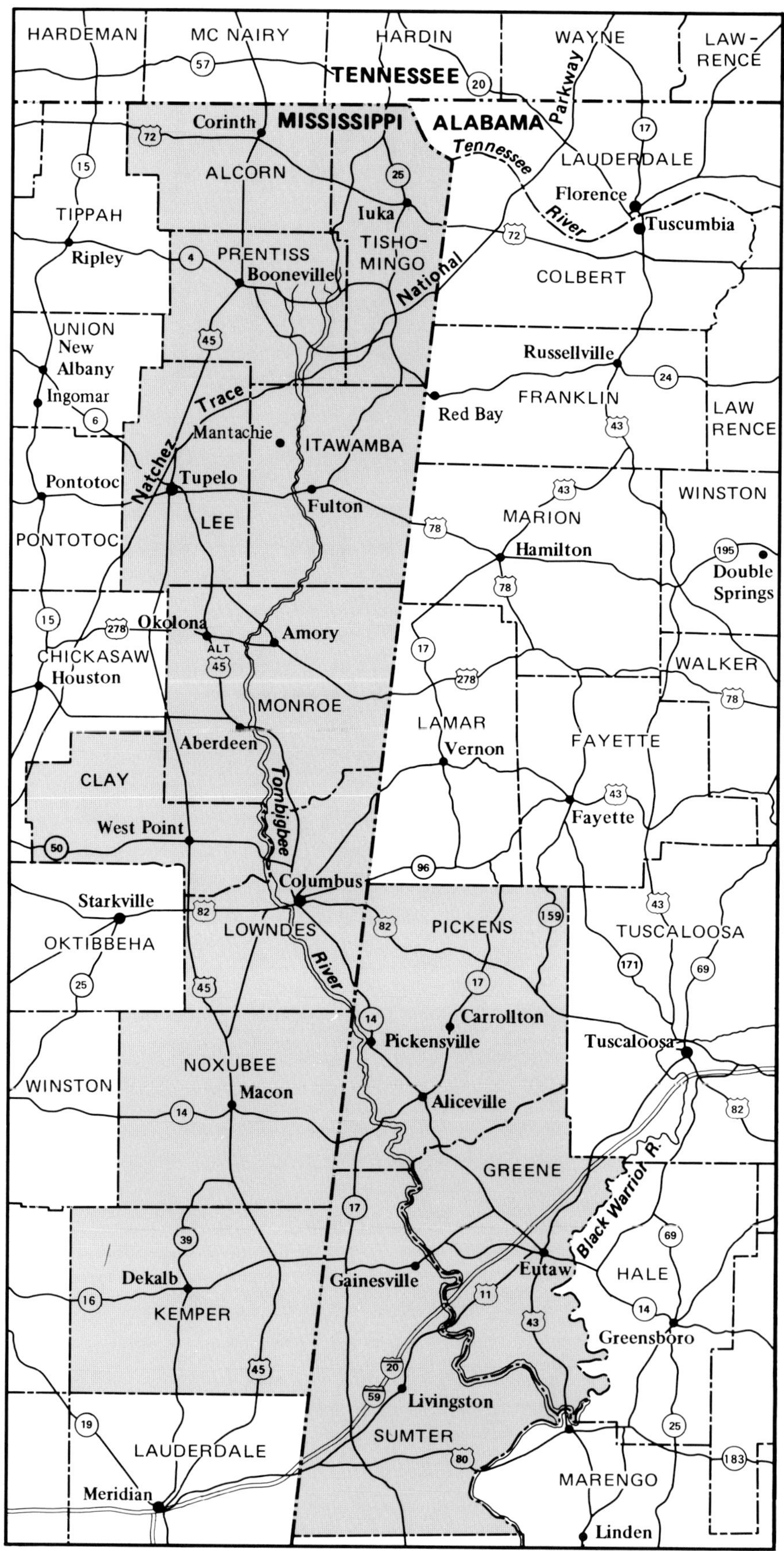

TENN-TOM COUNTRY

The Upper Tombigbee Valley

James F. Doster
and
David C. Weaver

THE UNIVERSITY OF ALABAMA PRESS

Copyright © 1987 by
The University of Alabama Press
Tuscaloosa, Alabama 35487
All rights reserved
Manufactured in the United States of America

Library of Congress Cataloging in Publication Data

Doster, James Fletcher, 1912–
    Tenn-Tom country.

    Bibliography: p.
    Includes index.
    1. Tombigbee River Valley (Miss. and Ala.)—History.
I. Weaver, David C., 1942–   . II. Title.
F332.T6D67 1987   976.1′2   85-13974
ISBN 0-8173-0279-4 (alk. paper)

Contents

Illustrations

Tables

Preface

So many people and organizations helped the authors in the pleasant task of preparing *Tenn-Tom Country* that full and detailed acknowledgments are impossible. Many persons were interviewed and consulted who are not quoted in the text. The scholars who made substantial contributions include Charles G. Summersell, Eugene M. Wilson, John T. Nichols, Jack D. Elliott, Jr., Jerry C. Oldshue, W. Stuart Harris, Warner O. Moore, Kit C. Carter, Carey B. Oakley, and Ned J. Jenkins. Grady McWhiney, our former colleague, contributed most of the statistical work and was a valuable consultant on the Civil War story. The late Kenneth R. Wesson, our esteemed research associate, worked with us full time for a year with fidelity, reliability, and efficiency. William M. Stennett of Tupelo's Community Development Council gave freely of his time and even took some of the pictures for us. Librarians in many institutions responded energetically and intelligently to our inquiries and aided us in our searches for information, as is their usual practice. Engineer Byron N. Schilling at Burnsville was especially helpful. Cartographer Craig Remington spent many hours drafting maps and figures. The University of Alabama generously supported our efforts in several ways.

Family members have rendered invaluable service. Some reviewed preliminary drafts of the text and gave us detailed criticisms. A large part of the photography was done by Jan Weaver, who not only did the laboratory work but also struggled with the authors through knee-deep mud on the bottom of the divide cut among plunging construction vehicles and visited many quieter locations to get good pictures. Various libraries, archives, and individuals have given us access to and use of their collections.

We also thank the many persons not here mentioned by name who have helped us.

JAMES F. DOSTER
DAVID C. WEAVER

TENN-TOM COUNTRY

Introduction

THE BUILDING of the Tennessee-Tombigbee Waterway, commonly known as "Tenn-Tom," has brought national attention to the Upper Tombigbee Valley of Mississippi and Alabama. This vast project was embroiled for twenty years in prominent controversies involving environmental protection, economic development, big government, excessive public spending, and transportation policy. The investigations and debates focused on technical details of law, engineering, economics, finance, and environmental systems. They did not address the human character of the area in which the waterway was being built or the people and landscape to be most directly affected by it.

What is the country like? What kind of people live there? What has been their story through time? What were the results of previous attempts to foster economic development in the region, and what has been done to protect and preserve its historic heritage? Answers to these questions are of vital interest to people who live in the valley and who must deal with the waterway and its impacts. They should also appeal to many who live at a distance and who have followed the debates of recent years without knowing the region. Providing answers to the questions is the main object of this book.

To deal with every point of interest is impossible, and we have not attempted it, but we hope that our readers who finish the book will obtain a broad and meaningful picture of the Tenn-Tom country and its people and of the changes that have occurred there through time. These pages offer a picture of life, even a kind of epic, with many themes. We have sought mainly to describe, but our own views and interpretations have deliberately been allowed to creep in to give meaning and impact to the text. To expand the range of coverage, we have selected representative individuals and have included their stories, often in their own words.

To facilitate understanding by the reader, numerous maps and photographs have been included. For readers who may wish to probe deeply, we have added statistical tables that add a new dimension of their own, but most of these have been put into an appendix well out of the general reader's way.

The Upper Tombigbee Valley was inhabited by human beings 10,000 years ago. More recently, it was the home of historic Indians. Then came the white settlers and black slaves. These new Americans and their descendants have known high prosperity, civil war, an unfriendly federal government, doldrum days and destructive economic forces, hard times, and resuscitation under a benign and friendly but meddlesome federal government.

Dynamic leadership, under brightening economic skies, was bringing creative changes to the area long before Tenn-Tom became a fact. That leadership, in fact, against powerful and continuing opposition, led to the building of the waterway. Social and economic problems remain, but new opportunities are being opened for the future.

Preserving the Memories of Early Times

1

The *Eliza Battle*

The Upper Tombigbee River was at flood stage in late February 1858, when Captain Stone brought the *Eliza Battle* up to the landing at Columbus. She was a side-wheel steamboat on a regular run from Mobile. The river, the steamboats, and the thriving plantation economy of the region were still in their glory days.

At Columbus the vessel took on passengers and cotton for Mobile. The weather was unusually cold. Cabin passengers occupied the hurricane deck, while deck passengers had to make themselves as comfortable as possible below, sleeping on cotton bales or wherever they could find space among the deck hands and firemen. Wood fuel was stacked near the boilers and was replenished at woodyards along the way.

Advertised as a fast-running packet boat, the *Eliza Battle* was a splendid vessel by local standards, just right for the Columbus trade at high water. As she slithered with the current past Hairston's Bend and Ten Mile Shoals, there was little reason to fear snags and bars, for the water was deep and the captain knew his business. She took on more passengers and cotton bales at such little river ports as Nashville Ferry, Pickensville, Vienna, and Warsaw and occasionally at plantation landings.

After dark the vessel passed Demopolis, where the Black Warrior River joins the Upper Tombigbee and nearly doubles its size. With 1,400 bales of cotton aboard, she continued on her southerly course. It became bitterly cold as the night advanced, and the wind bore down from the north with a fierce determination. While the bartender was conducting an active trade, the pilot in the wheelhouse, high above the water, squinted through the darkness between the tall iron chimneys and steered his vessel by spinning the big wheel. A drum on the wheel's hub tugged at ropes running back under the hurricane deck to the tiller. Much wheel spinning and many signals to the engineer were needed to steer the ship around a sharp bend.

After midnight the northbound steamer *Black Warrior*, with sparks

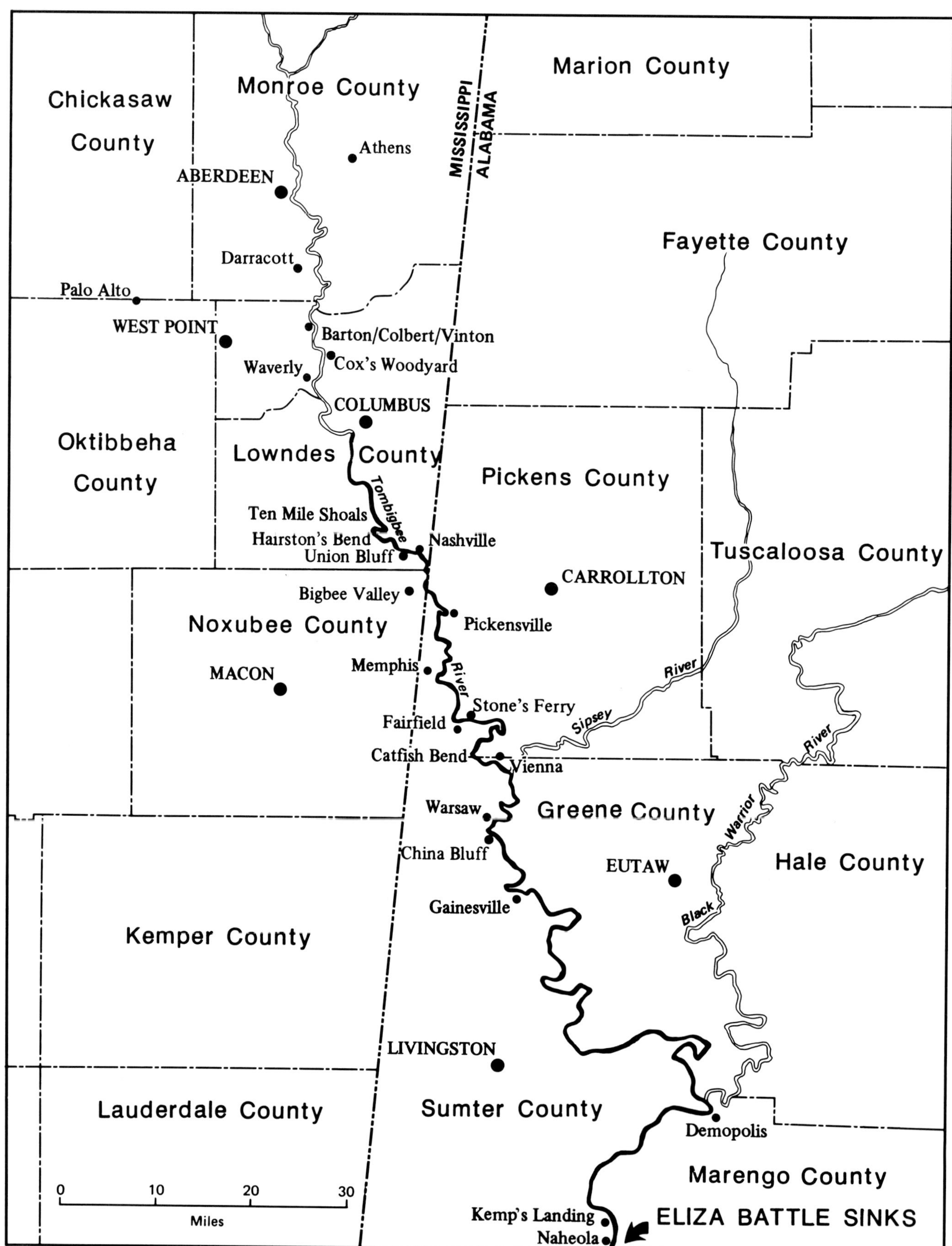

Map 2. Route of the *Eliza Battle*

blowing from her chimneys, passed to windward. Then between two and three o'clock in the morning, as Kemp's Landing fell behind, disaster struck. Cotton bales on the boiler deck suddenly took fire. The flames appeared in the after quarter, then moved quickly to the ladies' cabin and swept forward as the wind howled. Passengers rushed out in their nightclothes to launch the lifeboat and the yawl, but the flames thwarted their efforts.

Captain Stone headed for the bank, but the river was at flood stage and the water extended through the treetops into the swampy lowlands. Flames drove the engineers from their posts and burned through the tiller ropes. The boat crashed into a tree. Passengers and crew threw cotton bales and the landing stage overboard and jumped for their lives. Captain Stone was the last to leave. Some people clung to floating objects and others to tree limbs as the wind blew the flaming steamboat free and drove her across the swollen stream. The *Eliza Battle* sank just above Naheola.

The mate and some others floated downstream with the current, clinging to the bales and yelling for help. At length they roused the local inhabitants, who rescued them and hauled boats on wagons to the scene of the disaster. Four hours had passed before this help arrived. Meanwhile the people in the water clung to trees or to cotton bales and other floating objects as long as they could. Of a total of fifty or sixty people, at least twenty-nine perished during the night from exposure. Fifteen of the known dead were passengers and fourteen were members of the crew.

Passengers on the steamboat *Magnolia*, which happened along after a full day and night and carried the bodies of the dead to Mobile, conducted an investigation and wrote a report. According to their account, Mrs. B. Cromwell and child, of Sumter County, were frozen in a tree, and Mrs. H. G. Turner and child, of Washington County, met a like fate. W. T. Smith of Greene County and Augusta Jones of Columbus were also frozen to death. So were Messrs. Caradine and Willis of Chickasaw County, Dr. S. W. Clanton of Warsaw, a Mr. Martin from Kentucky, and an unidentified young man from Fairfield, on the river. Other people who perished from exposure included John Powell, the barkeeper, Jackson, the Negro barber, Barnett, a cook, and Nancy, a chambermaid. Several cabin boys and deck hands, who were Negro slaves, also died. Steamboat accidents were common, but the horrifying fate of the *Eliza Battle* is remembered above all other such events in Alabama and Mississippi.[1]

1. Most of the details of the *Eliza Battle* story are taken from the *Mobile Daily Advertiser* of March 4, 1858, which contains the report of the *Magnolia's* investigating committee. Also relied on is a brief account in the *Proceedings of the Seventh Annual Meeting of the Board of Supervising Inspectors (Appointed under the Act of Congress, Aug. 20, 1852) Held at Buffalo, New York. October 14, 1858* (Baltimore: 1858). Bad as the *Eliza Battle* disaster was, embellishments published in later times have created a legend larger than the fact. There is even a widely believed account, replete with details, of the voyage's beginning at Aberdeen, but no evidence has been found that the vessel went anywhere near Aberdeen in 1858. It may be true, however, that many years later a condemned criminal confessed to having set the blaze to conceal a robbery.

Welcome to Kirkwood! Roy Swayze puts out the welcome sign for visitors at the restored Eutaw mansion. Photo: Jan Weaver.

The *Eliza Battle* and her passengers belonged to the flourishing river-centered society of the Upper Tombigbee Valley at the peak of its prosperity. The tragedy was an omen of the future. Within a few months, the opening of a railroad to Mobile ruined the river trade. The Civil War shortly thereafter brought disaster to the whole region. The people struggled after the war to restore the valley's vitality, but the glory days became only a receding memory. Yet many people alive today cherish that memory and seek to preserve it.

The Swayzes of Kirkwood

Most of the notable events on the Upper Tombigbee, such as the wreck of the *Eliza Battle*, survive through oral, written, or pictorial records, but there are also more tangible reminders of the region's heyday in the form of large antebellum homes. Today many enthusiastic people are dedicating themselves to the restoration of these decaying but impressive monuments to a great culture of the past.

At Eutaw we meet Roy Swayze. "I was practicing law in Fairfax County, Virginia, just out of Washington, D.C.," he says, as he reclines in his work clothes on the front porch of his Kirkwood Mansion, "when I came down here with my wife to visit a friend. We happened to see this house sitting up on the hill, alone and deserted and crumbling down. It was overgrown with brush and had no paint. The cupola was missing, and there was no railing on the gallery. We asked the owner if we could look inside, just as a matter of curiosity. When I walked in the main door, the hallway, which is now light and airy, was as dark as a tomb. There was dust over everything, but I could see that the original furniture was still in the house. There were pictures on the walls, clothes in the closets, and mementos everywhere. I saw the portrait of the first owner of the house, Mr. Foster Kirksey, hanging on the wall. It really got to me, because I felt how terrible that this man, who was so proud of his town and of his own accomplishments and of his home, should in such a short period of time be forgotten entirely and the house allowed to fall down. By the time I got to the attic I had counted seventeen leather trunks filled with personal things and letters and documents. I realized that this was a treasure house, a slice of the history of the state of Alabama. I had no earthly reason to buy it. I had more than I could do in Virginia practicing law."

Swayze did buy the property, not knowing what he was going to do with it. Two months later he had a heart attack. Upon his recovery he retired from the law practice and moved to Eutaw with his wife, mother, son, and two daughters, to do what he wanted to do, which was to restore Kirkwood and bring it back to its place in history. That was in 1972. Nine years later he had almost fully restored the house and grounds. "Now," he says, "I am working hard on the restoration of the history of the people who lived here. It extends from the birth of Mr. Kirksey in 1817 until his death in 1906, and takes us from the days of Indian culture into the twentieth century."

"I believe," says Swayze, "that the history of this area clearly

This portrait of Foster M. Kirksey, Kirkwood's original owner, hangs over an original marble mantel at the mansion. Photo: Jan Weaver, courtesy of Roy Swayze.

defines the rise of the cotton kingdom and how it flourished, how fortunes were made, what people thought, how it all ended in the catastrophe of the Civil War, what happened to the people immediately thereafter, how they lived after that conflict, and how they adjusted to the twentieth century. The house itself and all its furnishings are artifacts of those days. With the Kirksey collection of documents [now in The University of Alabama Library] and with the artifacts which we have here, we can obtain a clear history of this upper-class Black Belt family. I want to write this little history as the last act of my restoration."

About himself Swayze says, "I grew up in Texas. I took a civil service job at the U.S. Supreme Court in Washington and went to law school at night. I enjoyed the practice of law, but I always liked to work with my hands, and I never had the opportunity, because there was never time. I did not even mow my own lawn. My father was a blacksmith in his younger days; then he became a steel contractor. I suppose it was in my blood to do that sort of thing. I saw the potential of Kirkwood, and my hands literally itched to do the work. Each detail of the house has become important to me, and there isn't an inch that I haven't gone over and tried to repair to the best of my ability. There were no public funds involved in the rebuilding of Kirkwood. Rebuilding the cupola took fourteen months. Of course we have had professional advice all along the line. Of the antebellum structures that once flourished here only a few remain. You are looking at the visible remnants of a unique society that existed in the Black Belt area of Alabama. We would like to preserve the feeling that Greene County, and the Black Belt area as a whole, was a very productive and pleasant place to live."

Swayze thinks it still is. He adds, "We must hold onto this past heritage, because if it disappears, the character of our once-lovely area disappears altogether. There are a number of young people who have come here and bought up old houses and are in the process of restoring them, spending their own money. We have called a halt to the destruction of the antebellum structures like this in the Black Belt area. In retirement I could not find a better place to live, because this is a warm, friendly community, with the old traditions still alive. The people still visit strangers and bring them flowers and preserves. We still have family entertainments, and family traditions are very strong. I think that a new society will develop here and that the old heritage will become an important keystone in that society."

At the moment of the interview Roy Swayze was preparing a barbecue for four hundred of his student daughter's friends from The University of Alabama. His restoration of Kirkwood was almost complete. A few months later, however, after another heart attack, he found it necessary to confine his further restoration efforts to the study of the documentary records of Kirkwood and of the Kirksey family.

The Snows of Waverly

Robert and Donna Snow live at Waverly Mansion, on the Tombigbee River, a few miles above Columbus. This monumental antebellum structure was once the center of a flourishing settlement. The Snows found it and bought it in 1962 after it had stood vacant for forty-nine years. Robert Snow, with a background in art, was an antique dealer and cattle rancher of Philadelphia, Mississippi. Says Snow, "We had always been interested in historic buildings. In October 1961 we came here to have a look. On a beautiful day we drove down to the ferry which had been operating at Waverly since before the Civil War and blew our horn. An old black man pulled the ferry over to the side of the river by hand with a cable, and we ran our automobile on. There were people sitting on the side of the ferry fishing, as it went back and forth across the river dragging their lines.

"We came up the Waverly river road, and here was the house, scarcely visible because the vegetation was like a jungle. We had to walk through all sorts of weeds and bushes. The house had vines growing over the roof. Windows and shutters were hanging helter-skelter on the walls. I went up on the fallen-in porch and peered through a broken bohemian glass window pane into the entrance hall. I looked up and I could see that sixty-five-foot observatory up there. I said I've got to buy this house, and Donna said I was crazy. We finally got around back and crawled in through a sidelight window. It was the most beautiful house I had ever seen, but the chandeliers had hay and sticks hanging where the birds had been nesting. There were squirrels and their nests over the door and window facings, just big stacks of hay. When you looked up to the dome, the ornamental plaster work up there was absolutely covered with dirt dauber mud all glued into it. When we got inside and observed the building, she wondered if we could ever repair it. I said sure, but of course we were twenty years younger then. Trees about eight or ten inches in diameter had grown up through the office next door. The front porch had fallen out on the ground and honeysuckle had covered it up."

Mrs. Snow adds, "A cow had got hung up in the honeysuckle. There was no walk, just bushes and beggarlice. It was a marvelous place for bats and wasps and things like that. Birds had nested in the house for years. The porches were rotting, and some of the marble steps were scattered out in the broomsedge. A mimosa tree had come up between two steps in the back and had pushed the steps aside."

Heirs were found, and after several months of legal complications, the Snows bought the house. They have lived in it and have restored it largely by their own work to something approaching its former grandeur, furnishing it tastefully with an abundance of period antiques. They still live in it and operate it as a tourist attraction. "The work never ends," says Donna. "You can cover the territory, but you never finish." Robert still operates a small antique business

Above: George Hampton Young, a wealthy planter and businessman, was the builder and original owner of Waverly Mansion. Photo: David C. Weaver, courtesy of Lucy Banks.

Right: Donna and Robert Snow in front of Waverly Mansion. They have restored the deteriorated structure to its original grandeur. Photo: Jan Weaver.

in the office building in the yard, but he has no time for restoring antiques anymore.

The Snows have two sons and two daughters: Allen, Gage, Melanie, and Cindy. Gage, the second son, was born at Waverly. Raising children in a museum posed some problems. Says Donna Snow, "The room up above here, where the great big bed is, is our son's room, and that is why the bedspread is always pulled right down to the floor. He has all his records and all that on the other side of the bed. We just pull the bedspread down and leave them there. They have been good about keeping their rooms roped off when they are not in there, or even when they are in there."

Waverly Mansion, finished in 1852, was built by George Hampton Young (1799–1880), a large slaveowner from Georgia, who grew cotton and was an agent for George G. Henry, a cotton factor and commission merchant of Mobile. Waverly is located at a site formerly known as Mullen's Bluff, where an Indian countryman named John Pitchlynn built a home in the early 1830s. At the nearby river landing are traces of warehouses, a gristmill and sawmill, a tannery, a cotton gin, a brick kiln, an ice house, a gas-lighting plant, and other establishments. This was the headquarters of a patriarchal domain.

The mansion itself is a frame building of Greek Revival design, dominated by a huge octagonal central hallway that extends upward into a cupola above the main roof. The upper floors are reached by curving stairways. Sixteen cupola windows at the top may be opened to facilitate ventilation in the central hall by permitting a constant upward movement of air warmed by the summer's heat. Not surprisingly, the house has attracted considerable attention from students of architecture. Its impressive features are legion. Much of the original equipment, such as gas-lighted chandeliers and pier mirrors, has survived the ravages of time.

Although the house has been thoroughly restored, the huge boxwoods in front have not to this day fully regained their proper shape after being subjected to decades of foraging livestock. The Snows grew smaller boxwoods along the front walk from cuttings.

In addition to Kirkwood and Waverly, dozens of other homes of antebellum vintage are still proudly occupied by their current owners in Livingston, Eutaw, Columbus, and Aberdeen, and some in rural districts (see chapter 6). The wealthy lived principally in the southern part of the Upper Tombigbee area, and the signs of opulence taper off gradually toward the north. Above Aberdeen large homes are scattered and isolated. The early homes of the poorer folk have not generally survived, but their characteristics were repeatedly expressed for many decades in the folk houses of the region, and a considerable number of these later offspring are extant.

Lucille Peacock

Not all of the individuals who have labored to preserve knowledge of the past have been concerned with buildings. At Aberdeen lives Lucille Peacock, who since 1933 has dedicated her best efforts to the locating and preserving of local documentary records. We find her at the W. A. Evans Memorial Library in Aberdeen amid great stacks of local records, a "retired" octogenarian. Let her tell her own story: "My grandfather Peacock fought with old Nathan Bedford Forrest. When the war was over, he was disgusted with the situation, so he joined a company going to South America. They were some forty-odd days going from New Orleans to Rio de Janeiro, and he married a young lady he met on that trip.

"My father, Elmo Palmiro Peacock, and two of his brothers were born in Brazil. But Grandpa came back and settled at Old Spring Hill in Alabama. I can see him now, in his eighties, riding his horse named Silver. My daddy was a farmer. He went to the Delta, where he managed a plantation near Greenville. He wanted to manage a big plantation, so he moved to Clover Hill, then to Modoc in Arkansas. But then came the big flood. We went to the levee and put up a tent and stayed there ten days. When it was over with, Daddy said we were going to the hills. Times were hard, and you hardly had clothes to wear and food to eat. He bought a little farm at Aberdeen and I still live on it."

Miss Peacock continues: "The Aberdeen Woman's Club members were getting tired of keeping the library open so the children could walk up there from the school and check out a book," and they wanted to employ someone to do it. "I had had library science at Peabody College, so I got the job and gradually became a full-time

Lucille Peacock, librarian of the Evans Memorial Library in Aberdeen, dedicated her life to the collection and protection of documents and artifacts relating to Monroe County. Photo: Jan Weaver.

Dr. William A. Evans, a Chicago physician, retired to his native Aberdeen and became an avid local historian and benefactor of the Aberdeen library which bears his name. Photo: Evans Memorial Library, Aberdeen.

librarian. That was in December 1933, and I have been working here ever since." As to local historical records, she says, "I started with one old land grant signed by President James Monroe, and five Indian arrow heads." Then came the big event: "I will always remember the Saturday afternoon in 1934, when a handsome old man came walking up the steps and said, 'I have decided to offer the City of Aberdeen a library.' I did not sleep much that night. The city accepted, and he built that main building out there."

The "handsome old man" was Dr. William A. Evans (1865–1948), a well-known Chicago physician and formerly the editor of a syndicated newspaper column. He had grown up in Aberdeen and had returned there to spend his declining years. Says Lucille Peacock: "He started the first health column in the entire United States, calling it 'How to Keep Well.' That bound volume over yonder on how to keep well contains all the treasure of his columns." Evans not only helped the library financially but was also a collector and a writer of local history.

"Little by little we began to grow," says Miss Peacock. "Some friends of Dr. Evans gave very generously, so that we could add to the library. Folks began to say, 'Well, I'll give you this,' and 'I'll give you that,' and I looked in many a trashcan and in many an attic and outhouse, gathering everything I could in the way of manuscripts. These included family records, genealogy, hotels, drugstores and all kinds of stores, and churches going back to 1819."

Now visible among the collections on display are numerous artifacts: guns, swords, preachers' saddlebags, dentists' tools, interesting knives, and Indian items. "I have had bushels of arrowheads," says Miss Peacock. An old lady out in the country called me and said she had the prettiest cowshead and just knew I wanted it. There it is!" Among her more interesting items is the F. S. McKnight collection of some fourteen thousand glass photographic negatives, which, unfortunately, is uncataloged.

"When Dr. Evans died in 1948," she says, "he left us a hundred thousand dollars invested. We still get the income. Of course the city had to agree to give certain amounts." The contributions of Evans and the dedicated efforts of Lucille Peacock have produced a treasure house for the study of local history. It may also be expected to provide future scholars with rare opportunities to study the local manifestations of broad trends and developments. The full value of her work of collecting and preserving cannot be estimated until systematic cataloging can be accomplished. She concludes, "Dr. Evans wanted his people to know their local history. That is what he tried to plan for. I just like history."

Emory Jones

At the Northeast Mississippi Junior College at Booneville, Emory Jones, who teaches English, is determined to lay the basis for a native literature among Mississippi people. Born at Starkville, he has lived

Professor Emory Jones stands in front of the Old Tishomingo County Court House at Jacinto. Photo: Jan Weaver.

in Iuka since he was seven. He has deep roots in the local culture, which is far different from that of the old plantation country to the south. He accepts change as inevitable and appreciates its benefits, and he takes a friendly attitude toward newcomers. He deeply believes, however, that the old roots should not be severed. His way of nourishing the native virtue is by identifying and developing local literary talent. New Albany, the birthplace of William Faulkner, the novelist, is not far down the road.

Jones's doctoral dissertation at the University of Mississippi focused on the Southern Literary Festival, which was started in 1936 by Charles D. Johnson at Blue Mountain College in Tippah County, Mississippi, to encourage creative writing on college campuses. In 1978 Emory Jones attended a meeting of the festival at Southeastern Louisiana University. When he returned he helped establish the Mississippi Junior College Creative Writing Association. The association has instituted prizes for meritorious writing in several categories, and it publishes the *Junior College Writer* to provide a showcase for the work of students and local residents. Jones's own school produces the *Flambeau* with a similar purpose. Says Jones, "We conduct a contest in our five-county area of twenty-five high schools and offer a scholarship at Northeast to the first-place winner in the categories of essay, short story, and poetry. We have had a tremendous response, and I am already seeing the results at the college level now, with these winners coming through from the high schools. We felt that we had talent and that we had writers, but we didn't have any outlet for them, and we didn't have any motivation for them. We don't have any published writers yet except in our local journals. This sort of thing is very hard to judge, but I think some are going to publish later on a regional or national scale." Jones's heavy teaching load and his own graduate studies have occupied most of his time, but he is now polishing his own productions for publication.

Emory Jones has written a series of articles in the local newspapers on the history of Tishomingo County, on the Bay Springs area, on Iuka, and on the educational institutions around Iuka. He has also contributed to historical preservation by serving on the Old Tishomingo Courthouse Museum Committee. "The old courthouse at Iuka," says Jones, "just went into disrepair and degenerated. We plan to have a community hall in the old courtroom upstairs, as well as housing for a museum and a development association office. I am sort of a sentimentalist, I guess. I want Iuka still to have the flavor of small-town Mississippi." The county seat of old Tishomingo County before it was split in 1870 into three counties was in the tiny settlement of Jacinto (locally pronounced "Jay-centah"). There we find an even earlier courthouse, a beautiful relic of early times, which is now fully repaired and restored.

Hilda Hill

Hilda L. Hill, who lives on a farm at Ingomar near New Albany, is no ordinary farm wife. Her husband, Charles Gaston Hill, a graduate of Mississippi State University, raises soybeans, cattle, and grain for cattle feed. Hilda graduated from Blue Mountain College for women and obtained a master's degree from the University of Mississippi. She did further graduate work at Mississippi State University and the University of Southern Mississippi. Says she: "My Master's was in theater. This is a real unusual combination, but we live on a farm, and I have a love of the land. I have one son who is a wildlife biologist and one who is a landscape architect. We started farming on good land at Lapatubby Bottom. Charlie and I decided that we would teach our children that the hills and hollows in the Lapatubby Bottom were the greatest place in the world."

Mrs. Hill began teaching school at Ingomar. She later taught speech and theater at the Northeast Mississippi Junior College and is now the director of the North Mississippi Environmental Education Consortium, which is supported by several colleges and other public agencies in the area. She conducts workshops and zealously promotes the training of teachers in environmental education. "The small farmers have vanished," she says, "and the people have changed. They are working in furniture factories. When the children come in from school, all they know to do is turn on the television. I feel that our students don't understand our region. Our people are getting away from families and roots and background. It is important to us that we instill into our youth a pride in their land. The more they understand of the history and background and roots of the region, the more they can have something important to say. Our purpose is to create an informed citizenry. When you know what you have, you are able to make wise decisions down the line. There is a difference between way-out environmentalism and environmental education. Those people are extremists. We are not at all. We are not the emotional type." The building of the Tennessee-Tombigbee Waterway has given Mrs. Hill and her consortium a golden opportunity to build the Crow's Neck environmental education center to implement the concepts which she sets forth.

Jack Elliott

Today no one lives at the little settlement of Palo Alto in western Clay County but the Elliotts, who run a store and raise a few cattle. Their eldest son, Jack, grew up with much curiosity about his surroundings. As he tells it: "When I was a kid, I was always fossil hunting or looking for Indian projectile points. I found quite a few around Palo Alto. I would put signs in the window of my father's country store advertising that I would buy projectile points for a dime apiece. I got to researching the documentary records relating to Palo Alto and found it had been a considerable settlement at one time, with a population of 100 to 125, quite a little center for frontier times. Most of the old town had been plowed over. After the buildings had been abandoned, the sites had been put into cotton production. You can walk out almost anywhere and find pieces of broken ceramics, nails, and brick fragments dating from the heyday of Palo Alto."

Continues Elliott, "My interest spread out geographically in concentric circles to the neighboring settlements. When I began thinking of going to college, I wanted to study archaeology. Mississippi State was an obvious choice because of its proximity to my home. I went into anthropology because it was the only discipline that really focused on the prehistoric archaeology of the southeastern United States."

Elliott participated in various archaeological digs at prehistoric sites along the Upper Tombigbee River and developed skill in site excavation, but his main interests centered on historic times. As he explains, "It occurred to me that there were quite a few historic sites along the river, particularly abandoned town sites, that were not being given any emphasis in the salvage work along the Tennessee-Tombigbee Waterway. Then I started writing letters to the Corps of Engineers informing them of these sites. The ones I was particularly

Environmental education and the understanding of and appreciation for the native culture are the great interests of Hilda L. Hill of Ingomar. The Crow's Neck Center on Bay Springs Lake has been her special project. Photo: courtesy of Mrs. Hilda L. Hill.

Jack D. Elliott, Jr., of Palo Alto, as a young man was a local historian, genealogist, and archaeologist with a deep commitment to the preservation of the region's cultural resources. Photo: Jan Weaver.

interested in at first were Colbert, Barton, and Vinton. Then I began to realize the importance of Waverly, Plymouth, and Cotton Gin Port. The Corps replied that it would look into them, and in the meantime I had instigated putting Colbert and Barton on the National Register through the Department of Archives and History in Jackson. In 1976 I was asked to help on an archaeological survey of the waterway, which would concentrate upon specific construction areas and proposed spoil dumps. We were looking for archaeological sites which had not been theretofore identified, both historic and prehistoric. We examined edges of old river runs and prominent-looking knolls where Indians might have lived. We also did background research, looking for indications of historic occupations. Out of that survey came our two-volume report."

Asked, "What are you doing all this for?" Elliott replies, "A more joyful and meaningful life, I suppose. A sense of fulfillment out of studying the past. I enjoy understanding the complexity of historic relationships, social and economic. There is such a wide variety of data available, and in many cases not much has been done. The archaeological data base is of help, but its contribution to our knowledge of nineteenth-century and early twentieth-century life in this area is fairly minimal. There are many more aspects of knowledge that we can get into with archival material."

Elliott tries to make the best use of each kind of material, one to complement the other. He has also found oral history in the twentieth century useful for the reconstruction of settlement patterns and the distribution of building sites. "Using an intensive survey of these river towns," he says, "you can locate all the occupation areas in the town and get a pretty good idea about how these people were distributed and relate that to relic roads and streets." Elliott has a low opinion of the building of boat ramps and picnic grounds to mitigate the damage to cultural resources caused by construction of the waterway, but he favors the protection of town sites and river ports as much as possible to permit future study and possibly later reconstruction as exemplifications of the fading culture of the region.

Swayze, Kirksey, Snow, Young, Peacock, Evans, Hill, and Jones are but a few of the names of the energetic and interesting people of strong character and personality who have shaped and preserved the life and culture of the Tenn-Tom country. Others who have also played prominent and colorful roles will appear in the chapters to follow.

The Natural Heritage

Nature has endowed the Upper Tombigbee Valley with a great variety of physical features which have helped to shape its cultural characteristics and its history. The geologic formations lie in parallel, crescent-shaped bands, sweeping from northeastern Mississippi southward and then eastward across central Alabama toward Georgia. The strata of sedimentary rock trend downward toward the south and west, each being covered by successive later deposits and each having its own parallel outcropping band. As the Tombigbee River moves southward from northeast Mississippi into western Alabama, it crosses the bands of the crescent.

The Tuscaloosa formation is the oldest of the Cretaceous formations that outcrop in the counties most closely associated with the Upper Tombigbee River. It lies above the Paleozoic rocks, some of which are exposed in the northeast corner of Tishomingo County. The Tuscaloosa formation has a thickness of about three hundred feet in northeast Mississippi and as much as a thousand feet in western Alabama. It consists of dark clays, thin seams of lignite, purple, red, orange, and yellow sands, iron-cemented sands, gravels, and in the lower part a white-gray clay. In Mississippi the formation is exposed in a belt five to fifteen miles wide.

The Eutaw formation overlies the Tuscaloosa, with deposits ranging from 90 feet to as many as 390 feet in thickness. The lower portion of the Eutaw consists largely of blue, dark red, orange, and yellow sands. The deposits are discontinuous, and no stratum can be traced for any long distance. The upper portion of the Eutaw, called the Tombigbee Sand, is characterized by fine-grained micaceous sands, calcareous sands, and greensand. The outcrop of the Tombigbee Sand is in a narrow belt extending from northwestern Tishomingo County into Pickens and Greene counties in Alabama.

Complicating the above designations are deposits of Lafayette, or Orange, sand, which consist of well-rounded gravels and sands of the eroded Appalachian highlands carried southward into the

Map 3. Major physiographic regions

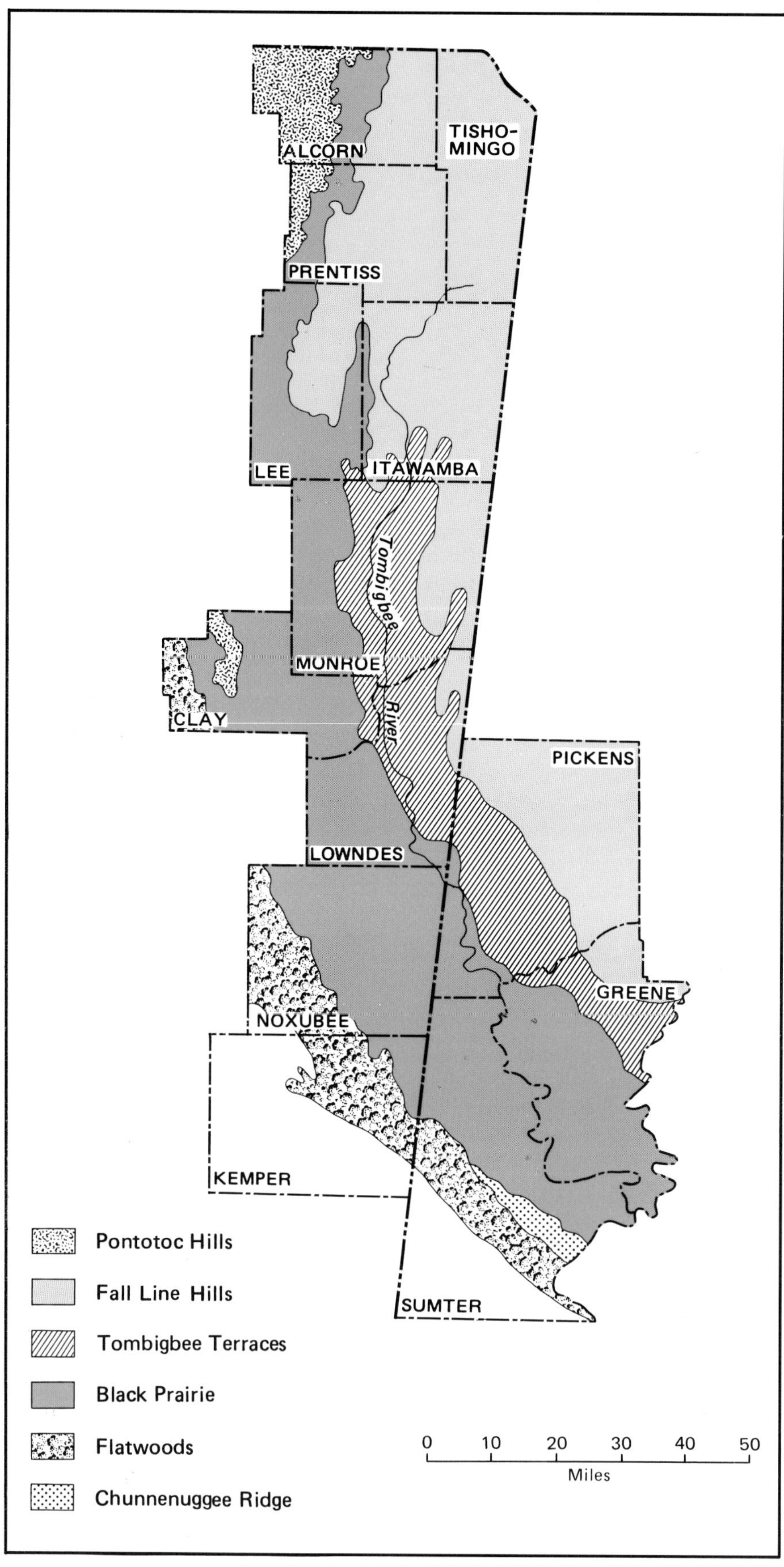

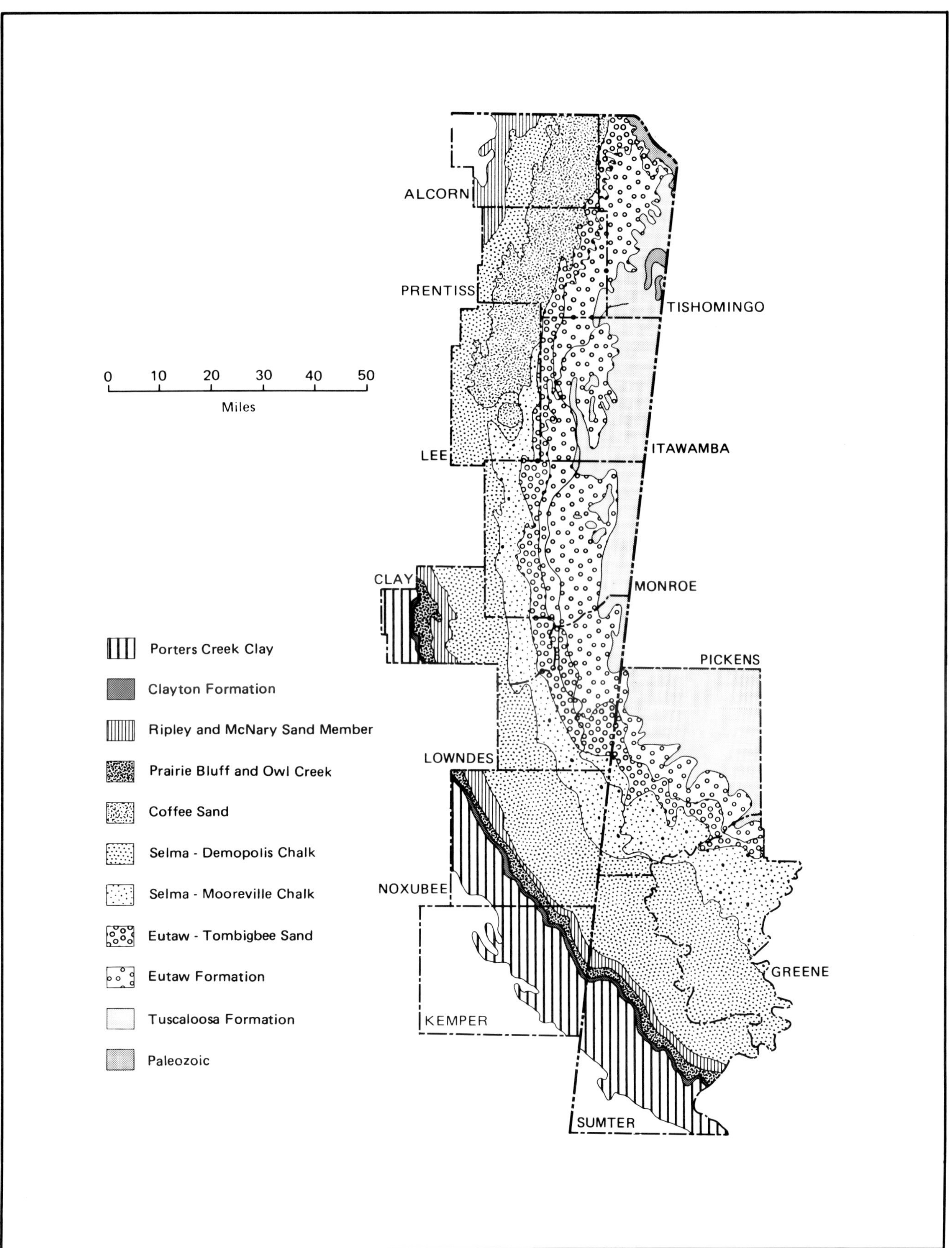

Map 4. Geological formations

adjacent inner coastal plain margin by ancient streams. Modern streams have entrenched the surface, leaving this old alluvium (water-deposited soil) as a discontinuous deposit that now covers hilltops and ridges, often at some distance from the present stream channels. The upper portions consist of fairly homogeneous red to orange sand overlying a bed of gravel. The latter is commonly well cemented by iron precipitated in groundwater.

Probably the most striking characteristics of the Tombigbee area are found in the Black Prairie (or Black Belt, as it is called in Alabama), a band which runs north and south at some distance to the west of the Upper Tombigbee River, then swings to the east over the river in an arc through Pickens County and crosses Alabama to the south of Montgomery. The chalky deposits of this calcareous region degrade into a sticky, dark-colored soil, which gives the area its name.

The basic material of the Black Belt is the Selma Chalk formation. It overlies the Tombigbee Sand, as does its sandy equivalent in the north, the Coffee Sand. The band of exposure of the Selma reaches a width of about twenty-five miles in Sumter, Greene, and Noxubee counties but grows narrower in its northern extension, which reaches into Tennessee. Variations in the hardness and the purity of the chalk and of its admixture with other materials have caused distinct elements in the formation to be separately identified by subdivisions. The lower part, known as the Mooreville member, is thin-bedded and chalky, with sandy clay or marl, and is generally covered with residual soil and terrace material (older alluvium) redeposited by the Tombigbee River and its tributary streams. In the north the Mooreville loses its identity by merging with the Coffee Sand. Above the Mooreville is a very thin layer of porous and relatively hard limestone, called Arcola. While its outcrops are not extensive, there are places where its resistance to erosion has led to the development of low flat-topped hills.

The main body of the Selma Chalk lies above the Arcola and is known as the Demopolis Chalk. Its lowest portion consists of sand and limey clay. The middle part, outcropping in the central part of the Black Belt, is particularly rich in clay and has been known locally in Mississippi as "Blue Rock." The upper layers of the Demopolis contain much less clay. The overall thickness of the Selma Chalk ranges from 350 feet in northeast Mississippi near the Tennessee line to about 1,200 feet at the Alabama-Mississippi line.

The Black Prairie is generally coterminous with the outcrop of the various subdivisions of the Selma Chalk. At places it appears to be almost flat, but the northern and western portions tend to be rolling or even hilly. Local relief generally has a range of ten to fifty feet. Streams originating in the prairie region tend to be seasonal in response to surface runoff, for the underlying chalk is not permeable and supplies no groundwater. Streams that cross the prairie and have their origin elsewhere are less subject to seasonal extremes in their flow. In earlier times dense forests and canebrakes filled the floodplain areas, and swamps constituted serious barriers to trans-

portation. So much ditching and drainage work has been done in northeastern Mississippi that few streams today retain their natural channels within the floodplains.

The scarcity of groundwater makes springs rare in the prairie region, where shallow water supplies are hard to find and often dry up in the summer. The impervious nature of the chalk and the downward slope of the underlying strata, however, have created an excellent situation for artesian wells fed by groundwater from the hills to the east and north. To reach that water it is usually necessary to drill through several hundred feet of chalk. If the result is a free-flowing well, the effort is well spent. While drilling deep wells was impracticable for the earliest settlers, such wells were being put down through the chalk long before the Civil War. Even a mill was once operated on artesian water near Demopolis. When the pressure brings water to within a few feet of the surface, it is sometimes feasible to hollow out in the chalk a cistern in which water will accumulate and from which it can easily be raised to the surface by means of buckets or pumps. Old wells of this type can be found in the Livingston area.

The Black Prairie is distinctive because of its low relief, its dark,

The outcrop of the Demopolis Chalk formation in a high bluff at Epes on the Tombigbee River. Here a highway bridge and a railroad bridge cross the river. To the right on the far bank, not here visible, is the site of old Forts Tombecbé and Confederación. Photo: Corps of Engineers.

clay-rich soils, its natural vegetation, and its annual precipitation, which is lower than that of the adjacent belts of hills on either side. Calcium from the weathered limestone and from the marl of the Selma Chalk fixes the organic remains of plants, especially of the grasses, so that the soil is very dark. It was originally very fertile.

The Coffee Sand formation reaches northward from the area of Tupelo into Tennessee in a band twelve to fifteen miles wide. It is equivalent to the Mooreville in age and is described as light gray sand, sandy clay, and calcareous sandstone. Some of it has a distinct coffee color.

The Ripley formation lies atop the Selma Chalk. It consists of alternating strata of coarse sandstone, limestone, clay, unconsolidated sand, phosphatic greensand, and lime-rich clay or marl. Fossils are common in some strata. The Ripley is represented in the Pontotoc Ridge, or Ripley Cuesta, in northeast Mississippi, a belt of low hills rising above the western and southern edge of the Black Belt. It is nearly absent as a feature between Houston and Shuqualac, but it expands to a considerable width (Chunnennuggee Ridge) in central Alabama. The Pontotoc hills were sought out early as an area of fertility and a desirable place for settlement, for the hills are not high, and much land in the wide intervening bottoms was attractive to an agricultural people.

The Prairie Bluff Chalk, the uppermost Cretaceous formation, lies above the Ripley. It is a hard, brittle, sandy chalk in its southernmost area, but to the north it contains large quantities of sand and clay. In Clay County, its thickness runs to seventy or eighty feet, and it is relatively sandy. The Prairie Bluff outcrop is locally considered a part of the Black Belt.

In large areas the various outcropping strata just described have been covered by deposits of alluvium (water-deposited soil), which has gradually been washed into low-lying areas along the creeks and rivers where wide swamps and canebrakes once interfered with transportation and settlement. There are also wide terraces of older alluvial deposits lying above the level of the floodplains of the Tombigbee and various of its tributaries. These terraces, or benches, are remnants of older floodplains formed by streams that occupied the valley during earlier stages of development. The ancient streams eroded to lower levels, leaving part of their former floodplains at higher elevations as terraces. Along Tibbee Creek there are in places two or three terraces extending as much as six miles back from the creek. Terrace areas as wide as six miles also occur on the eastern side of the Tombigbee in Lowndes County. The terrace belt extends northward through Monroe County into Itawamba, becoming gradually narrower. As one pursues the river northward, up the East Fork and Mackey's Creek, the streams become smaller and more crooked. Although the fall per mile becomes progressively greater, there are extensive stream terraces.

The topography of the Upper Tombigbee Valley includes a broad band of Fall Line Hills on the eastern and northern side, elevated two hundred to three hundred feet above the Black Prairie. Except in

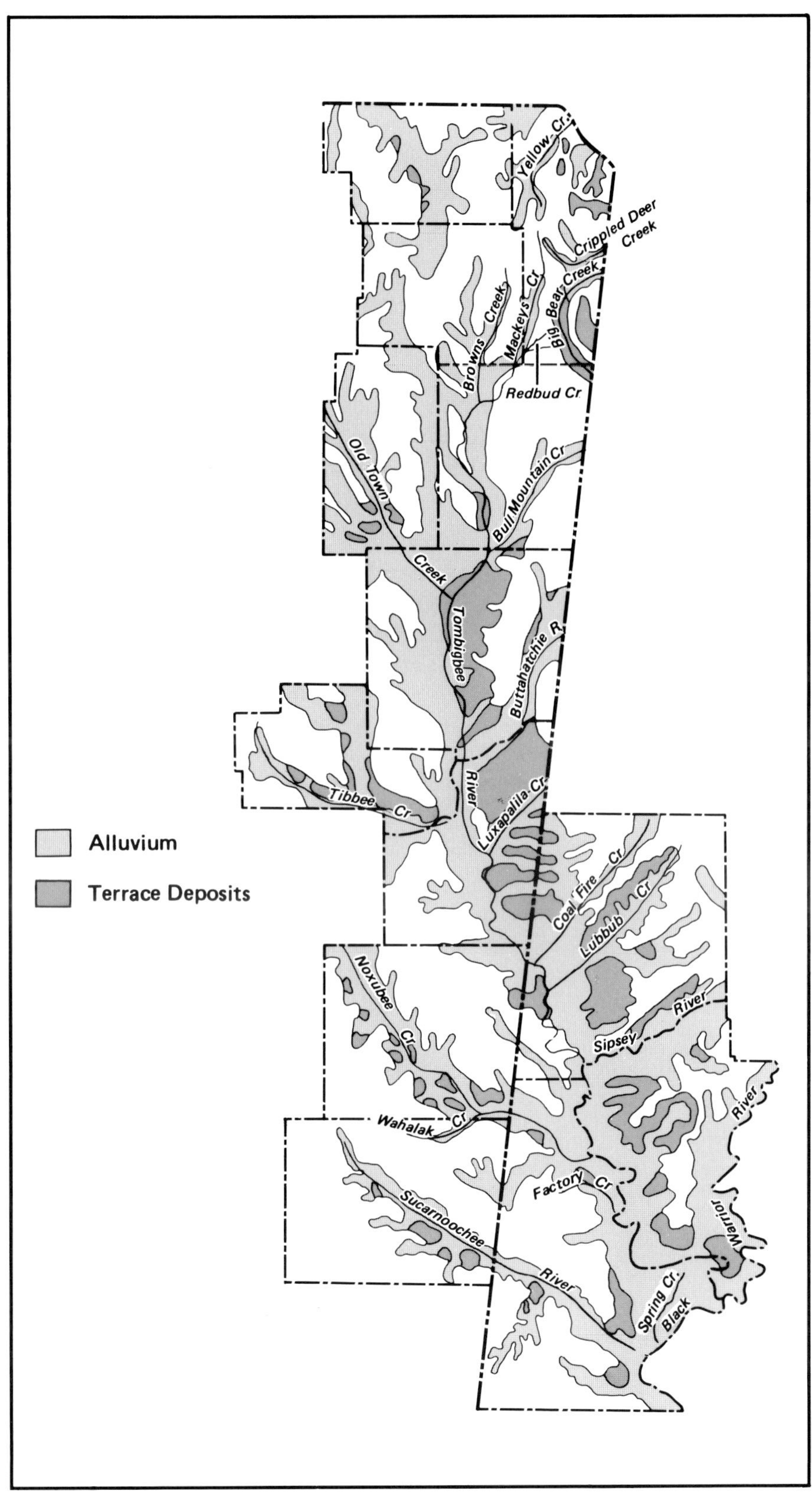

Map 5. Major streams and alluvial deposits

Merle W. Myers, a Methodist minister's son from Illinois, made one of the first analytical studies of the Upper Tombigbee Valley. A skilled cartographer, he interspersed his text with detailed maps. Although he has now retired from the department of geography at Mississippi State University at Starkville, Myers retains a deep interest in the region. His two-volume doctoral dissertation, "Geography of the Mississippi Black Prairie" (Clark University, 1949), provides a valuable foundation for the geographic study of an important part of the Upper Tombigbee Valley. Photo: Jan Weaver.

portions relatively close to the Tombigbee River, the hill area is well dissected by stream erosion, and the valleys are too small to provide an extensive basis for agriculture. There is too much fall in the streams to permit much navigation. At the northern extreme, Tishomingo County, which contains the Tennessee-Tombigbee dividing ridge, is hilly, but it contains some surprises. Merle W. Myers, the principal geographer of the area, classes 4 percent of Tishomingo County as terrace.

Floodplains along the streams add to the level land in the Tombigbee and Tennessee river hills. In Itawamba County, floodplains more than a mile wide border Bull Mountain Creek and the East Fork of the Tombigbee. Despite notable areas of fertility to the east and north of the Tombigbee, however, it is the western and southern alluvial areas, the Black Prairie, and the Pontotoc Ridge that have provided the most extensive regions attractive to agriculture.

The primary vegetation of the Fall Line Hills area is a mixed pine-hardwood forest. In its undisturbed state this forest is thought to have consisted primarily of hardwoods, with pines appearing singly or in clusters. The fact that pines quickly form essentially pure stands following disturbances such as cultivation or fire has meant that scattered stands of pine are a common feature of this area. In the absence of further disturbances, however, these stands are eventually replaced by a mixed oak-hickory forest. Its dominant species include butternut, mockernut, and pignut hickories; white oak, post oak, and northern and southern red oak; and loblolly and short-leaf pine. On drier ridges, especially in the northern portion, Virginia pine and scarlet oak are dominant. On wetter sites yellow poplar, shumard oak, willow oak, live oak, and bay magnolia occur frequently. The abundance of tree species has provided the basis for lumbering operations of various kinds, which have dominated the economy in many parts of this physiographic region. The natural vegetation of the upper terraces resembles that of the Fall Line Hills, but the vegetation of the lower terraces and particularly of the floodplains is typical of the river floodplains throughout the Gulf Southeast.

Close to the rivers the water table tends to be at or very near the surface, creating saturated conditions, which many plants tolerate with difficulty. The floodplain forest follows the streams and remains distinct as they pass through the Fall Line Hills and the Black Prairie. It is typically dominated by Tupelo gum, bald cypress, pecan, and several species of oak, particularly shumard oak, overcup oak, water oak, willow oak, laurel oak, and swamp chestnut oak. Other species that are common in this forest include swamp privet, red bay, water elm, American elm, cabbage palm, sugarberry, and rattan vine. The combination of dense vegetation, saturated ground, and subjectivity to flooding has made the lower alluvial lands and floodplains unattractive to residential settlement.

The natural vegetation of the Black Prairie reflects the high calcium content of the soil. The dark, heavy clay soil supports a flora with many elements in common with the prairies of the Midwest. In areas where the soil is relatively deep, a rich forest develops, comprising species found primarily on limestone sites: red cedar, overcup oak, shumard oak, chinquapin oak, durand oak, laurel oak, and nutmeg hickory. Where the soil is very thin, the forest is replaced by gladelike areas that in many respects resemble prairies, with shrubs and herbs as the dominant plant forms.

Traces of Early Man

Human occupation of the Upper Tombigbee Valley dates back thousands of years. By the study of artifacts (objects made by human hands) in the area of the Tenn-Tom Waterway, archaeologists have recently contributed heavily to our understanding of early man in North America. Table 1 lists the various time periods and stages of development.

PALEO INDIAN STAGE, 10,000–8000 B.C.

The presence of the Paleo Indian in the Upper Tombigbee Valley between 10,000 B.C. and 8000 B.C. has been extensively documented by the discovery of lithic (stone) artifacts, the dates being extrapolated from the radiocarbon dating of sites in the dry states of the West, where similar artifacts have been found. The Paleo Indians were hunters and gatherers who wandered about in small bands, following the food supply. They used crafted stone spear points, knives, and adzes and hunted big game animals such as mammoth, bison, and deer. Little else is known about their lives.

ARCHAIC STAGE, 8000–1000 B.C.

The Archaic stage, beginning about 8000 B.C., saw important climatic changes which affected the plant and animal species of the region, but the human inhabitants nevertheless show a cultural continuity with their counterparts in the preceding Paleo Indian stage. Deer and smaller animals, supplemented by hickory nuts and acorns, were important sources of food. Gradual changes in the shapes and sizes of projectile points have given archaeologists a basis for dividing the Archaic stage into early, middle, and late periods and for comparing the dates of habitation sites.

Social organization continued to be characterized by wandering bands, as it had in earlier times, but during the late Archaic period, people were beginning to live in larger, semipermanent camps in the summer and fall, dispersing each year into smaller groups to hunt and gather wild foods. In the dry seasons shellfish were extensively exploited on the shoals of the Tombigbee River. The middle Archaic tool kit included scrapers, knives, drills, choppers, adzes, spoke shaves, hammers, and anvil stones. At late Archaic sites found along the Tombigbee River, ground and polished stone implements and a wide variety of bone tools such as awls, needles, and pins have been unearthed.

The presence of lithic materials from distant locations has led

Paleo Indian spear points are evidence of human occupancy of the Tenn-Tom country probably as long as 10,000 years ago. Photo: James F. Doster, courtesy of Mississippi State Historical Museum, Division of Mississippi Department of Archives and History.

Table 1. Human Occupation of the Upper Tombigbee Valley (After Ned J. Jenkins)

Period	Stage	Description
B.C. 10,000–8000	Paleo Indian	Sparse nomadic population. Large, lanceolate, fluted, projectile points suited to hunting large game.
8000–1000	Archaic	Substantial change in climate and plant and animal species. Evolution of new kinds of projectile points and tools. Deer, smaller animals, and plants are important sources of food, as are hickory nuts and acorns. Semi-permanent camps in summer and fall, dispersion into small groups in winter and spring to hunt and to gather wild foods.
1000–100	Gulf Formational	A concept developed by Ned J. Jenkins from studies made in Gainesville Lake area. Late Archaic life-style remains unchanged. Cultural interchange. Introduction of pottery making.
100 B.C.–A.D. 1100	Woodland	A new and distinct culture or cultural group moved into Tombigbee Valley from north. Larger, more permanent villages, burial mounds, production of corn in small quantities. Small, triangular projectile points suggest use of bow and arrow after A.D. 600. Primarily a hunting and gathering culture.
A.D. 1100–1540	Mississippian	Mounds used for burials and ceremonies. Permanent settlements. Bow and arrow hunting. Large-scale corn production and storage. Stratified society. Larger populations.
1540–	Historic	Spaniard de Soto's army, 1540–1541, seized corn supplies, introduced European diseases, left behind a starving, disease-ridden population. Historic knowledge thereafter is sketchy until arrival of French Bienville in 1736. At that time Choctaws lived south of Tibbee Creek and Chickasaws to the north.

Source: Authors.

archaeologists to infer the existence of a Gulf Coastal Plain cultural tradition (with affiliations to the south) and an Upland Plateau tradition (with affiliations to the northeast). These different patterns of cultural adaptation converged and overlapped in the Upper Tombigbee Valley, particularly in the area between Demopolis and Columbus. A network of social, economic, and perhaps ideological ties existed within and between these areas throughout the Archaic period.

GULF FORMATIONAL STAGE, 1000–100 B.C.

The Gulf Formational stage represents a lifestyle modified by trade and cultural exchange in the late Archaic and early Woodland periods in the Gulf Coastal Plain. Fiber-tempered pottery-making was introduced into the Upper Tombigbee Valley, and pottery, with its evolving composition, shapes, and decorations, has from that time provided archaeologists with a tool for identifying cultural associations and dates. The appearance and exclusive use of Gulf tradition ceramics (pottery) mark the beginning of the Gulf Formational stage at different times in different areas. Artifacts collected from a large base camp in the prairie area at the Broken Pumpkin Creek site, eight miles from the Tombigbee River and southwest of Aberdeen, suggest that the local population spent part of the year at a settlement and the rest wandering in search of food. Acorns from prairie oaks in the fall and herbaceous plants in the spring supported deer, an important source of human food. The lithic technology continued Archaic patterns. The late Gulf Formational stage in the upper reaches of the Tenn-Tom country saw a remarkable florescence in pottery styles, with lithic technology in general continuing to exhibit Archaic traits.

WOODLAND STAGE, 100 B.C.–A.D. 1100

The early Woodland culture of the Upper Tombigbee seems to have originated in the Ohio Valley region. Whether it was accompanied by a considerable movement of peoples is unclear. Within the Upper Tombigbee drainage area, the Woodland stage begins with the middle Woodland period about 100 B.C. and lasts to the end of late Woodland about A.D. 1100. The Woodland stage is defined by the appearance of cord- and fabric-marked pottery, elaborate burial ceremonies, a marked increase in trade and barter, a wide distribution of art styles, and the introduction of agriculture. In the Upper Tombigbee Valley burial mounds resembling those found in the Ohio Valley accompanied the appearance of the new pottery styles. The dominant culture of the valley, known as the Miller I–III phases, has been defined from archaeological studies along the Natchez Trace in northeast Mississippi, where the Bynum and Pharr mounds are found. The Miller culture covered roughly the area of Upper Tombigbee drainage and extended a few miles south of Demopolis and a few miles up the Black Warrior River. Base camps, transitory camps, and ceremonial centers have been identified, and some have been excavated. Base camp sites have been found both in the river floodplain and on creeks some distance from the river. During the sedentary season, presumably the late summer and fall, subsistence depended on efficient exploitation of floodplain forest products and deer, supplemented by fish, shellfish, and turtles from the river and sloughs. Base camps may have been occupied throughout the year by parts of the population. In the winter and spring, the larger groups broke up into small bands to hunt game and search for wild foods.

The late Woodland period, Miller III phase, was marked by the abrupt emergence of a new projectile point style, a small triangular form that probably originated elsewhere and perhaps marked the introduction of the bow and arrow. Corn also appeared for the first time. Although it was consistently used, it did not yet become a main element of the diet. Hickory nuts and acorns continued to be important food sources. The large Miller III base camps were concentrated in the river floodplain of an area extending from Demopolis north to a point just above Columbus, corresponding roughly to the crossing of the Black Prairie by the Tombigbee. Transitory camps were located both in the Fall Line Hills to the east and in the prairie to the west. Between A.D. 600 and A.D. 700, population substantially increased. The deer population declined, and smaller mammals became more important in the human diet, as also did fish, turtles, and shellfish. By A.D. 1100 the central Tombigbee Valley had reached its maximum human support capacity at the Woodland level of technology. Population pressure is reflected in human skeletal remains, studies of which indicate a high incidence of violence and nutritional stresses. Religious ceremonialism appears to have declined, and mounds ceased to be built.

MISSISSIPPIAN STAGE, A.D. 1100–1540

About A.D. 1000 a new culture type, known as Mississippian, appeared in the Tombigbee and Warrior river valleys, perhaps introduced from the central Mississippi Valley by intrusions of people with a more efficient technology and social and political organization. Notable was the more extensive production of corn and more effective organization for its storage and distribution. Most of the developments seem to have been in place rather than introduced, with a wide variety of local adaptations and developments. Mississippians continued to hunt deer and small animals and to eat hickory nuts, acorns, fish, and shellfish, but corn served as their basic storable food supply. Population grew and a political structure developed, with power resting on the authority to redistribute stored corn. A religious structure also developed to regulate the ceremonies associated with the growing and harvesting of corn. The settlement system consisted of permanent nuclear centers, with surrounding villages and farmsteads. Ceramic art reached a high state of development. Social stratifications were notable, and the Mississippians built mounds for religious and ceremonial purposes and to support the houses of prominent religious and political leaders. The overlap between Mississippian culture and Woodland culture, lasting perhaps a century in the Upper Tombigbee Valley, suggests that the accompanying conflicts may have given prestige and power to a rising warrior class.

The best-known Mississippian ceremonial and political center was at Moundville, on the Warrior River, but there was another on the Tombigbee at the mouth of Lubbub Creek, a few miles west of present Aliceville. Still another was at Lyons Bluff on Tibbee Creek, some fifteen miles from the Tombigbee River. Both the Lubbub and Lyons Bluff sites have recently been extensively excavated and studied, so that we have a newly expanded knowledge of the Mississippian people in the valley. By 1500 their social and political structure seems to have been in a state of decline.

HISTORIC STAGE, A.D. 1540–

The coming of the Spanish explorer and conquistador Hernando de Soto to the Tombigbee area in 1540, with a considerable Spanish army, produced a fleeting documentary record of the aboriginal population under stress. De Soto found the Chickasaw Indians already permanently based in the prairie of the Tupelo-Pontotoc area, where they cultivated great fields of maize. He seized corn supplies that had been stored for the winter, held local chiefs hostage as he moved from village to village, and introduced European diseases to which the Indians had no acquired immunity. The impact of the de Soto expedition on the Indian cultures cannot easily be measured, but the Spaniards introduced superior tools, weapons, and military tactics as well as that useful animal the horse. They also upset a delicately balanced system and left behind a starving, disease-ridden population. Between the 1540s and the eighteenth century the historic record is tenuous and awaits amplification from archaeological explorations not yet made. In this protohistoric period European contact altered the late Mississippian culture.

SUBSISTENCE PATTERNS

Environmental factors and advancing technology affected the lives of the early people in the Upper Tombigbee Valley. Their numbers were limited by food supply. Their way of life from early Archaic times necessarily included nomadic movements to follow the seasonal requirements of hunting and gathering until efficient corn agriculture produced a storable and reliable food for sedentary people. Base camps in the Tombigbee River floodplains had access in the summer and fall to fish and shellfish, acorns, hickory nuts, deer, and small game. These camps might be occupied during the whole year by a part of the population. In the winter and spring small bands would range widely from the base camps into the prairie and the Fall Line Hills in search of food while they lived in temporary camps.

Although the prairie offered obstacles to permanent occupation, there were places at its edge where base camps were practical. Along the permanent streams in the prairie, oak trees produced acorns that attracted deer in the fall as well as turkey and squirrel. Hickory nuts, however, were limited mainly to terraces of the Tombigbee and other streams. There were in the prairie numerous wide swamps filled with cane, which deer could eat during the winter; these are now gone. The prairie also offered herbaceous forage for deer in the spring and summer and produced cottontail rabbits, which were most plentiful in the fall. Bears could be found in the canebrakes.

In Mississippian and historic times, the extensive production of corn changed the patterns of habitation. A part of the population remained sedentary to produce corn while the hunters roamed at large. Women, children, and old men tended to remain in permanent abodes during the winter. The great celebration and social gathering of the year came at the time of the green corn feast in July or August, after which migratory activities might be resumed for a time.

NEW INVESTIGATORS OF THE DISTANT PAST

At the beginning of the twentieth century, hardly a line of the above account could have been written. It is so fresh now that some of the reports on which it is based are not yet publicly available. An account of a few of the people who developed it makes an interesting story in itself.

Clarence Bloomfield Moore, a Philadelphian of inherited wealth, made a lifetime career of world travel and of archaeological explorations in the Southeast. Moore utilized a flat-bottomed steamboat, the *Gopher*, for his water transportation. His captain would examine in advance the territory that Moore wished to explore and would obtain permission to investigate it from the owners of the land. During the winter of 1901, Moore explored sites along the Upper Tombigbee River from Columbus to Demopolis. He located and listed various mounds and campsites but uncovered few artifacts and failed to note the real richness of the area in prehistoric sites. In 1905 and 1906 he made the first explorations at Moundville and laid the groundwork for more thorough and more professional excavations. After Moore no one made a systematic study of the Upper Tombigbee Valley for many years.

In the 1920s Walter B. Jones, the state geologist of Alabama, who had served on a federal commission to locate the route followed by the explorer Hernando de Soto, became interested in Moundville. Beginning in 1929, he conducted excavations at the mounds over a period of several years, on behalf of the Alabama Museum at the University of Alabama. Assisting him was an exuberant young man named David DeJarnette, who in the course of years became increasingly determined to unearth the story of early man in the Southeast. War and the search for a livelihood took him away from his native Alabama, but he returned to become curator of Mound State Park at Moundville and taught archaeology at the University of

Left: The steamboat *Gopher* (foreground), at Columbus in 1901, belonged to archaeologist Clarence Bloomfield Moore. The vessel in the background is the locally owned *Vienna*, which burned in 1907 and was the last regular steam packet vessel on the Upper Tombigbee. Photo: courtesy of Lowndes County Library.

Below, left: Excavation of the Pharr Mounds (ca. 1970), on the Natchez Trace Parkway southwest of the Bay Springs lock, added to the knowledge of early man in the Tenn-Tom country. Photo: David C. Weaver.

Below: David DeJarnette, an influential pioneer in Alabama archaeology, blazed the trail for others to follow. Photo: Office of Archaeological Research, University of Alabama.

Alabama. DeJarnette spent his summers in archaeological digs at many sites and trained a host of enthusiastic young men and women who followed in his footsteps.

In the 1930s Jesse Jennings and others made extensive archaeological investigations in Mississippi along the route of the Natchez Trace and in the Tupelo area. It was Jennings who investigated the Miller site and defined the Miller phases. Others have more recently excavated the Pharr and Bynum mounds, located near the present Tenn-Tom Waterway on the Natchez Trace.

In 1970 DeJarnette directed a survey of archaeological sites in the area of the future Gainesville Lake. The Corps of Engineers, pressed to mitigate the damage it was about to do to the traces of early man, gave financial support to further explorations. Under contracts with the National Park Service and the Corps, additional surveys of archaeological resources were made in the Tenn-Tom areas by the University of Alabama, Mississippi State University, the University of West Florida, and other agencies.

By 1977 the surveys had identified 682 sites in the Tenn-Tom area, with the following components (more numerous than the sites):

Paleo Indian	2
Archaic	284
Woodland	682
Mississippian	118

Less than half lay within impacted areas. An elaborate plan was adopted, financed by the Corps, to "mitigate" the expected damage by selecting the most promising sites in impacted areas for archaeological investigation before work on the waterway destroyed them forever. Sites selected for further investigation were those likely to yield information on subjects about which little was known, such as settlement patterns, subsistence, mortuary practices, and material culture development. While the Upper Tombigbee area was not, of course, the exclusive home of early man, it was an important center of occupation and of traffic, and the extensive artifacts systematically unearthed have contributed to the advance of knowledge of prehistoric man in America.

Much of the work of mitigation has been conducted by the Office of Archaeological Research of the University of Alabama at Moundville on the Warrior River, where David DeJarnette, the founder and patron saint of Alabama archaeology, once presided. From a well-equipped laboratory at this vantage point, Carey B. Oakley now conducts an active program of archaeological research in the Upper Tombigbee Valley that is mostly financed by the Corps of Engineers. Says Oakley, "In 1976 this office negotiated probably the first archaeological contract with the Corps of Engineers. Under Ned Jenkins as supervisor we excavated five prehistoric sites. Other sites and other universities were soon involved. The University of Alabama did a testing program of 58 archaeological sites reaching all the way from Aliceville, Alabama, up to Bay Springs in northeastern Mississippi."

The excavations close to the river in the area of the Gainesville Lake, particularly at Lubbub Creek, a few miles west of Aliceville, have been of outstanding value. "I think Lubbub was a unique ceremonial center," says Oakley. "Although not as large as Moundville, it nevertheless shows the regional expression of that particular culture. Prehistoric Indians gravitated close to water, and the Tombigbee Valley was a major thoroughfare for mobile populations and ideas. We have been able to pretty systematically reconstruct the life ways of both prehistoric and historic populations in a period of, say, eight thousand years. We can still go into different groups coming in, different groups going out, their subsistence, how they lived, where they lived, their settlement patterns, and the character of their communities."

Carey B. Oakley, director of the Office of Archaeological Research of the University of Alabama, has headquarters at Moundville. His organization has done extensive archaeological work in the Upper Tombigbee Valley under contracts with the Corps of Engineers and other government agencies. Photo: Office of Archaeological Research, University of Alabama.

Not all of the archaeological explorations of the Upper Tombigbee area have been conducted by professionals. There are amateurs with burning zeal. A striking personality is that of James William ("Bill") Furr, Jr., a Columbus electronics technician. He says, "When I was a child, my mama would take us to Indian mounds in the country. I have been actively collecting night and day since 1970. Even in winter rain and cold, I have been on the river in my little boat miles from Columbus, exhuming Indian fossil remains. I have often stayed up into the early hours washing my finds in the driveway, so I could bring them into the basement. I have a lot of drive, and I stay with what I start on. They say by 2000 all the sites will be gone, and all that archaeologists will have to study will be what has been found already. I am amassing a tremendous amount of archaeological, cultural, and river history material that scholars a hundred years after I am dead and gone will be going through, sorting the pieces out."

Furr continues, "My Tennessee-Tombigbee Waterway museum has material from both rivers, and is a complete waterway museum with everything from cannons to dugout canoes to cranials to murals to fossils. I have also been into the Alabama hills working on different creeks, mostly at Archaic sites. My oldest material is Paleozoic, 300 million years old, but most material around here is middle Archaic. I have early and late Archaic, as well as Mississippian and Woodland artifacts, a large conglomeration of everything. I have actually got the first arrow points that I started with when I was a little boy. I know exactly which ones they are and where they came from. Most of the

Above: Investigations at Lubbub Creek near the Tombigbee River in Pickens County by the University of Michigan. Photo: Office of Archaeological Research, University of Alabama.
Below: James William Furr, Jr., an amateur archaeologist of Columbus, studies prehistory with great zeal. Photo: Jan Weaver.

material is memorized in my head. In the museum I have very little written down. It is all in my memory."

Furr's collection is quite impressive, not so much for Archaic items as for those of more recent times. He considers it priceless and wants someone to provide a fireproof building in which to display it. The Mississippi University for Women in Columbus, he says, may in time help him to provide a safe display.

Between Furr and the professional archaeologists there has been considerable enmity. They have called him a "pothunter," which appellation he bitterly resents, and have harassed him for alleged destruction of archaeological sites. Furr has identified river sites only to find himself denied excavation permits by the Corps of Engineers. He claims the Corps has destroyed the identified sites by clumsy methods of exploration and excavation. Furr seeks artifacts for their own sake, while the professional archaeologists are more concerned with patterns of development in the culture of early man; to them the location, the strata, and the associated materials where artifacts are found are of critical importance. While Furr and the archaeologists accuse each other of being destroyers of sites (and in some sense both parties are), the main culprits have been the Corps of Engineers, the highway builders, and the real estate developers.

3

Indians and Indian Countrymen, 1540–1820

According to sketchy records, the Spanish expedition under Hernando de Soto, coming north from Mauvilla, in Clarke County, Alabama, crossed the Warrior River at Stephens Bluff on Melton's Bend. On December 16, 1540, in the face of Indian opposition, it crossed the Tombigbee, probably near Aberdeen. A party on horseback, sent to outflank the Indians, crossed farther north, possibly at Cotton Gin Port. Up to this point the Indian towns mentioned by de Soto's scribes have Choctaw names, but the Tombigbee River is referred to as the "River of the Chickasaws."

For the next century, European contacts with the local aborigines were few. When the French Père Marquette descended the Mississippi River in 1673, however, he met Chickasaws who possessed axes, hoes, knives, beads, and double glass bottles for their powder, articles which they had obtained from tribes to the east, who had in turn gotten them from English colonists on the Atlantic seaboard.

Soon afterward English traders and English goods reached the Chickasaws and Choctaws directly. In the late seventeenth and early eighteenth centuries the new colony of South Carolina provided a firm base for English trade with the Chickasaws using well-established trails.

The French established bases in the early eighteenth century at Mobile and New Orleans from which they could extend their influence into the southern Indian country. In 1717 they built Fort Toulouse in the country of the Creek Indians, where the Coosa and Tallapoosa rivers flow together to form the Alabama. Then in 1736 the Sieur de Bienville set out from Mobile with a French force to chastise the Chickasaws. He moved up the Tombigbee River, entered the Upper Tombigbee at Demopolis, and established Fort Tombecbé on the white chalk cliff (Jones Bluff) near present Epes. He moved on up the river in boats to Plymouth Bluff at the mouth of Tibbee Creek. Obtaining help from the Choctaws, between whom and the Chickasaws there was a deep-seated enmity, he continued upstream and erected a temporary fortification near the later Cotton Gin Port.

Reinforced by Indian allies, Bienville then moved overland to

Top: Hernando de Soto was the leader of a Spanish expedition which crossed the Upper Tombigbee River in December 1540 and left its mark on the native population of the area.

Above: The Sieur de Bienville, the French founder of Mobile and New Orleans, built Fort Tombecbé at Epes and attacked the Chickasaws in 1736.

Photos by Jan Weaver, courtesy of Agee Collection, University of Alabama Library.

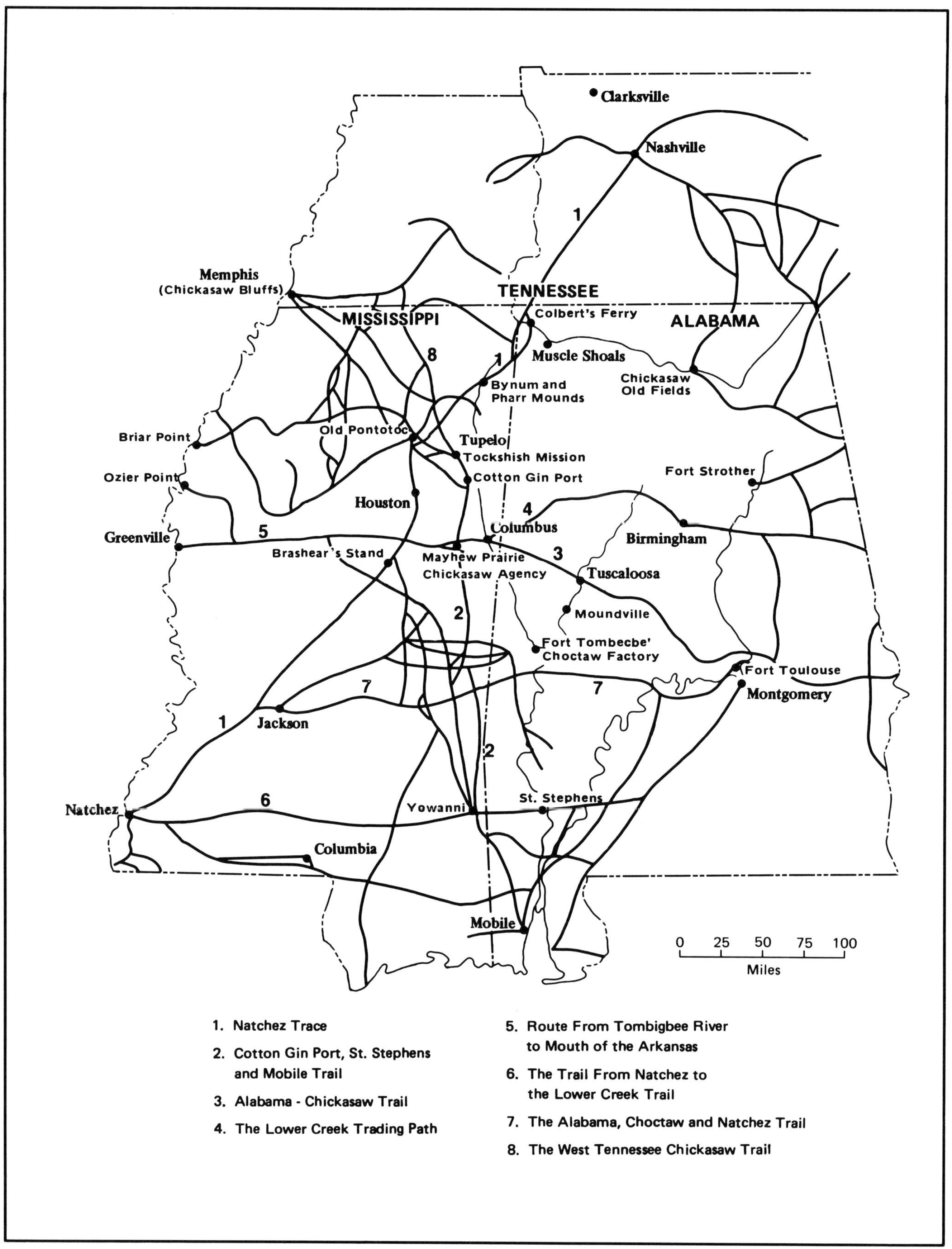

1. Natchez Trace
2. Cotton Gin Port, St. Stephens and Mobile Trail
3. Alabama - Chickasaw Trail
4. The Lower Creek Trading Path
5. Route From Tombigbee River to Mouth of the Arkansas
6. The Trail From Natchez to the Lower Creek Trail
7. The Alabama, Choctaw and Natchez Trail
8. The West Tennessee Chickasaw Trail

Map 6. Indian trails and related settlements

attack the Chickasaw towns near present Pontotoc. The Chickasaws had been provided by English traders with arms and ammunition and with advice on fortifications. Having defeated a French force from the Mississippi River a few days earlier, they proceeded to inflict a disastrous defeat on Bienville and his Choctaw allies. He fell back to Cotton Gin Port and hastily departed with his boats. The French war with the Chickasaws continued intermittently for a great many years, but the record is scanty. Letters of Chickasaw traders in the South Carolina Indian records frequently mention the French but are not very informative.

The conflict between the French and English was developing on a broad scale. The French and Indian War, supposedly beginning with George Washington's unsuccessful expedition against Fort Duquesne in Pennsylvania in 1754, was actually an extension of a conflict that had been under way for many years in the Indian country, where both sides sought to use the Indians as surrogates in an imperial struggle. The British of South Carolina were firm allies of the Chickasaws, against whom there were various French or French-inspired military movements between 1752 and 1754. The South Carolinians struggled to wean the Choctaws away from the French and succeeded with part of these Indians. In the war period the new and rather weak colony of Georgia also exerted some influence. British Indian superintendent Edmond Atkin gave support to South Carolina and Georgia and in 1759 negotiated several treaties with the Chickasaws, Choctaws, and Creeks.

As an outcome of the war, which ended in 1763, the French yielded to the British all claims to the areas east of the Mississippi River except for the Island of New Orleans. To Spain France ceded the Louisiana Territory, which included the Island of New Orleans and a huge area extending west of the Mississippi River. The Spanish had lost to the British all their claims to the Floridas. The southern Indians, who had been skillful in playing off one European nation against another, were not pleased with the outcome of the war, which had ended in a worldwide English victory.

The British government appointed John Stuart of South Carolina as Indian superintendent to succeed Atkin and sought to develop measures for dealing with the Indians without resorting to expensive wars. A part of the new Indian policy was to establish boundary lines with the Indians and to restrain activities across such lines that might tend to bring conflict. Some of the Indians were deeply attached to the French, and powerful Indian elements distrusted the English. Major General Thomas Gage, the British commander in North America, with headquarters in New York, had to reduce his forces for reasons of economy, and he disliked the Indians' maintenance of military posts too remote from their bases to be supported or reinforced in case of hostile actions. Reluctantly he consented to British occupation of the French Fort Tombecbé. His first object was to provide a base for trade with the Choctaws and possibly to some extent with the Chickasaws. The second object was to support the subtle efforts of Stuart's agents to keep a war going between the

Choctaws and Creeks and thereby to discourage the Creeks from attacking the English.

Stuart negotiated treaties with the Indians in which definite boundary lines were delineated. Standard prices on trade goods were agreed upon, and provisions were made for the licensing and regulating of traders. Among the treaties were those negotiated with the Choctaws and Chickasaws at Mobile in 1765. The establishment of the Indian boundary brought bitter opposition from frontiersmen and land speculators. Imperial regulation of trade and traders aroused resentment in the traders and jealousy in the colonial governors. The governors proceeded to appoint selected traders as colonial agents among the Indians. Stuart lost much of his influence and control, and disorderly conditions came to prevail.

In organizing their newly acquired territories the British established the colony of East Florida, with its capital at St. Augustine, and the colony of West Florida, with its capital at Pensacola. English West Florida extended from the Chattahoochee and Apalachicola rivers on the east to the Mississippi on the west and from the Gulf of Mexico on the south to latitude 32° 28' on the north. Accompanying the troops sent to occupy the new province of West Florida were two traders, John McGillivray and Daniel Ward, who established at Mobile their headquarters for trade with the Choctaws and Chickasaws, a trade in which both had evidently been engaged in earlier times from less convenient places. Superintendent Stuart handed out liberal presents to the Indians on treaty occasions (see table 2) and rewarded friendly chiefs with great medals and small medals, as the French had done.

Sloop navigation was possible on the lower Tombigbee as far north as present Jackson, Alabama, and keelboats and canoes could navigate farther upstream. On the Upper Tombigbee their progress depended on the season, the stage of the river, and occasional obstructions, and the voyage could be hazardous. While the Indians had canoes and used them for crossing streams and for short trips, they did not generally take to the water for long excursions. The Indian trade was conducted primarily with the use of pack horses. Horse paths tended to follow the ridges, avoiding swampy areas, and crossing streams as infrequently as possible. Necessary stream crossings were accomplished at shallow fords or by means of a precarious footing for the traveler on a fallen tree, while his horses had to swim.

The logistics of horse transportation in the southern Indian country needs some explanation. A well-fed horse was a wonderful asset, but pasturage was good only at certain seasons except in the ranges along the streams. It was not the custom to raise food for horses, and the animals had to rough it in range pastures. A horse was not a good beast of burden unless well fed, and he required food daily. Horses in the Indian country were reported by travelers often to be "too pore" for use. The wise traveler picked the season when food for horses was plentiful. Getting fresh ones involved trading with people living along the way. For one reason or another many a horse had to be left

Table 2. Indian Presents Distributed by the British to the Choctaws and Chickasaws at Mobile, December 1771–January 1772

Strouds	Combs
Duffiles	Duffil coats
Guns	Hawks bells
Riffled guns	Pea buttons
Powder	Awl blades
Ball	Fire steels
Flints	Needles
Gun locks	Thread
Tomahawks	Brass wire
Hatchets	Laced hatts
Gun worms	Plain hats
Saddles	White Linen
Bridles	Striped flannel
Vermillion	Terrelinge
Great coats	Ribbon
Ruffled shirts	Scarlet suits
Gartering & Caddice	Shoes
Callico	Stockings
Hoes	Buckles
Belts	Salt
Tin potts	Gorgets
Brass kettles	Arm plates
Gilt trunks	Wrist plates
Barley corn	Carrots tobacco
Knives	Leaf tobacco
Scissors	Scarlet cloath
Razors	Silver earbobs
Nonso pretties	Handkfs [Handkerchiefs]
Common beads	Axes
Skirts	

Source: Library of Congress Transcripts, PRO:CO 5/73.

behind, and horses were returned to their owners by a process reminiscent of the return movement of railroad freight cars to their owners—sometimes there were delays, and sometimes the route was circuitous. Stealing horses ("borrowing," as the Indians called it) was very common and to an Indian could be a form of sport just dangerous enough to be interesting. Horse stealing was the source of many bitter conflicts on the frontier.

The logistics of Indian warfare was difficult for white military men to grasp. An Indian army might travel hundreds of miles without boats, horses, or wagons. The warrior carried most of his possessions on his person. If he had a gun and ammunition, he could stop to hunt whenever he needed food, but he carried little food with him. An Indian army expended ammunition steadily without even seeing an enemy, something difficult for European military men to understand. The range of an expedition was limited primarily by the ammunition available for hunting.

Indian hunters might be away from home for months, especially in the winter. They transported meat home on their own backs or on those of horses. Although they stored food, the danger of running out was an ever-present source of dread. By Indian custom people with food supplied people without.

The Choctaws, a tribe comparable to the Creeks in size, lived in villages or towns, clustered in several parts of Mississippi, mostly westward from Jones Bluff. They seem to have had no permanent settlements on or east of the Black Prairie. Besides being hunters, they were farmers, raising corn, peas, beans, pumpkins, tobacco, sweet potatoes, leeks, cabbage, garlic, and sunflowers. They also collected wild food, such as hickory nuts, walnuts, pecans, wild strawberries and blackberries, and other wild fruits.

The Chickasaws were hunters, but they also engaged in agriculture. Many of them lived on the edge of the Black Prairie near Tupelo, where they raised crops similar to those of the Choctaws, but they were far less numerous than the Choctaws. The Chickasaws were of such mixed Indian ancestry that they were known to traders in the eighteenth century as the "Breeds." At different times they had had a settlement among the Creeks and another on the Savannah River among the Cherokees, each place being known as "Breed Camp."

The southern Indians commonly lived along the streams, but there is scant record of Chickasaws living anywhere on the Upper Tombigbee in historic times. Archaeologist Carey B. Oakley says, "I cannot think of one single, verifiable historic Chickasaw town within five miles of Tenn-Tom." This situation stands in marked contrast with that in the Alabama, Coosa, and Tallapoosa river areas in Alabama, where evidence remains of dozens of historic Indian towns along the streams. The center of the Chickasaw settlements was west of present Tupelo, on the prairie, where horses and cattle thrived.

Bernard Romans, who visited the Chickasaws in 1771, observed: "They live nearly in the center of a very large and somewhat uneven savannah, of a diameter of above three miles . . . and . . . get their water out of holes or wells dug near the town. . . . They have . . . what might be called one town, or rather an assemblage of hutts, of length about one mile and a half and very narrow and irregular; this however they divided into seven . . . [towns], . . . formerly inclosed in palisadoes, and thus well fortified . . . but it now lays open."[1] The division between Chickasaw and Choctaw territory was traditionally along Tibbee Creek and then northwestward by an indistinct line. A trading path between the two nations crossed the creek a couple of miles from the Tombigbee. The Choctaws lived in central and southern Mississippi, but in earlier times they had had a few villages on the lower Tombigbee. Romans observed numerous old fields along the river in present Pickens and Greene counties. Probably the Choctaw-Creek war, which was raging as Romans descended the river, had something to do with the abandonment. The Creeks, whose settlements were scattered over Alabama and Geor-

---

1. Bernard Romans, *A Concise Natural History of East and West Florida* (Philadelphia: R. Aitken, 1776), p. 62.

gia, claimed land as far west as the Tombigbee River in Alabama and Mississippi, but the boundary was long a source of bitter controversy and warfare. The Choctaws in 1805 sold to the United States lands east of the Tombigbee claimed by the Creeks, and in 1816 they sold lands already ceded by the Creeks. Indians seldom occupied the area between the Warrior and Tombigbee rivers in historic times, although they used it for hunting.

In the American Revolution, John Stuart, the British superintendent, worked until his death in 1779 to keep the friendship of the Indians for the British, while the Continental agent, George Galphin, worked to neutralize his efforts. The Chickasaws, supposedly loyal to the British, were sent by them to guard the Mississippi River. They proved ineffective guardians, although John McIntosh, Stuart's deputy, was stationed among them. The Choctaws were under British influence initially, but they were tampered with by the Spanish at New Orleans, and they did not prove very helpful as allies to the British.

The Spanish entered the war in 1779 and promptly captured the British garrison at Natchez; they took Mobile in 1780 and Pensacola in 1781. By the peace treaties of Paris of 1783 Spain kept British West Florida and obtained East Florida as well. It will be remembered that West Florida's northern boundary was latitude 32° 28' from the Chattahoochee to the Mississippi, but the new American nation claimed as far south as 31°.

The southern Indians, before 1783 primarily pro-British, hastened to make terms with the victorious Spanish. The Choctaws and Chickasaws did so by treaties entered into at Mobile in 1783 and the Creeks by the Treaty of Pensacola of 1784. A critical problem for the Indians was trade, which had been heavily interdicted during the war. Agreements ancillary to the treaties provided for regulation of trade, traders, and the prices of trade goods. The Indians supplied deerskins, but they required a great variety and quantity of European trade goods, not the least of which were guns and ammunition, desperately needed for hunting. The Spanish were not prepared to handle Indian relations effectively, nor did they have an established source of supply for the trade goods. The British firm of Panton, Leslie and Company, operating out of St. Augustine, Pensacola, and Mobile under Spanish license, came to dominate the trade. Among the Choctaws and Chickasaws lived various old French traders, who were at least nominally converted into Spaniards. There remained also several independent traders of British origin with Indian wives, such as James Colbert, John Pitchlynn, and Benjamin James, who had extensive influence among the Indians.

The growing influence of the United States in the southern Indian country is observable in the Hopewell (South Carolina) treaties of 1785–1786 with the Cherokees, Choctaws, and Chickasaws, which defined boundaries, forbade Americans to settle on Indian lands, and allowed the United States to regulate trade with the Indians. Until Congress acted to regulate trade, however, citizens of the United States could freely enter the Indian country to trade. By a treaty at Hopewell with the Chickasaws in 1786, the United States

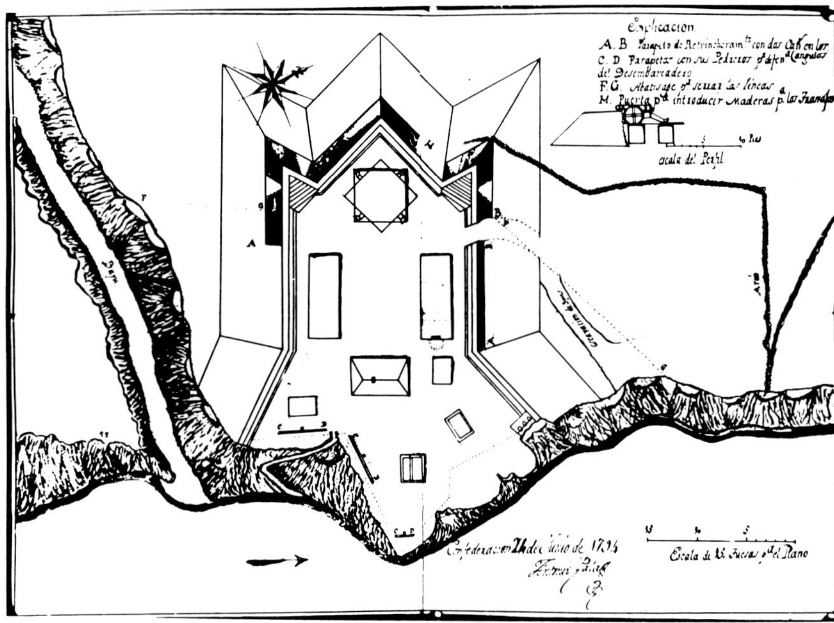

Above: James P. Pate of Livingston University, who directed the excavation of the site of Forts Tombecbé and Confederación at Epes, with hard chalk blocks removed from the site. Photo: Jan Weaver.

Above, right: A drawing by Spanish engineer Palao, dated June 24, 1794, of the plans for Fort Confederación. Photo: Archivo General de Indias, Seville.

acquired a reservation five miles in diameter on the Tennessee River at the lower part of Muscle Shoals in Alabama. In 1790 came the treaty of New York between the United States and the Creeks.

While Spanish power was declining, the aggressiveness of Spanish officials was not. In 1794 the Spanish governor Carondelet proceeded to occupy the old site of Fort Tombecbé at Epes and to build there the new Fort Confederación. Efforts of the Spanish to expand their influence and authority in the Indian country were checked by the Treaty of San Lorenzo (Pinckney's Treaty) of 1795, in which Spain recognized latitude 31° as its boundary with the United States. Spain evacuated Fort Confederación in 1799 but remained in control of all of the Gulf Coast and the Louisiana Territory. Spain was reduced to near impotence, however, by the wars of the French Revolution.

When James P. Pate, a professor of history and dean of the College of General Studies at Livingston University, went there to teach, he decided to combine historical with archaeological skills in a study of the site of old forts Tombecbé and Confederación. His doctoral dissertation at Mississippi State University had been on the Chickamauga Indians, and he was interested in the relations between Indians and Spaniards. Pate obtained plans of the French and Spanish forts from the Archivo General de Indias in Seville. With financial help from the Alabama Historical Commission and Livingston University, he employed James Parker, an experienced historical archaeologist, as field supervisor and undertook excavations with student aid. They found only fragmentary artifacts but they stirred great interest in the site, which is right on the Tenn-Tom Waterway. Says Pate, "We think that most of the large artifacts had been carried off by metal-detector hunters, weekend diggers, and amateur archaeologists, who probably destroyed much of what we might have found there. There are a lot of plans for industrial development along the river," he continues, "and the site could be further impacted in a negative way if we are not very careful. I would like to see something done on the fort site, some type of restoration, certainly the preservation of the site."

To extend its influence among the Indians, the United States in the early nineteenth century established several public trading factories. One of these, primarily for the Chickasaws, was put at Chickasaw Bluffs (Memphis, Tennessee) in 1802. It was closed for a period during the War of 1812, and permanently in 1818, partly because of competition from private traders and failure to make a profit. In 1804, a factory was opened at Fort Stoddert, primarily for the Choctaws. It was soon moved to St. Stephens, on the Tombigbee near present Jackson, Alabama. After the Creek war it was again moved to Factory Creek, near Jones Bluff on the Upper Tombigbee. It operated until the Indian factory system was abolished in 1822, and it was associated through most of its existence with the honesty, reliability, and kindness of George S. Gaines, the factor.

Both the Indians and the white traders used trails that pack horses could follow. Short trails connected villages, and long trails linked the nations. There were others to salt licks, bodies of water, and trading posts. These trails set a pattern for the first wagon roads in the region. Trails leading from southwest to northeast through the Chickasaw country were used by flatboat men returning from Natchez and New Orleans. In order to open a road from Nashville to Natchez, agents of the United States in 1801 negotiated a treaty with the Chickasaws and another with the Choctaws. Then in 1802 Lieutenant Edmund P. Gaines surveyed a route from Nashville to Natchez through the Chickasaw country. Following the survey, a road was opened that became known as the Natchez Trace and for the next several years was more or less passable for wagons at some seasons.

The acquisition of the Louisiana Territory and of the Island of New Orleans by the United States in 1803 created an urgent need for better transportation and communication between the eastern seaboard of the United States and New Orleans. This meant the opening of roads and water courses through the Indian country. Growing numbers of frontiersmen were pressing upon the Indian country and tending to occupy the Indian lands illegally, although the federal government removed many of them from time to time. The Indians feared that the use of roads and water courses would bring disputes, thefts, and murders, for which the Indians would be held responsible and punished, so they resisted and delayed the projects.

In 1811 the United States decided to push the opening of the roads whether the Indians consented or not. One route lay across the Creek country from Georgia to Fort Stoddert on the Mobile River; another ran from Fort Stoddert to New Orleans. A third was to follow the line of Gaines's survey from Muscle Shoals to Cotton Gin Port, then move down the Tombigbee Valley to Fort Stoddert. The roads were opened in the fall of 1811 except for that along the Tombigbee, the completion of which was somewhat delayed. At various times the Natchez Trace was improved, but it remained a bad road for wagons.

Top: George S. Gaines, a brother of Edmund P. Gaines, headed the U.S. Indian trading factory at St. Stephens, later moved to a site near Epes. Photo: Jan Weaver, courtesy of Alabama Historical Commission.

Above: Edmund P. Gaines, a brother of George S. Gaines, laid out the Natchez Trace and Gaines's Trace when he was a young officer. In the 1820s and 1830s he was one of the two principal officers of the U.S. Army. Photo: Library of Congress.

The Natchez Trace Parkway, shown here in Tishomingo County near the Alabama line, crosses the Tenn-Tom Waterway within sight of the Bay Springs lock. Following the route of the old Natchez Trace, it runs from Nashville to Natchez. Photo: John Mohlhenrich, National Park Service.

Pushmataha, a famed chief of the Choctaws and a steadfast friend of the United States, was praised by Gideon Lincecum, Andrew Jackson, and George S. Gaines. Photo: Jan Weaver, courtesy of Alabama Historical Commission.

All of the roads could be difficult in wet weather. South of Plymouth transportation depended heavily on the Tombigbee River, but the river was difficult to navigate at most seasons.

As a result of the War of 1812 between the United States and England (1812–1815) and the war with the Creeks (1812–1814), Indian resistance to the penetration of the Indian country by the United States was broken. Extensive Indian land cessions opened the way for the survey and sale of the newly acquired lands by the government. Some sales of public lands had been made between 1809 and 1811 on the lower Tombigbee and the Mobile River. Between 1810 and 1813 Spanish West Florida was seized by the United States, thus opening the way to free navigation of the Mobile River and its tributaries.

With war at an end and vast new lands in the South and West available, settlers poured in. In 1816 the Choctaws and Chickasaws surrendered their claims to all lands on the eastern side of the Tombigbee south of Gaines's Trace. Soon the lands there were surveyed and offered for sale at auction. In 1817 the Alabama Territory was formed from the eastern part of the Mississippi Territory, the western part being admitted to the Union as the state of Mississippi. These events were accompanied by a rapid influx of people primarily from the states to the east, who were anxious to acquire productive lands cheaply. It was initially thought that all the lands east of the Tombigbee were in Alabama.

Gaines's Trace from the Tennessee River reached the Tombigbee at Cotton Gin Port. Both the river and the trace became parts of the boundary of the United States with the Chickasaws under the Chickasaw treaty of 1816, which restricted the entry of white traders into Indian lands. Cotton Gin Port became an important Indian

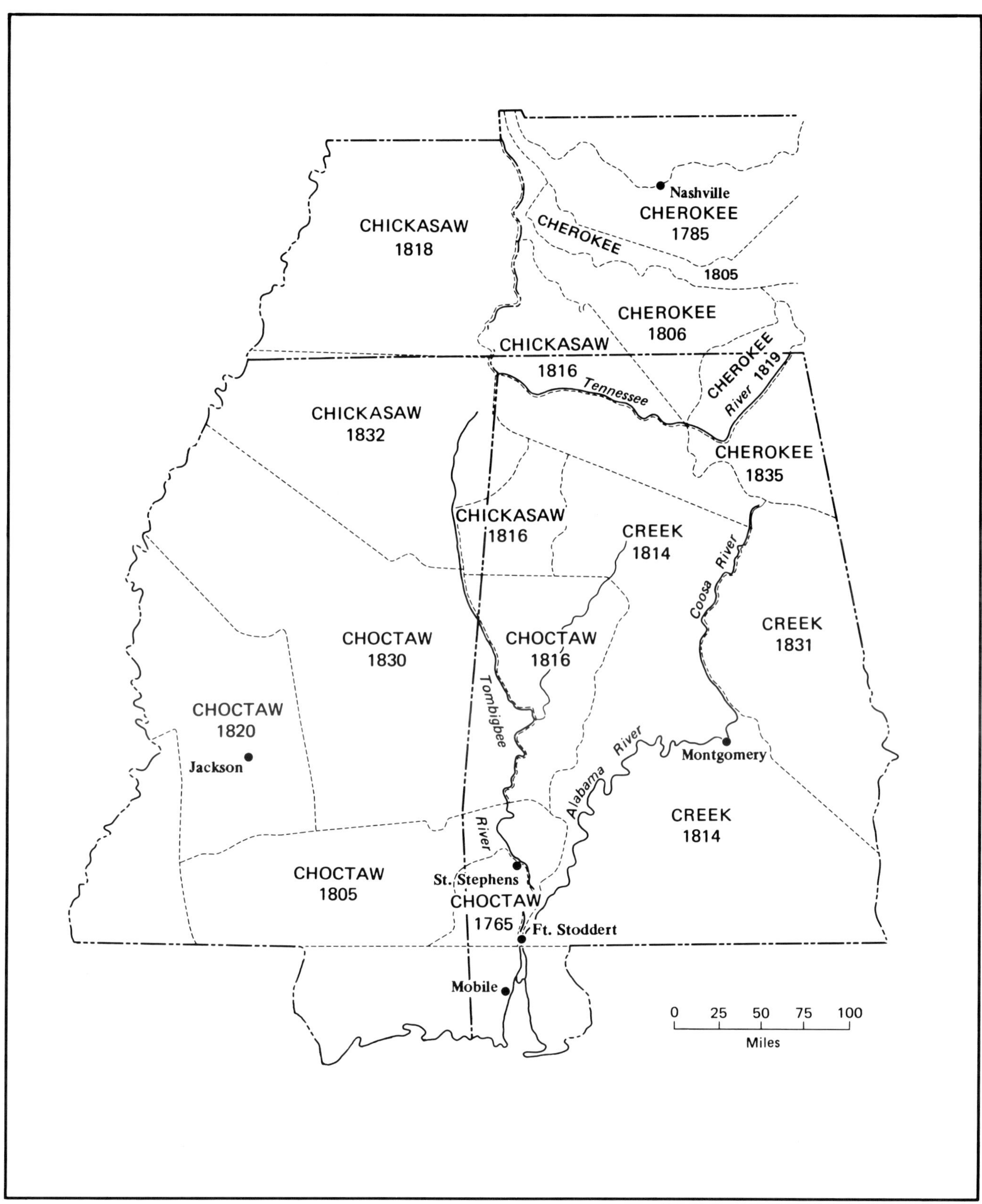

Map 7. Indian land cessions

trading center. By 1820 it had a population of forty-six whites and three blacks and by 1823 an inn, a ferry, and a mill of some kind. John Breeding had a nearby store at a spot called Breeding's Landing. On April 13, 1824, the Cotton Gin Land Company was formed to plat the town.

In the early nineteenth century the United States brought strong influence to bear on the Indians to induce them to adopt the white man's methods in plant and animal husbandry. The response was strong but uneven and created stresses among the Indians. Most Indians continued to live with a minimum of shelter, clothing, and household utensils. Fragmentary archaeological evidence observed by the authors at the Creek Indian sites at Tuckabatchee and Tensaw, however, indicates that wealthy Indians lived very much as did the wealthy white frontiersmen. In the 1820s the Choctaws and Chickasaws moved in great numbers from their relatively concentrated settlements to dispersed individual farms.

The area about Columbus, on the east side of the Tombigbee, was of early interest to white settlers. The best early account of it comes from a pioneer settler named Gideon Lincecum, who moved there from Tuscaloosa in 1818. He engaged in rafting logs on the Tombigbee River and in a wide variety of other activities, some of which he wrote about.

> The State line had not been run, and we were supposed to be in Alabama [but] we found ourselves fifteen miles from the line on the Mississippi side, 200 miles from the other portion of the State. And thus cut off from the law, we were there 18 months before we saw an officer of any kind.
>
> At length the Legislature recognized us as a portion of the State. They appointed me chief justice, with authority to appoint all the officers necessary to organize the county. The Legislature appointed me chairman of school commissioners, with power to appoint four associates; also to lay off the town and lease the lots for the term of 99 years, renewable forever.
>
> Holding the courts, appointing the officers, surveying the town lots, appointing and regulating school commissioners at town, and all the other school sections in the county, procuring teachers, engaging workmen for the academies and opening the mail six times a week, consumed so much of my time, that my own business was badly neglected.
>
> I went over the river and entered into partnership with John Pitchlynn, Junior, a half-breed Choctaw. He was a highly educated man and a very clever fellow; but a most incorrigible drunkard.
>
> In the knowledge of all outsiders, I occupied the position of a superintending clerk. Pitchlynn had a pretty good storehouse at the ferry landing opposite Columbus, and four or five thousand dollars' worth of goods. I had about the same amount. We put them together. I moved my family into a large two story building he had commenced, and took possession of the goods and storehouse and ferry.
>
> Pitchlynn's residence was two miles from the store, a circumstance favorable to our business; for he was, when drunk, so abusive, and so often drunk, that he was not popular with the Indians.
>
> I bartered with them for every kind of produce, consisting of cow-

hides, deer skins, all kinds of fur, skins, buck horns, cow horns, peas, beans, peanuts, pecans, shellbarks, hickory nuts, honey, beeswax, blowguns and blowgun arrows, bacon and venison hams and big gobblers. I made it a rule to purchase, at some price, everything they brought to the store.

I made frequent trips to Mobile. There I laid in my groceries, sugar, coffee, whiskey, etc., but all my dry goods came from the house of Dallas & Wilcox [in Philadelphia].

It was a fine place for business; and I should in a short time have accumulated sufficient wealth to satisfy me, if we could have been healthy there. But one or more of the family was sick all the time. My wife and I both came very near dying of fever two or three times. The children were sick, so were our servants.

Great as was this location for making money, we were so unhealthy that we were forced to leave it. Pitchlynn, without my knowledge, had gone up to Cotton Gin Port, rented a house, set up a $5,000 stock of goods, and engaged a drunken fellow by the name of Morrison to superintend the selling of them to the Chickasaw people, who dwelt opposite. Pitchlynn spent most of his time at that place where he could drink free of my interference. It, however, suited the drunken Morrison and they had a grand time of it.

After a while, Pitchlynn came and told me, that Morrison had made way with the greater part of the Cotton Gin goods, and that he wanted me to go up there, take possession and save what I could of them. I finally consented. It was entirely an Indian business and many of the names were so badly spelled that I could not make out who they were.

I went to the hill country and selected a quarter section of public land, entered it, built some houses on it, and moved my family upon it as soon as possible. Here among the clean, uncropped grass, in high dry open woods, timbered with oak, hickory, chestnut and tall pines, with a gushing spring of pure, good, cool water, the children soon recovered their health.[2]

Lincecum spent much of his time with the Choctaw Indians, with whose language he became familiar. He studied their ways, habits, and adaptations to life on the frontier. He rather extravagantly sympathized with them against other white intruders, who generally regarded the Indian as a nuisance to be removed as soon as possible. The Chickasaw treaty of 1816 provided, at the request of the Indians, that, since peddlers from the United States created disputes and misunderstandings and perpetrated frauds, the United States would grant no more licenses to white traders in the Chickasaw Nation. The penalty for trading without a license was confiscation of the goods. As a result, people wishing to trade with the Chickasaws found it convenient to do so on the east bank of the Tombigbee, outside the Indian territory. Cotton Gin Port was particularly well suited to be a center of the Chickasaw trade during the 1820s, being the closest point for legal trade with the principal Chickasaw settlements. Half-breeds, classed as Indians, might very profitably serve as traders in the Indian country itself. It was in a similar situation with the Choc-

2. The Lincecum quotations are abridged excerpts from the "Autobiography of Gideon Lincecum," in *Publications of the Mississippi Historical Society*, vol. 8 (Oxford: Mississippi Historical Society, 1904), pp. 474–478.

taws that the Lincecum-Pitchlynn partnership had operated in the area west of Columbus.

In 1817 Congress appropriated money to build a road from Reynoldsburg, on the Tennessee River, south along the eastern edge of the Black Prairie to join the Natchez Trace near the Chickasaw towns. With the aid of congressional appropriations the United States constructed between 1817 and 1820 what became known as the Military Road or Jackson's Military Road. It extended from Tuscumbia, Alabama, on the Tennessee River, southwestward to a crossing of the Tombigbee River at Columbus, then southwestward across the prairies of present Lowndes and Noxubee counties, crossing the Noxubee River a little above Macon. The portion of this road west of the Tombigbee, however, quickly deteriorated from neglect, almost to the point of uselessness.

In 1820 the Mayhew Mission was founded west of Columbus in the northwest corner of present Oktibbeha County in the Black Prairie, the particular area being known as the "Mayhew Prairie." It soon became a focal point of roads and trails through a fertile region. In the 1820s a road was opened that ran from Athens, a new settlement in Monroe County, west across the Tombigbee below the site of the later town of Aberdeen, to a crossing of Tibbee Creek near Mayhew Mission, and on to Doak's Stand on the Natchez Trace north of Jackson. It was known as Doak's Road. East of the Tombigbee, in areas open to white settlement, roads radiated out from Columbus to Pickensville, Hamilton, Athens, Cotton Gin Port, and eastward to Tuscaloosa. Another road of the 1820s ran west from Cotton Gin Port to Tokshish Mission, the Chickasaw Agency, and the Chickasaw settlements in the Tupelo-Pontotoc area. There were still other roads.

The land surveyors in 1820 revealed that a considerable area east of the Tombigbee lay within the state of Mississippi. From it in 1821 the legislature created the county of Monroe, with a county seat about halfway between Cotton Gin Port and Possum Town (incorporated as Columbus in 1822). The site of the courthouse, on Henry Willis's farm a mile or so east of the Tombigbee and two miles north of the Buttahatchee River, became known as Hamilton. (Present Hamilton is a new town, about five miles away.) In 1822 a courthouse and jail were finished, and in 1825 the town was surveyed into lots. The new county was isolated from the rest of the Mississippi settlements by the Tombigbee River and extensive Indian territories (see map 8).

The growth of Columbus encouraged Congress in 1821 to provide for a road from that village westward to the Natchez Trace at Brashear's Stand, thus connecting isolated Monroe County with the rest of the state by a route through the Indian country. The Robinson Road, as it became known, did not follow the ridges but crossed extensive wet bottomlands. It was kept in repair. The opening of the Military Road and the Robinson Road made possible by the mid-1820s continuous stagecoach service from Washington to New Orleans by way of Natchez. By 1830 there were ten stands or stages (places for feeding horses) on the Robinson Road. Columbus, situated well above the floods, on the east side of the Tombigbee, was

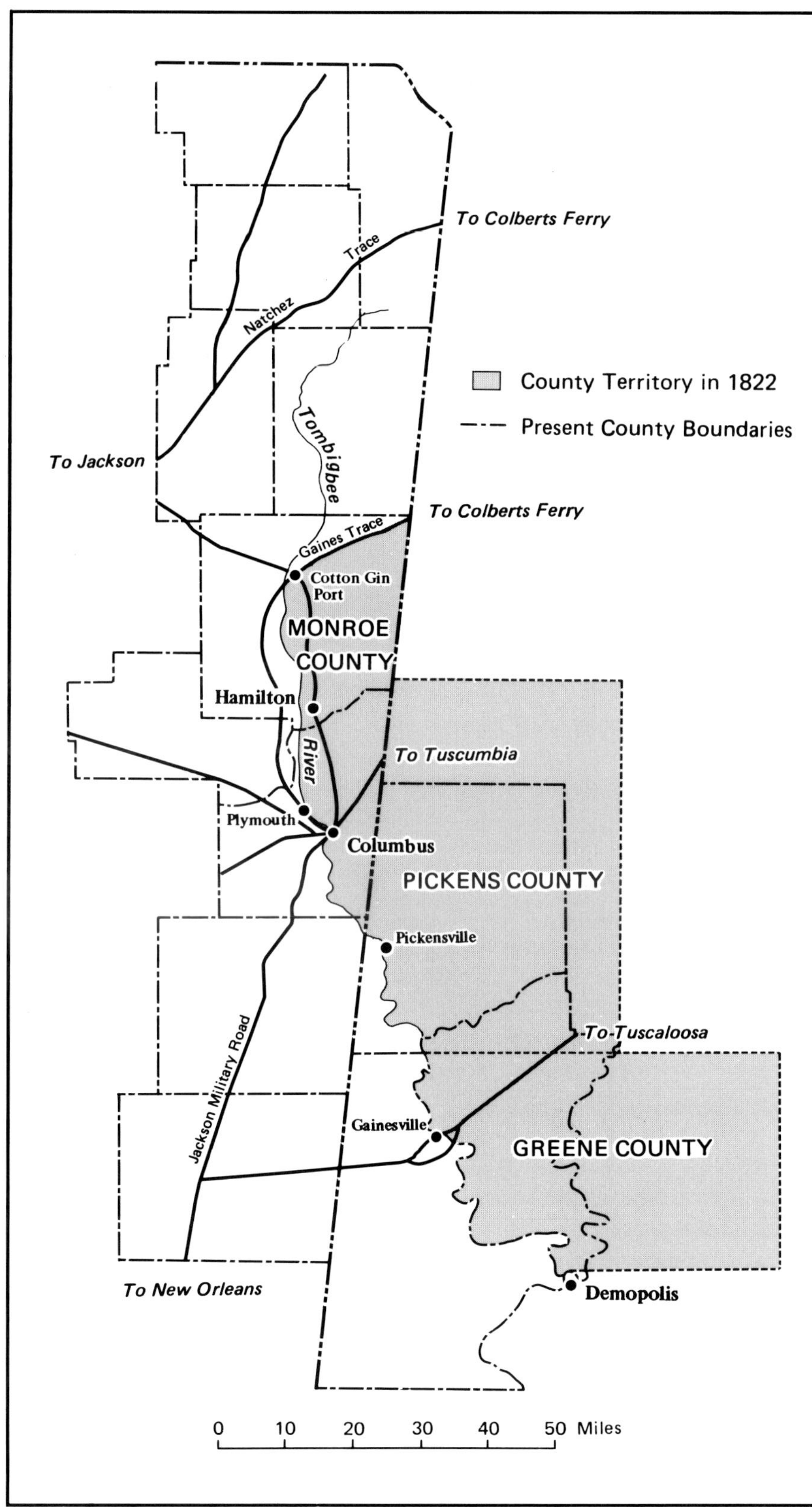

Map 8. Counties and roads in the 1820s

now connected by river with Mobile and by road with Nashville, Natchez, and New Orleans. It was thus in a good position to develop as a commercial center.

The physical structure that was to govern the patterns of early settlement was well laid before the great flow of population into the area got under way. The extensive country of best agricultural promise lay west of the Tombigbee and still belonged to the Indians. It was beginning to be probed by white pioneers, however, and the trickle of settlers would soon surge into a flood.

4

White Planters and Black Slaves, 1820–1840

The Coming of the White Settlers

The lands east of the Tombigbee in Alabama and Mississippi that had been obtained by treaties with the Creeks, Choctaws, and Chickasaws were brought to market between 1820 and 1828. Lands around Pickensville and Nashville were offered at auction in 1821, those at Columbus, Hamilton, and Cotton Gin Port in 1824. Lands offered but not sold at auction subsequently became available at "private sale" for $1.25 per acre.

The small settlements on the east side of the Tombigbee served as bases in the preparations for occupation and exploitation of the lands to the west of the Tombigbee as soon as the Indians should yield them. The Choctaws and Chickasaws, subjected intensively to the white man's ideas and finding their hunting progressively impaired, spread out from their villages and built homes and farms much like those of the frontier whites. They raised livestock and wanted the same kind of range lands that the whites did. Their agriculture became more intensive, and some of them grew considerable amounts of cotton, a few with Negro slave labor. They used the white man's money, and some opened fields and pasture lands near the Tombigbee.

The Indians were becoming more like the whites; in fact, some members of Indian society were whites, and many others were of mixed blood. Many had English names and a few were literate. Indians of white blood took the lead in developing individual farms and trying to acquire wealth. Some of them raised cattle, horses, hogs, sheep, and poultry. Some, in fact, owned slaves and produced cotton commercially. The Indians were increasingly surrounded by whites who wanted their lands, however. In 1829 Mississippi extended legal process to the Indian country, and in 1830 it extended Mississippi laws over the Indians.

In the Treaty of Dancing Rabbit Creek in 1830, the Choctaws, yielding to pressure from the federal government, ceded their lands west of the Tombigbee to the United States, promising to remove to

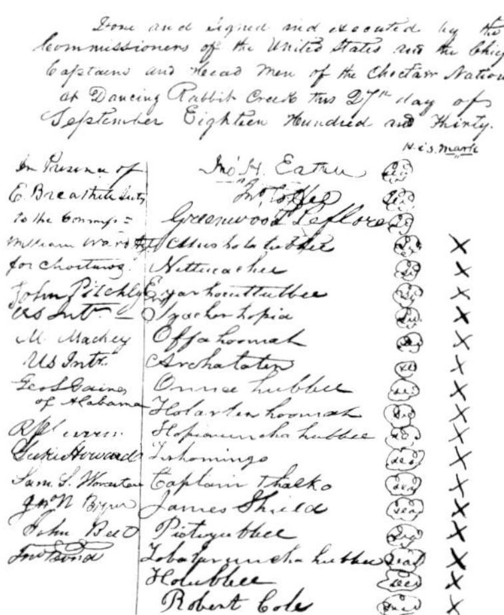

Signatures on the Treaty of Dancing Rabbit Creek, September 27, 1830. The principal signers for the United States were John H. Eaton, the secretary of war, and John Coffee, both intimate associates of President Andrew Jackson. The principal signer for the Choctaws was a chief named Greenwood Leflore. Several pages of Indian signatures (not shown) follow, mostly by mark, with the signatures of several half-breeds, some of which are also by mark. The witnesses included John Pitchlynn and George S. Gaines. Photo: National Archives.

lands to be purchased beyond the Mississippi River. The treaty provided that liberal land grants in fee simple would be made to individual Indians who chose to remain. No white settlements were to be permitted before the main body of the Indians had removed to the West. On the surface it appeared that the Indians had made a very good deal for themselves, but in practice they fared badly. White settlers moved in despite the prohibitions of the treaty. The Indians were generally swindled out of their property, and nearly all, including those of mixed blood, departed within a few years. Some townships west of the Tombigbee were surveyed in 1833–1834 and were offered for sale at auction in 1834.

The Chickasaws stayed longer, but in 1832, in the Treaty of Pontotoc, they too agreed to go to the West, saying they found themselves oppressed in their present situation because they were subject to the laws of the states in which they resided yet ignorant of the language and laws of the white men, which they could not understand or obey. The treaty provided that the ceded lands should be surveyed and sold by the United States and the proceeds turned over to the tribe. Individuals were to be paid separately for their respective improvements.

The Chickasaws were slow in obtaining suitable lands in the West, and in the meantime, despite the treaty provisions, the whites moved in, set up stores, and sought out good lands for purchase. By the Treaty of Washington in 1834, it was agreed that the United States would keep intruders out of the Chickasaw lands and would protect allotments to individual Indians. The remaining lands would be surveyed and sold under the established land system, but the price of lands not taken after one year would be reduced to $1.00 per acre, after two years to $0.50, after three years to $0.25, and after four years to $0.125. The lands were surveyed, and very extensive areas, including those along the Tombigbee River, were covered with Indian allotments, on which the United States issued patents in the early 1840s to individual Indians. Land sales in the Chickasaw cession began in 1836. Whites managed to buy up most of the Indian allotments in Mississippi, usually rather cheaply, but a few chiefs of mixed blood, with large allotments, did very well.

Establishment of County Seats

In Mississippi in 1830, a large area west of the Tombigbee was added to old Monroe County, and the county seat was moved from Hamilton to Athens. At the same time, the southern part was split off to form the new county of Lowndes, with Columbus as its seat. In Alabama in 1832, Sumter County was created from the lands west of the Tombigbee and Pickens County was expanded to the Mississippi line. New counties of convenient size were formed as the state legislatures extended their jurisdiction over the former Indian territory. Taverns, inns, stores, and private houses were used as the sites for judicial and for other government functions until permanent seats could be selected and buildings erected. The county seat was usually placed near the center of the county's population.

When the selection was controlled by other factors, or when there was a population shift or county redivision, the county seat was likely to be moved soon. When Chickasaw territory was added to Monroe County, Athens lost out to Aberdeen and then disappeared from the map. Jacinto was near the geographic center of old Tishomingo County, but when the county was subdivided, the government was moved and the town lost its vitality. Pickensville, the center of an early settlement on the Tombigbee, became the first seat of Pickens County, but as other parts of the county gained population, the seat was moved to Carrollton, a location convenient to more people. Macon's position as a county seat was strengthened by the coming of the Mobile and Ohio Railroad.

Settlements West of the Tombigbee

A considerable tide of white settlers crossed the Tombigbee in the 1830s. They came from North and South Carolina, Tennessee, Alabama, Georgia, and Virginia. Prices bid on land at public auctions were generally unimpressive, but speculators reportedly did considerable buying. As far as the public record shows, however, actual settlers did most of the speculating, and extensive lands continued to be available at the minimum price of $1.25 per acre. At this price a hundred dollars in cash would buy an eighty-acre tract.

Settlers were later in moving into the Chickasaw cession than they were into the former lands of the Choctaws, for the Chickasaws were slower in moving to the West. Settlers in the Chickasaw country found fertile bottomlands and were also attracted to the Pontotoc Ridge and the Black Prairie. In 1836 the town of Aberdeen was settled on the west bank of the Tombigbee. It quickly became a rival of Columbus.

Some of the settlers who acquired fertile lands were wealthy enough to purchase whole sections (640 acres) or even thousands of acres either directly from the government or from land speculators. Some brought large numbers of slaves with them. Other settlers had smaller holdings and some none at all.

Cultural Traditions and Settlement Patterns

The lowland and upland cultural traditions of the South, tracing their respective origins to European backgrounds, were both strongly represented among the early settlers in the Upper Tombigbee area. Blacks arriving as slaves constituted a third element. The lowland tradition was associated with plantation agriculture and production for market, the upland tradition with stock raising and self-sufficient farming. In the eighteenth century both had become well established in the southern colonies, and each had evolved its own peculiar character through the progressive adaptation of old European life-styles to the physical environment of the interior South. Although the traditions overlapped and were not uniform in their characteristics, their distinctiveness and persistence are evident. Both contributed heavily to the cultural origins of the Tombigbee settlements, where the two mingled but did not form an amalgam.

Migrating southern colonists sought out familiar cultural and physical features in the landscape. For them traditional ways of maintaining life had been tried and proven, and experimentation with new forms involved substantial risk. Stability and psychological comfort were provided by familiar vegetation and the soil types it represented, by the construction of dwellings of familiar types with familiar wood, and by the location of a site near good water with suitable land for cultivation, space for other settlers, range for livestock, and so on. On meeting the physical geography of the Upper Tombigbee Valley, the upland people found the Fall Line Hills section a natural extension of their Appalachian and Piedmont habitats and readily made themselves at home.

The Black Prairie constituted a novel terrain for prospective colonists, for it differed radically in topography, soils, and hydrology from any previous environmental medium in their experience. In general, upland southerners bypassed and neglected the Black Prairie as a place of settlement, but settlers of lowland tradition proved willing to experiment in making it productive, bringing with them their preference for the plantation lifestyle and introducing slavery and cotton cultivation on a large scale.

In both traditions, there seems to have been a subconscious drive selectively to recreate and maintain accustomed patterns. The inherited concepts and ways of doing things were constantly being tested, however, and were reluctantly modified or rejected as experience gave a measure of their appropriateness to the new frontier environment. Innovation based strictly upon local conditions was not conspicuous, and conditions were too varied and time was too limited to permit much growth of peculiarly indigenous patterns. The physiographic and cultural divisions of the Tenn-Tom country tended to be associated more with the extensive contiguous outside areas than with each other. There developed no "Tombigbee culture," although a pattern of Black Belt–Black Prairie mores did evolve that resists change to this day.

The black slave immigrants to the Tombigbee Valley in the early years of settlement generally came from the older plantation areas of the Atlantic seaboard; perhaps a few came directly from Africa. They lived largely in the place and after the fashion that their owners determined. While blacks possessed many cultural traits distinct from those of whites, their material culture came to reflect strongly the elements of the Euro-American lifestyle with which they were required to harmonize.

The problems of a settler in finding a suitable place for settlement and the issues and choices involved are illustrated in letters that James Nance of Pickensville wrote to his father in North Carolina. He passed the summer of 1832 in examining lands in various places. In July he made an eight-day trip alone into the Choctaw Nation to look for a place to settle. For two days he saw only Indians, whose language he could not understand. Viewing the prairie, he said:

> It looks like some ocean, not a tree nor a shrub only once and a while some scrubby blackjack, and is covered in grape and weeds from knee to six feet high and take the country generally though very rich lands enough to make any man leave home.

> But the disadvantage in this is no water at this season of the year. . . . In places I rode from morning until night before I got a drop and then not good and camped with the Indians. In winter the muddiest country you ever saw and most disagreeable. . . . If government was to give me one thousand acres, I could not be satisfied to move there in my opinion for I think it will be a sickly place. Let others make the trial before me.

> Great many disadvantages will and does attend that country tho the richest land I ever saw it is more than as good again as any land on Swift Creek. You cannot manure any land in Wake County [in North Carolina?] equal to it. I have no doubt but that it will bring 1500 weight of cotton to the acre and not a single tree upon it.[1]

Others were already moving into the prairie, but Nance went to the land office at Tuscaloosa and bought 160 acres of rich land on the east side of the Tombigbee and began clearing it. "The disadvantage," he said, "is that it is subject to overflow in large freshets. . . . We cannot live nearer than one mile and half with safety for health tho I have seen people live in worse places than that." Much land along the river was subject to flooding, in other words, and mosquito-borne diseases were a menace in swampy areas. Nance observed that he had gone to a cow-selling. He had killed four wildcats and four deer. Along the river, where the cane was thick, he had been frightened by a bear. He described his living arrangements in 1832 as follows: "The house we live in is a small house built of logs with a shed on each side and pyazer [piazza] on the ends, no shutters or doors, a part of the floor is split pieces of poplar. I live at home and owe nothing."

Nance soon sold his North Carolina farm and borrowed additional money to buy slaves and land near the Tombigbee. In 1833 he wrote his father:

Canebrakes like this one deterred settlement in some places along the Tombigbee River margins. The young canes provided forage for livestock, however, especially in winter, when food was scarce. In such a thicket James Nance met a bear. Photo: Roland Harper Collection, University of Alabama Library.

1. The Nance quotations, here abridged, are from typed copies of Nance's original letters. The copies are owned by Catherine Spell of Carrollton. The authors' thanks are due to Jack D. Elliott, Jr., Sanders Huff, and Mrs. Spell for making the copies available. The originals are not extant.

> We have eighteen in family, now we require your greasy meat
> sticks. . . . My heaviest hog weighed 248 lbs. and I bought the hogs
> from the Indians in August at 4 dollars a piece. . . . I have 20 hogs for
> another year I also have 9 head of cattle 4 head of horses. I made a
> planty of corn to serve my need tho I bought 52 bushels. . . . I bought it
> four [for] a debt that was owing to me at 50 cents per bushel. . . . I
> made 2800 lbs. of cotton and only had 20 acres. . . . This is a plentiful
> country to them that use industry.

In April 1833 Nance went to Mobile on a steamboat with his cotton, where, he said, "I purchased all my necessarys such as sugar, coffee, flour, fish, molasses, irons, blacksmith tools, sawmill irons and when I quit I owed them three hundred and forty-seven dollars." He made a good cotton crop in 1833 and sought to buy more land, but the price in his neighborhood was fifteen to twenty dollars per acre, so he sought lands elsewhere at the government's minimum price. He must have prospered, for Nance's Ferry across the Tombigbee and Nance's steam mills on the western side have left their mark on the map, as have Nance's brick kilns. Nance's descendants lived long in the area. While Nance was no literary artist, the fragmentary observations in his letters tell us much about the country on the Tombigbee in which he lived in the early 1830s. Living too close to the river was highly undesirable, but some years of experience alone could indicate a safe distance.

Mary J. Welsh, who was born at St. Stephens on the lower Tombigbee in 1823, moved with her parents in February 1834 up the river to Gainesville, then overland twenty miles northwest to the border of the prairie country, where the family joined her father's brother, who had moved there the year before. She tells her own story:

> The road through the woods followed the newly made blazes, forded
> Bodka creek and crossed a section of Wild Horse prairie, leading in a
> northwesterly direction. . . . The trip I made on horseback, behind my
> mother. . . . This was my introduction to pioneer life, which I after
> wards enjoyed to the full measure of a child's capacity. . . .

> The earliest settlers were of various degrees of wealth, but all men of
> strictly moral and religious sentiment, which gave a healthy tone to the
> whole community infinitely more valuable than any amount of material
> wealth with out it. . . . They built a school house and churches and
> procured the services of a teacher and pastors respectively. . . .

> Most of the land in our immediate neighborhood was heavily tim-
> bered with a dense undergrowth. As the "clearing," fencing and pre-
> paring for a crop had to be accomplished by manual labor, one stroke at
> a time, it was slow and heavy work. But the soil was fertile and amply
> repaid the laborers in the yield of corn, cotton, potatoes and peas, the
> crops generally raised. . . . The early cotton crops were so heavy that

the larger boys were stopped from school every fall to help pick it out.
New land was cleared for many years.

The scarcity of water was the most serious difficulty the pioneers had
to encounter. The only water courses within available distance were
Noxubee and Wahalak creeks. Many wells were sunk, but only a few
outlasted the wet season. Stock was driven to the creeks every few days
in summer. Every week or two the family washing was carried there.
Rainwater was caught and treasured. Not a drop of clean water was ever
thrown on the ground. . . . I often wonder now how we managed to
get along with so little water.[2]

Settlers of the Nance and Welsh types were numerous, and some
of them had greater resources. These people were clearly not like
Lincecum. They were small-scale slaveowners, who carefully selected good lands. They were frugal, they educated their children,
and they prospered. Others, without slaves and with lesser assets,
sought to make it strictly by their own labor and that of their families.
They had to concentrate on subsistence until they could produce a
surplus of a marketable crop.

Concerning the early settlers, historian Frank L. Owsley has this
to say:

The method of migration and settlement in the South was fairly uniform during the pioneer period. Friends and relatives living in the same
or neighboring communities formed one or more parties and moved
out together, and when they had reached the promised land they
constituted a new community, which was called a "settle-ment,"—and
still is so called. Settlements were frequently miles apart, and the
inhabitants of a single settlement would be more scattered than they
had been in the old community in the East; and other settlers would
come in after the first trek in smaller groups or in single families and fill
in the interstices. These later comers would often be relatives or friends
of those who had come first, or friends of their friends. Frequently
church congregations would move in a body.[3]

Some of these migrants would prosper and some would not. Concerning what was to happen to them Owsley adds:

Those agricultural immigrants who had deliberately shunned the fertile
but tough clay and lime soils and had settled upon inferior sandy-loam
lands placed limitations . . . upon their future economic prosperity in a
way similar to the piney wood and mountain folk. While many became
well-to-do, few became rich, for the economic level of an agricultural

2. The Welsh quotations in this chapter are abridged from Mary J. Welsh, "Recollections of Pioneer Life in Mississippi," in *Publications of the Mississippi Historical
Society*, vol. 4 (Oxford: Mississippi Historical Society, 1901), pp. 342–356.
3. The Owsley quotations are from Frank L. Owsley [Sr.], "The Pattern of Migration and Settlement on the Southern Frontier," *Journal of Southern History*, 11 (1945):
162, 171, 175–176.

people can rise but little above the fertility of the soil. On such lands were many large farmers and small planters with ten or fifteen slaves, but there were few if any large planters. Those agricultural migrants who moved into the rich lands were the most fortunate; for, while most who settled in the black belt were possessed of only moderate means at the time of settlement, nearly all rose greatly in the economic scale and many who were poor in the beginning became immensely wealthy before 1860. There were thus several regions differing greatly in fertility of soil, and consequently in wealth. As between these regions there was segregation; but within each region there was very little. In the black belt, for example, the property of the non-slaveholders and the great planters lay intermingled, and the census and tax lists show that the values of their lands and their agricultural productions per acre were about the same.

There was still another class of settlers, however, with a different background and way of life. The herdsmen, men of the upland tradition, raised cattle and hogs and sometimes other livestock on vast ranges which they did not own. These people were generally not literate, and the accounts of them come primarily from the occasional observations of others. Since they produced few written records, historians have tended to ignore them. They were usually squatters on public land or Indian land—or anybody's land. They required large areas for range pastures; such areas were available in the mountains, hills, and the piney woods, and particularly attractive were the canebrakes of the river and creek floodplains in Alabama and Mississippi, where all-year pasture was available. Owsley observes that "grazing as distinct from livestock feeding was of greater relative importance in the antebellum South than in any other part of the United States. Indeed, the South produced a larger number of mules, swine, and beef cattle in proportion to population than any [other] section until 1860."

The best pasture lands were also those best suited to agriculture, and the herdsmen moved into those parts of the public domain that land-buying farmers would soon acquire. It was inevitable that they would in time be crowded out, as they had been from the more easterly pastures. As we shall see in a later chapter, the coincident dynamics of time, geography, and circumstance would seal their fate. As Owsley explains it: "As long as the pine belt and highlands were not overcrowded by man and beast, the range remained good and these semi-pastoral folk lived well and possessed a strong sense of security. They were certainly not poor whites as a class; but neither were many of them wealthy. Eventually, when these regions began to be crowded—and this was happening in a few places prior to the Civil War—the people would be compelled to graze fewer cattle and cultivate more and more land until they would find themselves farmers cultivating poor soil without much knowledge of agriculture."

The pastoral people were an ever-present factor in the early settlement of the Upper Tombigbee Valley. They raised corn and vegetables for home consumption, and, where the fertility of their little valleys permitted, grew rather extensive amounts of corn for animal feed. The cotton farmers and planters who settled on the new lands also had livestock, but their main emphasis was on plant husbandry.

Self-sufficiency

Several factors tended to impose a high degree of self-sufficiency on pioneer society. One was the difficulty of transporting needed articles to the settler's home. Even greater difficulty was experienced in transporting the heavy and bulky products of fields and forests to market. Distances were great, the roads were bad when not impassable, and distant markets usually had closer and more accessible sources of supply. Furthermore, pioneer settlers were so preoccupied with the problems of survival and subduing the wilderness that producing for market tended to be difficult. "Living at home" was the general rule of the frontier. There remained, however, some necessities which had to be bought: axes, hoes, pots and pans, guns and ammunition, and numerous small articles of household and farm equipment. To obtain money with which to buy these items, even the small frontier farmer had to market something.

Pioneers with sufficient capital, education, and experience, and with slaves for labor, showed a general determination to prosper. The successful ones acquired fertile lands and made their plantations not only largely self-sufficient but also efficient producers of cotton, which was by all measures the principal market crop of the region. Cotton was needed as a raw material by manufacturers in England and by the growing industries of New England. Employment of slaves in eastern Virginia had lost much of its profitability, and a surplus of slaves from Virginia and other parts of the southern Atlantic seaboard was available for purchase by the planters of Alabama and Mississippi. Enterprising planters borrowed money when they could get it, for conditions seemed to promise prosperity. The panics of 1837 and 1839 seriously upset their headway, but boom times were to come in the years ahead.

The agricultural establishments in the Black Prairie, in the fertile bottoms, and on Pontotoc Ridge in the 1830s ranged from single-family homesteads without slaves to plantations with a hundred or more. Not all farms in the fertile regions were plantations, but many smaller farmers tended toward the plantation economy and became small planters. The plantation and large farm dominated social and political life. A planter society emerged, transplanted from the states to the east. A considerable number of the immigrants were members of professions, such as lawyers, doctors, ministers, and newspaper editors, but most of these people engaged in agriculture in addition to pursuing their professions. They were plantation oriented. While time was required to develop the facilities for living in the fertile plantation districts in the 1830s, rapidly expanding production for market lay ahead. During the 1830s characteristics developed that were to predominate during the next two decades.

The northeastern part of the Chickasaw cession was particularly attractive to herdsmen, who found there not only good grazing in the hills but also very fertile, although somewhat limited, bottomlands that were good for corn. The population in the northeastern counties did not become as dense as that of the more southerly valley counties, and the general character of their settlements differed. (County statistics appear in the appendix.) Land sales lagged notably, and the prices paid for later purchases were made very low by the application of the graduation principle. But the bounty of nature was considerable. Wild game could be hunted, and fish abounded in many of the streams. Cattle and hogs largely raised themselves. A house could be built with much labor but little expense. A suitable location for a corn patch and garden was not hard to find and "clearing" of new land could be accomplished by merely girdling the trees with an axe and leaving the dead limbs to rain down in windstorms over the next twenty years. Leather could be obtained from locally grown cattle. Home-produced wool and cotton could be spun and woven into cloth for clothing.

Earliest transportation into the Upper Tombigbee Valley was by pack horse, aided in season by small boats on the Tombigbee and sometimes on its tributaries. As we have seen in a previous chapter, an early system of trails developed and later came roads for wagon transportation. In order to avoid the numerous creek and river swamps, the roads tended to follow the ridges, and often the routes were circuitous. Swamps had to be crossed, but sometimes floods made passage impossible for months. Horses and oxen were used to pull carriages and wagons, and often large teams were required. Horses could become mired in the muck of the Black Belt and might even pull off a hoof.

People who hoped to prosper had to turn out large quantities of marketable products and get them to market, so the demand for transportation and marketing facilities became great. Existing transportation routes, especially that of the Tombigbee River, deeply affected the pattern of settlement.

A great many bars in the Tombigbee provided fords during six to eight months of the year. Ferries were established for crossing the river and its tributary streams, but they tended to be spaced far apart and to be inoperable at high water. Ferry services were provided by private owners under license. The boats were propelled by muscle power with the aid of a rope stretched across the river or lying on its bottom. They were built as scows with flat sides and in earlier times were known as "flats." Getting on and off with a team and wagon or carriage could be a dangerous undertaking, for skittish horses could plunge into the river with the vehicle. Even with a ferry it was troublesome to take livestock across the river. Besides this, the ferryman charged a fee, which people with very little money found irksome.

In a country where settlements were widely scattered and transportation was difficult, most people led an isolated life. The social effect was only one of the problems. Markets were distant, and the

The Waverly ferry in this twentieth-century photograph looks much as it did in antebellum times. Such ferries were generally operated by hand-drawn lines. Embarking and disembarking with teams and livestock could be dangerous. Photo: Lowndes County Public Library.

swamps and bad roads sharply limited the range of commercial traffic by wagon, especially in the rainy season, yet agricultural products required cheap transportation to distant markets. Cotton, the principal product of the area, happened to be rather valuable in proportion to its weight, compared with corn or other grains, but transporting it was still full of problems. The late summer and early fall constituted the dry season best suited to wagon traffic, but the rainy season had arrived by the time the cotton had been harvested, the seeds removed with a gin, and the lint baled.

The age-old way of transporting livestock to market was to let the animals walk. Cattle could be driven considerable distances, and in antebellum times great numbers of hogs were moved from middle Tennessee southwestward through Tishomingo County to the farms and plantations of Mississippi. Farmers in that county produced corn for sale to the drovers. The importance of better roads was generally recognized, but the magnitude of the task of providing a newly settled region with transportation facilities adequate to its needs often seemed overwhelming. When the states extended their government over the lands of the Choctaws and Chickasaws in the 1830s, the legislatures created various new counties. The county governments could require all able-bodied men to contribute several days of service each year to the building and maintenance of roads, but roads remained bad.

In the Tombigbee River and its branches there was a natural transportation system which had its primary focus in Mobile. The navigability of the streams generally varied in accordance with the distance from that commercial center. The Upper Tombigbee was a small river, and its various tributaries were yet smaller. To get the cotton out, and sometimes logs and lumber and other products, it was often feasible to build simple vessels with flat sides called "flatboats." Propelled by the current and manipulated with long sweeps, they could be floated downstream at high water, but they could not readily come back. The smaller keelboats not only moved downstream but could also, with the aid of much muscle power, be poled slowly back upstream to the point of departure.

The keelboat *Cotton Gin Cutter* from Cotton Gin Port arrived at Mobile on January 5, 1820, and the barge *Southern Trader* arrived there from Columbus the next month. In 1821 low water made the river difficult to navigate, but the keelboat *Columbus Hornet* made the trip from Columbus to Mobile. During the 1820s there was little for a keelboat or flatboat to haul from the Upper Tombigbee except what was shipped from sparsely settled Monroe County through the landings at Cotton Gin Port, Hamilton, Columbus, and Pickensville. With the opening of the lands west of the Tombigbee in the 1830s, however, foundations were laid for a rapidly increasing commercial production, which required access to a market. Flatboats and keelboats were used on the Upper Tombigbee until the late years of the nineteenth century.

The tributary streams of the Tombigbee on the east were generally unsuited to navigation, with the possible exceptions of the Sipsey River and part of the Buttahatchee River, but there were many streams on the western side of sufficient volume and with little fall. Just above Gainesville the Noxubee River entered the Tombigbee. At high water it might be navigated all the way to Macon. Above Columbus, Tibbee Creek with its various branches offered interesting possibilities. Above Cotton Gin Port, the East Fork (Mackey's Creek) and West Fork (Old Town Creek) were usable for navigation, and there were smaller streams of more limited potential. All were clogged with logs and obstructed by overhanging trees, and the water was usually too low to float a boat over the obstructions. If the overhanging and fallen trees and an occasional snag could be removed, however, many of these streams could float a flatboat at high water.

Mill dams and fish traps presented obstructions on creeks, and conflicts developed because some people wanted to have the benefit of such facilities, while others wanted to operate boats. The county boards of police issued licenses for the building of mill dams in Mississippi. It was illegal to obstruct a creek declared navigable by state law.

Steamboats ascended the Tombigbee early in the 1820s, and Mobile became the emporium of the Upper Tombigbee trade. Beginning in 1831, the Mobile newspapers reported each year the names of steamboats engaging in traffic on the Upper Tombigbee. In that year they listed the *Marietta, Corsair, Wild Cat,* and *Sun* as being in the Columbus trade. On one trip in 1832 the *Marietta* brought to Mobile 465 bales of cotton, 37 bales of deerskins, 1,300 bales of cowhides, a box of furs, and 5 barrels of beeswax. This cargo seems to have been fairly representative of the commercial production of the upper country at that time.

Travel by steamboat, and flatboat too, was dangerous. There were sandbars and snags and overhanging trees, and the possibility of bursting steam pipes and boilers added to the risks. There was the ever-present chance of fire, and the possibility of falling overboard was not to be taken lightly. On May 16, 1825, the little 45-ton side-wheeler *Allegheny*, returning to Mobile from Hamilton, struck a snag twelve miles below Columbus and sank. On January 19, 1837, the 144-ton side-wheeler *Iowa* caught fire and sank at Fairfield in Pickens County. Other accidents were common, culminating in the *Eliza Battle* disaster in 1858. Carriages, wagons, horses, and oxen supplemented the river as carriers of passengers and freight, and when the water was low, they were the only means of transportation.

Early Homes

While early settlers in the Upper Tombigbee Valley varied in wealth and in geographic origins, on the frontier they experienced common immediate needs and tended to respond to similar problems in the same way. They invested much of their capital in land, and their labor capabilities were stretched by the urgency of preparing for agricultural production. The quality of rural housing, for both rich and poor, was a matter of generally secondary concern, and few men initially provided much more than basic shelter for their families.

The earliest homes were simple log structures made of material from the adjacent forest. Erecting them was the first major activity of newly arrived settlers, who commonly helped each other with construction. A log cabin for temporary protection against the elements could be built with one to three days of community labor. Notched logs were laid horizontally to form a rectangular crib, and the cracks were chinked with mud. Openings for doors, windows, and chimneys were cut after the log walls were up. The roof consisted of long, thin, overlapping slabs of wood. Window openings were small and mostly unprotected, although some were fitted with crude wooden shutters with leather hinges. Nails were helpful but not essential. Floors were of dirt or in some instances of wood slabs or split logs (puncheons). Poles might support a loft for storage and additional sleeping space.

The essential cabin was a single room, or pen, with sides measuring about sixteen feet. In it were conducted the family's domestic operations: cooking, eating, and sleeping. Furniture was simple and improvised. The table, if not a big stump, was half of a split log supported on four round legs, the bedstead a frame built into a corner. A few wooden pegs set into the log walls provided storage for tools and utensils. Crude porches and lean-to shelters might be added to front, back, or sides to provide more protected space.

Mary J. Welsh tells of her experience as a child at Old Wahalak, in the northeast corner of Kemper County, in 1834:

> The cabins were roughly built of logs, with stick and mud chimneys and clapboard roof. The cracks of dwelling houses were lined with

boards and daubed with mud. . . . The windows, if any [,] were openings about two feet square, closed by a curtain, or at best by a shutter, like the door. . . . The floor, if by good fortune it was of plank, was more costly than all the rest of the building. The only mill within reach was on Running Water creek about twenty miles away. . . . Sawed lumber was costly and could be used only in building the family room. It was put down loosely and when well shrunken was driven up tight and nailed. A few people, at a cost of much labor hewed out "puncheons" for floors; others built their cabins on the ground and lived there comfortably and contentedly with their families, waiting for better times. One man who had only enough plank to cover three-fourths of his floor left the other fourth open. As he had no slaves the one room served for kitchen, dining room, and living room. . . .

A few of these dwellings had two cabins with what we called a "passage" between them; others had a shed room, the frame of which was made of skinned poles, weatherboarded with clapboards. Most farmers were content however with one room for the first year. I remember one cabin [her own family's] was built with a view to having another put opposite to it, hence the roof was extended over the prospective "passage," and the sills protruded on both sides. The housewife placed a high-posted bedstead under this roof and hung thick homespun curtains around and over it, and thus made a private and pleasant sleeping place for two of her boys. . . . The next year they had a room across the "passage," but it had a dirt floor. In this same floorless room I took my first lesson in Natural History by watching a toad catch flies. . . . Of course, there was abundant ventilation in these houses and it was pure and healthful air from the woods. Fireplaces were large and wood plentiful, and it was heaped on without stint. As the years passed and facilities increased, many improvements were introduced. Large frame houses, elegantly furnished, dotted the country here and there, but down to the War between the States many of the people were content to dwell in log houses with modern improvements and furnishings. . . .

The furniture of these early cabins was scant. The long journeys in wagons from the older states prevented the bringing of anything but the bare necessities. Those provident housewives all brought their feather beds and bed clothing, a bedstead or two, a few chairs, a little table furniture, a few things for the kitchen, and the indispensable [spinning] wheel and cards. The few empty barrels and goods boxes they possessed were utilized as furniture.

As life and livelihood became more secure, and the critical pressures of settlement receded, the early settlers or their children replaced temporary dwellings with more substantial log houses, featuring larger size, hewn timbers, shingle roofs, stone chimneys, and glass windows. Iron hinges replaced the earlier leather and wood ones, and stairways were installed instead of crude slat ladders for access to loft space. In many instances the loft was enlarged to a full second floor, with either a half- or full-story roof. Floors were almost always of puncheons or wide plank. Cracks were chinked

This servant's house on the Thornhill plantation in Greene County in 1934 is an old slave cabin of single-pen log construction. Photo: Library of Congress.

with mud, and walls were commonly plastered. Such houses were far more comfortable than log cabins, and some have seen continuous use, with additions and modifications, down to the present.

The several adaptations emerging from crude cabins before 1840 provided the basis for the house designs which dominated the region for the next century. First was the single-pen house, the most direct derivative from the log cabin. It was rectangular, with one basic room, and was either one story or one and a half stories high. It generally measured about sixteen feet by twenty feet, with a gable roof, a rear door opposite the front, and side windows flanking an end chimney. When such a structure did not provide sufficient space for a growing family, the basic form had to be expanded. Apart from lean-to extensions at the front and back, there were three primary ways to add space: by internal rearrangement, by expansion to the side or rear, and by upward expansion. In the first case the basic one-room rectangle or square was divided by a light frame partition into two smaller rooms, usually a kitchen and a living area. In an existing house this division did not add more space.

While in some instances single-pen houses were enlarged by adding more wall logs to increase the height of the building by another story or half story, it was a more common practice to add a complete second room to one side. If the new room was put against the gable-end wall opposite the chimney, a hall-and-parlor double-pen house was created. If the new room was added to the chimney side, the result was a central-chimney double-pen building of the "saddlebag" type.

A third type of double house was created by the construction of two log rooms, leaving a central passage ten to twelve feet wide between them, the whole structure being under the same roof. A form of double house common in the Upper Tombigbee area was the "dogtrot," produced by keeping the central hallway open at front and back to provide air circulation. The dogtrot was especially suited to the local summer climate.

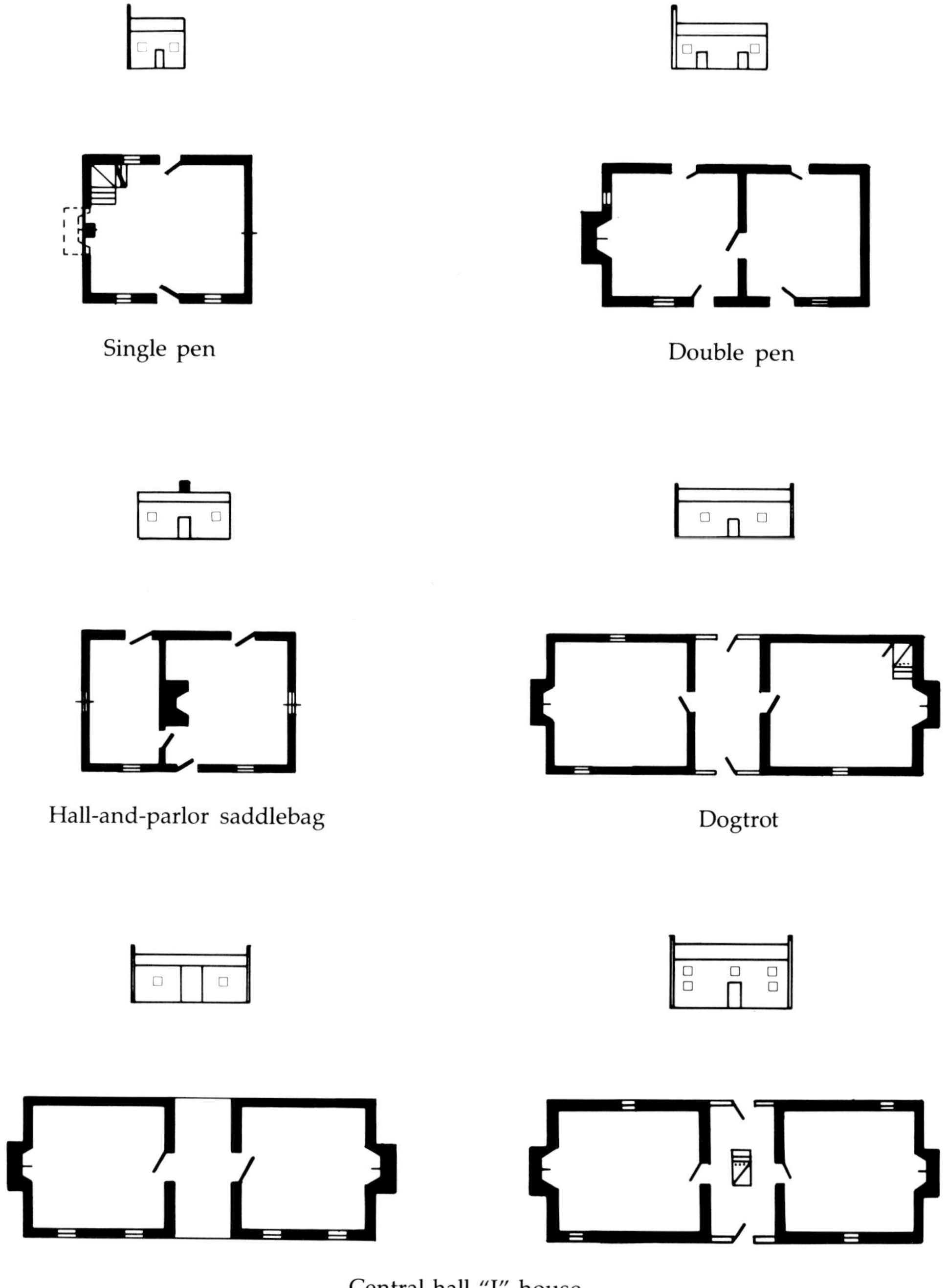

Figure 1. Regional "folk" house forms of the nineteenth century.

A combination log and frame dogtrot house near Sumterville in Sumter County illustrates the expansion of single-pen to double-pen house form. Photo: Roland Harper Collection, University of Alabama Library.

The Grassdale plantation house at Eutaw (late 1820s) is an excellent example of the "I" house style, with front porch and end additions. Photo: Roy Swayze.

The most visually impressive of the log structures emerged when the douple-pen or central-hall house was expanded by the addition of a full second story with a stairway from the lower to the upper hall. Such houses—one room deep, two rooms wide, and two stories high—were originally constructed on simple, clean lines without external embellishment. Partly because of their floor plan and shape, they are known to students of architecture as "I" houses, and some-times designated "plantation plain." Early examples had outside chimneys in the gables, often made of brick. There were several vari-ations of the basic "I" plan, usually incorporating lean-to structures to accommodate the desire for front or back porches, a kitchen, more storage space, or different locations for the chimneys. Such dwellings reflected the affluence of their owners. Immigrating men of sub-

The Old Inn at Darracott in Clay County served the main stagecoach line between Columbus and Aberdeen in the mid-nineteenth century. Photo: Evans Memorial Library, Aberdeen.

stance sometimes built them soon after arrival. Usually, however, prospering farmers created them by remodeling their existing single- or double-pen houses. Whatever the circumstances of its construction, the "I" house during the period 1830–1840 was the rural mansion of the Upper Tombigbee and the precursor of the much more ostentatious houses which proliferated after 1840.

Farm buildings of logs served as prototypes for schools, churches, courthouses, and stores. A home could be expanded into a tavern or an inn by the addition of a long, low porch, a room for public entertainment, a taproom, and rooms for lodging. To the basic log designs were gradually applied the advantages of sawn timber and frame construction as the restrictions of pioneer times were relaxed. Even into the twentieth century, use of log designs and their frame derivative allowed the poor man to build in remote districts where there was abundant timber.

From the designs of these simple houses and farm buildings, constructed quickly with local materials, tools, and skills, evolved the folk, or vernacular, architecture of the Upper Tombigee Valley. A compact, economic, and efficient layout was the rule, and practical use and comfort were the dominant considerations. Folk structures are usually distinguished by architectural historians from "academic" or "polite" housing, which is purposefully aimed at public taste and approval. These decorative styles were not locally created but were imported from other regions and other cultural settings. "Academic" housing characteristics which were in time to become significant in the Upper Tombigbee area were only beginning to be introduced in the 1830s. The regional florescence of "academic" housing is discussed in chapter 6.

5

Flush Times, 1840–1860

The Plantation Economy

In general the years between 1840 and 1860 represent flush times in the Tombigbee country. Having established their self-sufficiency, owners of slaves and fertile lands turned their attention increasingly to the production of crops for market, for that was the basic way to prosperity.

A large and well-developed plantation was a multifaceted operation and demanded considerable agricultural technology and skill in human relations in its management. There was usually an office close to the big house, and slave cabins were either scattered in shady locations or were arranged in rows extending back from the main building. A plantation might also contain buildings and equipment for several local service industries.

At first some of the soils were considered too rich for cotton, because they tended to promote the growth of the stalk at the expense of the boll and fiber. But after several years of cultivation in corn and other crops, these soils became better suited to cotton production. Repeated use without crop rotation tended to reduce the yields after a few more years, however, so there soon arose a demand for bringing in new land to sustain production.

It was difficult to plow the sticky prairie soils, especially with the plows then available. Cotton was planted in the spring by hand or with the aid of a drill on ridges formed by the plow. The plow and hoe were used for cultivation, and thinning had to be done with a hoe. Fertilizer was rarely used. Rust, rot, blight, and worms reduced plant yields and sometimes caused quite serious losses. In the late summer the crop was "laid by" (cultivation stopped), allowing some weeks of respite from heavy labor in "dog days," while the cotton bolls matured and opened. Picking followed, an arduous and tedious task. During the early winter, seeds were removed from the harvested cotton with the aid of a "gin" (short for "engine"), a machine which pulled off the lint.

Corn was an important crop on both plantation and farm, occupy-

Opposite, above: Gaineswood at Demopolis, of plastered brick, is one of America's architectural treasures. Built between 1843 and 1859 by General H. B. Whitfield, it has been restored by the Alabama Historical Commission. Photo: Jan Weaver.

Opposite, below: Waverly Mansion stands on a splendid setting near the Tombigbee River in Clay County. It is among the most grandiose of all Black Belt–Black Prairie homes. Photo: Jan Weaver.

Above: Rosemount in southern Greene County (1832) is located a mile off the country road between Boligee and Forkland. Some historians of art believe this to be the most grandly conceived mansion in Alabama. Photo: Jan Weaver.

This old slave house on the Thornhill plantation, photographed in 1934, is of mid-nineteenth century log dogtrot construction, with a wood shingle roof. Photo: Library of Congress.

ing a great deal of acreage and requiring much labor. It was grown on the rich prairie soils and bottomlands, on Pontotoc Ridge, and in the coves of the hill country. It could be consumed by people as fresh "ros'n ears" (roasting ears) or in the form of hominy and meal, and it could be fermented and distilled to make corn whiskey. It was also a staple animal feed. Most of the corn was consumed in the localities where it was produced, although some parts of the prairie produced a surplus. Corn was usually planted on ridges and was plowed and hoed several times. Sometimes the whole stalk and leaves were pulled green for fodder. In wooded areas where stumps and dead trees remained, cultivation with the hoe rather than the plow necessarily predominated. The main corn harvest came in the fall, after the ears had dried and hardened.

Wheat came to be grown in some areas, notably on Pontotoc Ridge, and other grains were produced to some extent, especially oats. Garden crops included peas and beans and potatoes. Some fields were also planted in peas and beans for direct consumption by livestock. The work stock, which had to be well fed to be efficient, included horses and oxen and a few mules. Riding and buggy horses were numerous, and considerable poultry was raised for home consumption.

The large size of landholdings, the high degree of self-sufficiency, and the smallness of the scattered population did not encourage village growth. There were little hamlets with a store or two and perhaps a blacksmith shop and a physician's house, often located where two roads crossed. Plantation owners made their principal purchases and sales through factors in Mobile, which they often visited in the winter.

The Tombigbee River with its steamboats and flatboats formed the main stem of commercial transportation, and wagon roads fanned out from the river landings. Steamboat navigation was possible dur-

The stagecoach inn at Forkland served travelers on the important early road between Demopolis, Pickensville, and Columbus. Photo: Jan Weaver.

ing only about five months of the year. It was supplemented, and in the dry seasons supplanted, by stagecoaches and wagons. In the upper parts of the Tenn-Tom country there was some overland trade with Memphis and by the Tennessee River with Nashville, but cotton and heavy goods nearly all moved down the Tombigbee lifeline to Mobile. People unable to make their own arrangements in Mobile depended upon more affluent neighbors and occasional country and town merchants to provide an intermediate market. The low floodplain of the river valley was in many places quite wide, and the river channel often ran close to the bluff on one side, leaving a floodplain extending a mile of two on the other, so that conditions of settlement and tillage might vary widely on opposite sides of the river.

The surge in agricultural production and the needs of trade stimulated the founding and growth of towns along the river. Names suggestive of grandeur appeared, such as Memphis, Warsaw, Vienna, Athens, Aberdeen, Columbus, and Waverly. Some of the river landings, however, had more down-to-earth appellations, such as Mrs. Cox's Woodyard and Catfish Bend. Of the towns Columbus was the most favorably situated and the most important, but there were times when its dominant position was challenged. After the Choctaw lands west of the river had been opened to settlement, landings along the western bank were more favorably located to serve the transportation and trade requirements of the settlers on the fertile prairies than was Columbus. Passage across the Tombigbee at Columbus involved expensive and troublesome ferriage and could be interrupted completely at high water. West Port, only a mile away, was on the west bank. Plymouth, below Lincecum's Shoals and just below the mouth of Tibbee Creek, seemed favorably located. Farther north, after the Chickasaw lands became available for settlement, Waverly and Colbert appeared to be attractive places where the trade of the prairies might meet the river. Merchants established ware-

Map 9. River ports and major
landings, 1840–1860

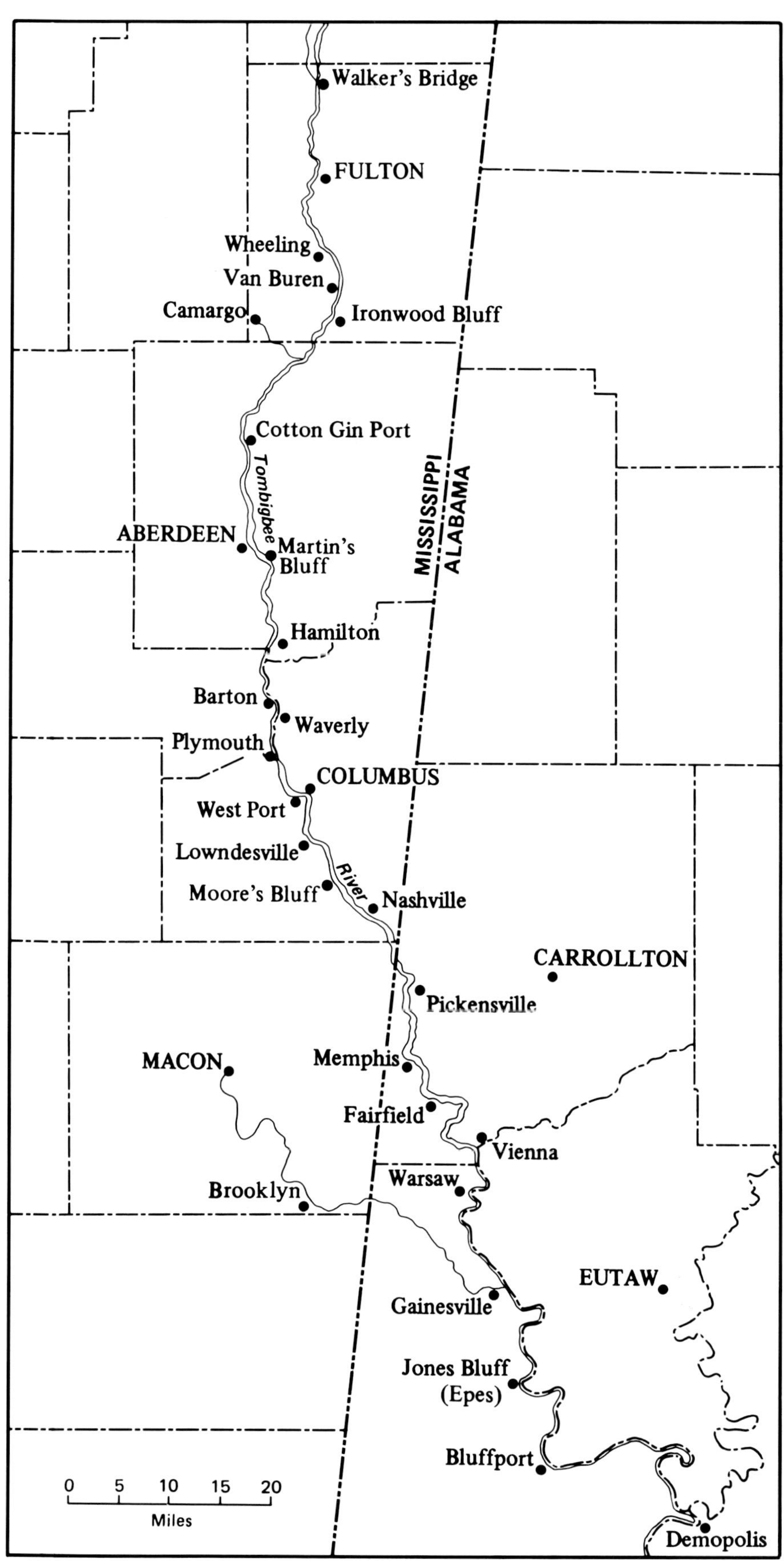

houses or sheds at the favored west bank locations, with facilities for camping and taking care of animals, to permit the cotton growers to bring in their loaded wagons, pulled by large ox teams struggling through the sticky gumbo of winter mud. After resting, the drivers and their slow-moving teams could return home, leaving the cotton in the custody of the merchants, whose sheds protected the bales from the weather until they could be picked up by a steamboat. South of Columbus there were river landings of importance at Moore's Bluff, Union Bluff, and, on the east bank, at Nashville, with a hinterland of increasing production behind each.

At Barton (successor to Colbert) in 1850 there were planters, merchants, carpenters, physicians, a ferryman, a millwright, clerks, steamboat men, a gunwright, a stage driver, a mechanic, a blacksmith, and a tailor. There were also fifty-seven slaves, sixteen of whom were owned by one planter and sixteen by another. No one claimed property worth more than four thousand dollars. At Barton-Vinton (successor to Barton) in 1860 the occupations were much the same, but a teacher and a minister, an Italian confectioner, a Negro manager, and six farm laborers also appeared. There were sixty-nine slaves, of whom one farmer owned thirty-three and two others nine each. One farmer listed sixty thousand dollars' worth of property and one merchant a like amount, an indication that wealth was accumulating in the hands of some of the people. As this was a rural community, a part of the tradesmen were in all probability also engaged in agricultural pursuits.

While Columbus had a head start on its smaller competitors, it had its ups and downs. After attaining a population of more than 1,600, it was hard hit by the financial panic of 1837 and the stagnation which followed. By 1846, however, flush times had rejuvenated Columbus. In the mid-1840s prosperous planters moved from the Black Prairie into the town, where they built fine homes and made the place a center of comfort, amenities, and prosperity. The little river towns on the west bank, with their warehouses convenient to the river and to the trade of the prairie, were subject to the ravages of high water. How high the water might rise could not easily be guessed, but experience in time proved that most of the bluffs on which the small ports were located were not high enough to give sure protection against peak floods. The flood of 1847 was particularly destructive, and it seems to have been the chief cause of the demise of the settlement at Nashville, below Columbus and near the Alabama line. Moore's Bluff and Union Bluff had similar troubles.

The construction of a free bridge over the Tombigbee at Columbus and the attractions of trade at the larger town worked to the disadvantage of the smaller places. Disease, probably malaria, seems to have been a prime factor in the demise of Plymouth. The little settlement of Colbert was transferred a short distance to the new settlement of Barton, which in time gave way to another new settlement nearby at Vinton, the shifts being mainly due to high water. The decline of the outports of Columbus is indicated by the discontinuance of their post offices. The post office at West Port was discon-

Map 10. Plat of the town of Warsaw, Sumter County, 1846 (Original in the Probate Court records, Sumter County, Ala., Deed Book D, p. 754)

Artist's conception of a steamboat at Martin's Bluff near Aberdeen in the mid-nineteenth century. Drawing by Richard A. Marshall, courtesy of Jack D. Elliott, Jr.

tinued in 1841, that at Nashville in 1852. The post office at Plymouth operated until 1855, that at Waverly until 1860. At Colbert the post office was transferred in 1848 to Barton. Ten years later it was moved to Vinton, where it was discontinued in 1862. There continued to be enough local business to sustain some of the little river ports on a small scale.

The story of Aberdeen is quite different from that of the Columbus outports. Settled in 1836 on the west bank of the Tombigbee, Aberdeen got off to a rapid start at a time when Columbus was suffering decline. The new town was farther upstream and somewhat more difficult to reach by steamboat, and its navigation season was shorter. Nevertheless, when the river was open, steamboats proceeded up to Aberdeen and offered regular packet service. Navigation above Aberdeen was difficult, but steamboats could reach Cotton Gin Port for short periods at high water and were even reported as far upstream as Camargo on Old Town Creek (West Fork). More practical, however, was the announcement in 1847 that the keelboat *Fulton* would ply regularly between Aberdeen and Fulton, on the East Fork, and sometimes points on the West Fork. This reasonable adaptation to local conditions worked to the advantage of Aberdeen merchants, who by means of local water transportation could reach out into the interior and bring the trade to Aberdeen as a primary center rather than to Mobile.

Aberdeen also became a hub for roads which radiated in several directions. Although they were often difficult to traverse, they reached a wide trade hinterland. As was the case with Columbus, many planters moved their places of residence from the prairie into Aberdeen, making the town a center of fine homes and cultural as well as commercial development. It became the center of a prosperous area, and its growth was accompanied by the decline of such places as Hamilton, Athens, and Cotton Gin Port, which were its early rivals. Aberdeen's position, however, had some weaknesses. Its warehouses near the river suffered from floods, and new ones had to be built on higher ground. The absence of a free ferry or free bridge

The Gainesville Bank, said to have been built in 1835, was moved to Tuscaloosa and restored in 1970. Photo: James F. Doster.

across the Tombigbee gave merchants of the older settlement at Martin's Bluff, a mile to the east, a distinct advantage in the trade of some nearby areas. Aberdeen's business was vitally dependent upon the uncertain navigation of the river—and unforeseen disasters lay ahead.

Eutaw and Macon were important centers of business, but both were some miles distant from the river. Demopolis, just outside the Upper Tombigbee area, was a focal point for the trade of the southern parts of Greene and Sumter counties. The only considerable town in Alabama that was directly on the Upper Tombigbee was Gainesville, which served as a center of residence and business for people of a plantation area of rich prairie and alluvial soils. Situated on a high bluff, it was immune to floods, except for its installations on the river. Several smaller river ports also maintained a local importance and had merchants and warehouses. Plantations near the river or thirty miles away, and even the town of Macon, might require their facilities. The little ports were located on relatively high bluffs next to the river, but all except Pickensville and Epes were subject to inundation by occasional floods. Even at Pickensville low warehouses might be flooded.

Epes, on a high chalk bluff, was close to the earlier sites of old Fort Tombecbé and the Choctaw trading factory. Pickensville, on the east side of the Tombigbee, got its start before 1820, when the lands across the river to the west belonged to the Choctaws. It was the first seat of the new county of Pickens. Vienna, also on the eastern side of the river, had a postmaster by 1834. Fairfield, on the western side, had one a year later, but Memphis and Warsaw had to wait until 1844. A plat of Warsaw was filed in 1840 and one of Memphis at some time before 1845. All of these towns survived the Civil War. Epes remains today as a little village on an important railroad line. Pickensville still has a store or two, and Memphis survives as a black residential community. Fairfield (now Cochrane) continues as a tiny settlement, and Gainesville is a town of reduced importance.

Steamboats served those minor ports regularly when business was available and the river was deep enough. Planters and merchants who lived at a considerable distance needed the custodial services of the merchants of the little port towns. There were a great many plantation landings, too, where boats stopped according to the requirements of passengers and cargo. Some of these also had cotton sheds.

As any little river port was on the wrong side of the river for many nearby people, ferries were provided at various places for their convenience. At Pickensville there were warehouses on both sides of the river, for west of that point was a considerable agricultural settlement known as Bigbee Valley, which retains some of its appearance to this day. The stagecoach route from Columbus to Tuscaloosa ran through Pickensville, where an inn served as an overnight stop. In 1850, according to the manuscript census, Pickensville had thirty-one dwellings and a population of 166, most of whom presumably lived on the little roads running into Pickensville rather than at the mercantile center itself. Carrollton, the county seat and not on the river, had forty-one dwellings and a white population of 208. Memphis had twenty dwellings and a white population of 100 (see table 3). There is very little evidence of cargo-handling facilities on the Upper Tombigbee, except for warehouses, cotton slides, and sometimes funicular tramways. The little river ports seem to have been remarkably uniform in character.

In the northwest corner of Greene County was the rural community of Pleasant Ridge, which bordered on the Tombigbee and Sipsey rivers. A ferry across the mouth of the Sipsey connected Pleasant Ridge with Vienna, and there was another ferry, across the Tombigbee, at the same place. Snedecor's map of 1856 shows a warehouse on the western side of the Tombigbee at the ferry crossing, which indicates that the place was a landing for steamboats (see map 11). A few miles to the south there was another ferry across the Tombigbee at Warsaw, on the west bank, so the river ports of Vienna and Warsaw and the landing at the mouth of the Sipsey were all accessible to Pleasant Ridge by road. The Pleasant Ridge precinct was made up of some 34,500 acres comprising portions of the Fall Line Hills, fertile high terraces, and swampy bottomlands subject to overflow. In 1860 its total population was about 1,300. The white population comprised sixty-seven households and 355 people, of whom 68 percent were native Alabamians; 15 percent were from South Carolina, and only 2 percent were born outside the South.

The primary occupation of Pleasant Ridge was agriculture. There were two or three stores. In 1860 several overseers resided there, an indication of absentee ownership. The population was rather scattered and not concentrated in a compact community. Pleasant Ridge is representative of a kind of rural community that existed along the Upper Tombigbee River. It seems probable that Bigbee Valley and various other places had quite similar characteristics.

Table 3. Occupations in Pickens County Towns, 1850

Pickensville	Carrollton	Memphis
3 carpenters	6 carpenters	2 carpenters
2 farmers	2 farmers	9 farmers
2 physicians	5 physicians	2 physicians
4 clerks	5 clerks	3 clerks
9 merchants	6 merchants	4 merchants
2 blacksmiths	1 blacksmith	1 blacksmith
1 cabinet workman	2 cabinet makers	1 gin maker
1 wheelwright	1 wagon maker	1 wagon maker
1 student	3 students	
2 teachers	3 teachers	
3 bootmakers	3 bootmakers	
1 Methodist clergyman	1 Baptist clergyman	
1 tailor	1 tailor	
2 hotel keepers	2 hotel keepers	
4 laborers	1 laborer	
2 lawyers	8 lawyers	
1 harness maker	1 harness maker	
1 tanner	4 tanners	
2 bookkeepers	1 circuit clerk	
1 druggist	1 corn merchant	
2 overseers	1 constable	
2 carriage makers	1 stage driver	
1 painter	2 seamstresses	
1 musician	1 editor	
1 boatman	1 judge of probate	
2 saddlers	5 printers	
	1 postmaster	
	6 [illegible]	

Source: Manuscript returns, U.S. Census, 1850.

Few, if any, persons of substantial wealth appear actually to have lived at Pleasant Ridge. The same was probably true of the other rural districts of Greene County. Eutaw, the county seat, was the home of the prosperous people, and it was there that fine homes and gracious living were concentrated. Eutaw was the center of trade. Its traffic with Mobile went through nearby landings on the Warrior River rather than the Tombigbee. It may be assumed that Pleasant Ridge plantation owners who lived in Eutaw commonly had other occupations and may also have owned plantations in other places than Pleasant Ridge. It is likely that some of the cotton crop of Pleasant Ridge was locally ginned and baled and shipped through the nearby Tombigbee ports or landings. That which went to Eutaw may be assumed to have moved down the Warrior River.

Macon, in Noxubee County, was another residential center for plantation owners. Being in the center of a cotton-producing county, it had a thriving trade. Unlike Eutaw, however, Macon depended heavily on the rather distant Tombigbee River, reached by an overland traffic to the little river ports such as Memphis, Fairfield, Warsaw, and the larger town of Gainesville. An inventory of the Macon

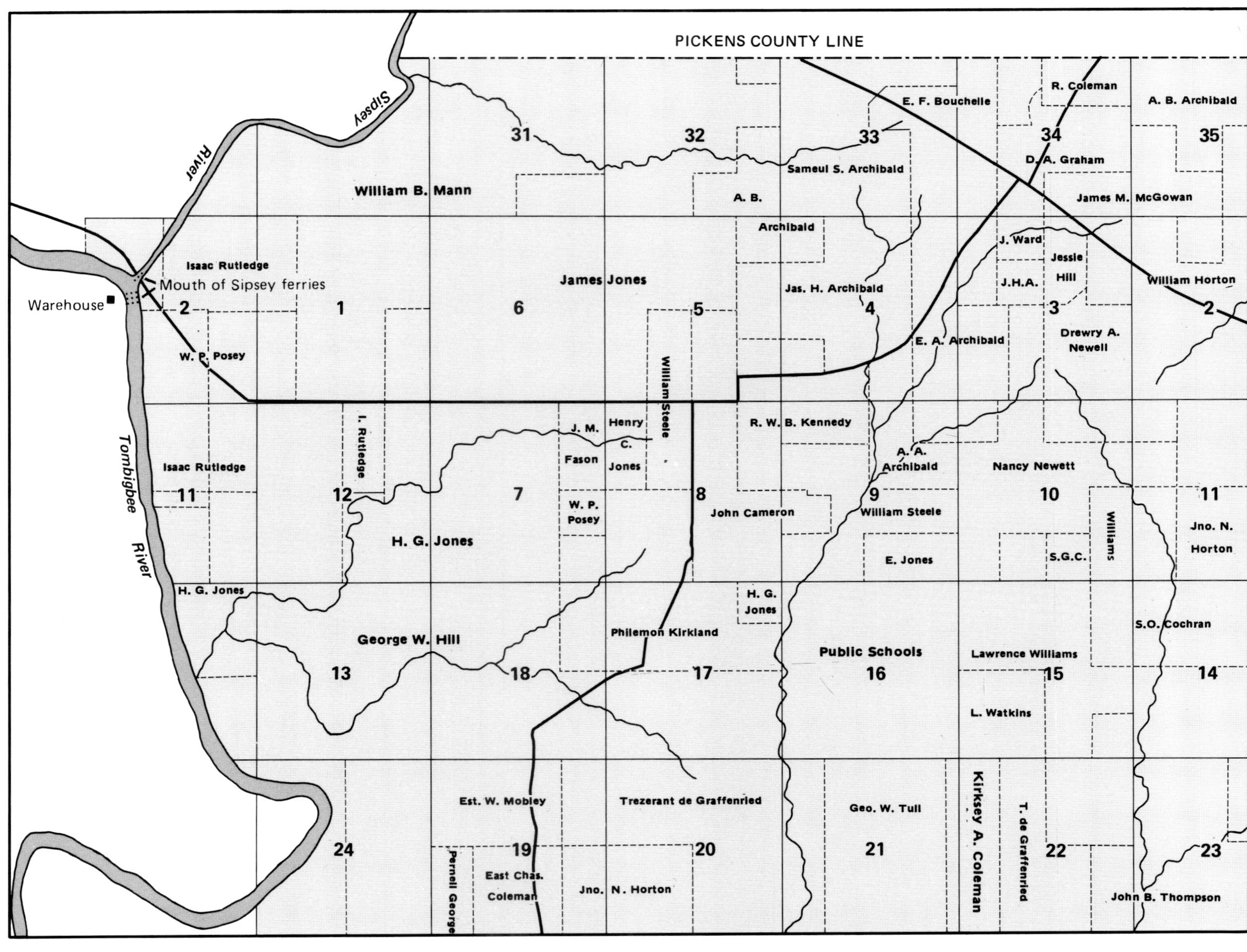

Map 11. Pleasant Ridge community, Greene County, 1856 (Abstracted from V. Gayle Snedecor's map of Greene County, Ala., 1856)

Table 4. Items in the Inventory of Smith and Jones, Merchants of Macon, January 1, 1846

Threads of many colors	Cravats
Cotton and silk hose	Socks
Ribbons	Netting
Suspenders	Carpets
Fans	Umbrellas
Hooks and eyes	Parasols
Bolts	Lace
Pins	Canes
Buttons	Hoes
Tapes	Plows
Thimbles	Nails
Gloves	Tobacco
Cloth: gingham, crape, silk,	Powder
satin, casmere [*sic*], tweed,	Gun cases and guns
muslin, linsey, flannel,	Collars
linen, and velvet	Bonnets
Jewelry	Looking glasses
Shawls	Trunks
Veils	Chests
Shoes	Salt
Boots	Ropes
Knives and forks	Coffee
Coats	Tea
Pants	Axes
Shirts	Scissors
Drawers	Plates
Books	Chains
Vests	Miscellaneous hardware

Source: Smith and Jones Invoice Book, 1844–49, manuscript in Duke University Library.

mercantile firm of Smith and Jones, given in table 4, shows some of the articles of trade in 1846. The firm appears to have done about three-quarters of its business in cloth and clothing. The initial inventory, at the beginning of 1846, was valued at $10,334.51, to which new stock costing $12,000.63 was soon added by purchase from merchants in Mobile and New York. By the end of the year all but $7,674 of the stock had been sold. Considering the usual markups, the store must have netted a handsome profit. Livingston, the seat of Sumter County, was another center of Black Belt trade, residence, and influence in a county that prospered in the flush times of the 1840s and 1850s.

The early pioneer knew how to live in the woods with the aid of simple but important tools. The axe, the hoe, the gun, the auger, the knife (and the two-handled knife, or drawing knife), the adze, the hammer, and the crosscut saw were all familiar to him. Blacksmith tools were well known, too. On the farm and plantation many activities were carried on that might be called industrial in nature. Sawmilling, gristmilling, cotton ginning, blacksmithing, brick making, spinning and weaving, leather tanning and the manufacture of saddles and harness, wagon and carriage making, wheel making,

The old well shelter at the James L. Parker home in Livingston, still in use when it was photographed in 1936, had fluted columns with capitals. Photo: Library of Congress.

boot and shoe making, slaughtering and food processing, distilling, earthenware manufacture, lime and plaster making, tin work, syrup making, furniture making, and soap making were all practiced on plantations but probably not all on any one plantation. Products of such household handicraft industries might be strictly for home use or might be traded in the community. There were skilled construction tradesmen, such as bricklayers, plasterers, and carpenters, many of whom were slaves. A craftsman on one farm or plantation served a wider constituency than his own establishment. Skilled slaves might be rented out. Sawmills, gristmills, and cotton gins were likely to serve a fairly wide constituency. There were specialist shops in the major towns and sometimes in the rural areas. A particularly important skill was blacksmithing, and the blacksmith shop was a source of many useful articles manufactured from iron. There was a small manufactory of hats in Columbus.

Power for light industries was available from three sources: water, steam, and animals. In most of the Upper Tombigbee Valley there were few sites for water mills near the river. In Itawamba and Tishomingo counties in the north, however, the terrain was rougher, the river valley narrower, and mill sites on tributary creeks near the main stream were more common. On Redbud Creek in southern Tishomingo County, for instance, water mills of the tub type were installed at several locations. Steam power was used close to the Tombigbee River at such places as Waverly and Bigbee Valley. Once the power source was in place, it might be used for several kinds of operations, so it was common to find a gristmill, a sawmill, and a cotton gin all at the same location.

While the industrial town and the factory system were almost unknown in the Upper Tombigbee Valley, an interesting exception is found at Bay Springs at The Narrows on Mackey's Creek (now covered by Bay Springs Lake) in Tishomingo County. Here was a creek with a considerable flow of water that rushed through a narrow gorge, with an excellent dam site. In the early 1840s George Gresham erected at The Narrows a sawmill and gristmill, powered by water at a mill dam. In 1851 Gresham's son, James F. Gresham, was joined by John Briggs, a prominent Eastport merchant, in erecting a mill for spinning cotton, which eventually had 744 spindles. Adjoining were a cotton gin, a gristmill, a blacksmith shop, and a general store and post office. Peak employment at the establishment was said to be between fifty and a hundred persons. Cotton yarn was the main product, although it is said that ropes were manufactured there in later years. Under new management, operations continued after the Civil War, apparently without much change. The market for the yarn seems to have been with the weavers in the neighborhood, who used hand looms. In 1885 or 1886 a fire, suspected to be of incendiary origin, destroyed the establishment, and it was not rebuilt.

The U.S. Census for 1850 and 1860 provides comprehensive data for measurement of the significant changes which were occurring in the 1850s in the Upper Tombigbee counties (a detailed analysis appears in the appendix). A threefold increase in production of cotton, the principal market crop, indicates a growing prosperity for the region. The population growth was relatively modest, but the decrease in the proportion of white population to black indicates a considerable growth in the number of Negro slaves. The number of acres per farm was becoming significantly larger, while the number of farms was decreasing. The impressive corn production and the large number of hogs, cattle, milk cows, and sheep per farm and per person indicate a high degree of self-sufficiency. A great increase in the total value of livestock but not in the number of animals suggests that relative scarcity was raising the prices of livestock as people concentrated on cotton. Another indication of growing prosperity is the impressive increase in the value of farms.

A study of the figures for individual counties shows a considerable diversity from one county to another. The average farm in Tishomingo County in 1860 produced only 8 bales of cotton, compared to 84 in Noxubee County, 80 in Lowndes, and 73 in Greene and Sumter each. Itawamba produced only 9. Likewise, in corn production per farm, Itawamba and Tishomingo lagged far behind the others. There was a notable decline in the number of hogs and beef cattle in the area generally.

The percentage of white population varied greatly among the counties, but in each there was a relative decline from 1850 to 1860, indicating a proportionally growing number of Negro slaves. In 1860, Itawamba and Tishomingo counties were about 80 percent white, as compared with 23.5 percent in Greene County and 24.6 percent in Sumter.

The side-wheel steamboat *Magnolia*, which came upon the scene of the *Eliza Battle* disaster in 1857, loading cotton bales at the bottom of a slide. Photo: Mobile Public Library, University of South Alabama Photographic Archives.

Steamboats

Before the Civil War most steamboats were side-wheelers, with the wheels located about two-thirds of the way back from the bow. The early models had only one deck and one boiler and chimney. Later models added an upper deck, a pilot house, and another boiler and chimney. As long as there were side wheels, the hull had to be relatively narrow. To protect the wheels the decks were extended on either side, these extensions being known as the "guards." They provided valuable additional deck space for stowing cargo and, if there was an upper deck, more space for a promenade for the cabin passengers. Deck passengers and deck hands remained on the main deck and slept wherever they could stretch out. Shallow draft was found desirable for navigating small rivers and even some places on large ones. Hulls underwent evolutionary changes which eliminated the keel and made the bottom nearly flat. A vessel of three hundred tons was about as large as was practical for use on the Upper Tombigbee River, and only two or three steamboats of more than four hundred tons were ever seen there.

There were a few stern-wheelers, but they were looked upon with disfavor, for they were not easy to handle, and the weight of the wheel suspended over the stern tended to make the center of the vessel rise up, an effect known as "hogging." In time various technical improvements made the stern-wheelers more attractive. Hogging was checked by the installation of heavy lateral chains or iron rods, known as "hog chains," one on each side, which extended up from the hull toward the center of the vessel at an angle and then were bent down horizontally and joined by turnbuckles. The difficulty of steering a stern-wheel vessel was solved by the use of multiple rudders just forward of the wheel, rudders which extended partly under the vessel and partly under the wheel and could be turned in parallel, giving excellent control. Power was applied to the paddle wheel by a double-acting steam cylinder on each side of the vessel, driving a crosshead, which in turn was coupled to a crank on the end of the wheel by a long wooden pitman (connecting rod). The stroke was long and relatively slow. The cranks were set ninety degrees apart, providing a smooth flow of power, and the wheel was made large and heavy enough to eliminate any need for a flywheel. Eliminating side wheels made possible a wider hull and a much shallower draft, suited to small and shallow rivers. Few stern-wheel vessels were seen on the Tombigbee before the Civil War, but after the war they gradually took over the steamboat business.

Wood provided good fuel for the boilers when it was dry, but it was bulky, and the boilers and propulsion equipment were inefficient. Frequent stops for wood had to be made. For pioneer steamboats the crew had to be sent out to cut the wood, but the practice arose among residents along the river of operating private woodyards as a business, so that steamboats could stop and buy their fuel as it was needed.

There were many controlling factors in the operation of steamboats, one of the most obvious of which was water depth. There were problems with snags at low water and with overhanging trees at high water. At low water the Upper Tombigbee River was a series of pools dammed up by sand bars and mud bars. The effective season for boating was generally limited to the months of December to June, but conditions varied widely from year to year. The inhabitants of the area adjusted to the fact that steamboating on this river was a high-water, seasonal business.

Steamboats were dangerous to travel on. There were usually no guard rails around the lower deck, and many a man fell overboard and was drowned. Snags, fire, and boiler explosions were an ever-present menace. Twelve steamboats are known to have been lost on the Upper Tombigbee River before 1860, besides the *Eliza Battle* and others that were destroyed after entering the lower Tombigbee at Demopolis. The *Iowa* was burned at Fairfield in 1837, but all the rest were apparently sunk by obstructions.

Steamboats were not generally operated by men of a saltwater background. Often their officers, and sometimes crew members, had been operators of flatboats and keelboats, and they knew the rivers and the traffic. The captain might be a part owner. The person who dealt with the public in the business of the boat was called the "clerk." For the comfort and convenience of passengers there also had to be cooks and stewards. Cargo was handled primarily by the deck crew, which had to move it on and off the boat by muscle power.

Techniques of operating steamboats at night were developed rather early, and it was customary for them to run both day and night except under especially difficult or unfamiliar conditions. Fog was a frequent menace on the rivers and could quickly force a boat to tie up to the bank until visibility improved.

A boat which operated on a regular schedule was known as a "packet." Many boats on the Tombigbee, however, did not follow a regular schedule but went where the traffic appeared to be. Since navigation of the Upper Tombigbee was seasonal, a boat would have to find work elsewhere during the low-water period or be laid up. Many of the boats entering the Upper Tombigbee came from distant places to operate for a limited season. Steamboating there was only a tiny fragment of a much larger picture in the operation of steamboats on American rivers. Many a boat came from the Mississippi River at New Orleans through the Mississippi Sound to operate on the Alabama rivers and even the upper reaches of the Tombigbee. Some boats well known on the Upper Tombigbee appeared also on the Apalachicola and Chattahoochee rivers.

A steamboat was constructed of wood and might be built almost anywhere: Mobile, Demopolis, or Columbus. Most of the boats on the Tombigbee, however, came from such distant places as Pittsburgh, Cincinnati, and Jeffersonville, on the Ohio River. Mobile was a principal center of ownership and operations, and a boat found on the Tombigbee one week might be on the Alabama River the next. The life of a steamboat was usually short. If it were not sunk by a snag or destroyed by fire or explosion, its hull would soon rot. Maintenance of steamboat hulls required frequent caulking and replanking. Boilers and engines for steamboats were not built anywhere near the Tombigbee River. Boats built along that river often utilized boilers and engines of other boats either scrapped or sunk. Many an engine was older than the boat which it propelled. Enrollment records in the National Archives in Washington make it possible to learn the construction details and the ownership of nearly every steamboat, but they have not been extensively used.

Steamboats competed with railroads in a violent and erratic manner. The economics of the two modes of transportation so differed that they could not operate well in harmony. When conditions were favorable, steamboats could carry more cheaply than railroads, which had to own and maintain their tracks, and the boats could charge lower rates between points they served. The railroads fought back with a variety of measures. The 1840s and 1850s saw the great day of the steamboats on the Upper Tombigbee. Although steamboats continued in use for local traffic after the Civil War, river towns without railroads tended to dry up.

The Mobile and Ohio Railroad

The inadequacy of the Tombigbee River as a transportation artery in serving the growing commercial needs of the Upper Tombigbee Valley led to various efforts to introduce railroads into the area. In the 1850s a line from New Orleans to Jackson, Mississippi, was under construction, and in 1852 Aberdeen and Monroe County subscribed heavily to stock of a company that was to lay a track from Jackson through Aberdeen to Nashville, Tennessee. Meanwhile, various interests were at work to construct the Memphis and Charleston Railroad to connect Chattanooga with Memphis in Tennessee by a route serving the highly productive Tennessee Valley in Alabama. The line, built in the 1850s, passed through Corinth and Iuka in northeast Mississippi.

Before the Civil War and for long afterward, however, the only railroad to have a deep influence upon the Tombigbee area was the Mobile and Ohio. Organized in 1848, this company moved firmly to the completion of its main plan, which was to open a line from Mobile through the fertile agricultural areas of northeast Mississippi and thence across Tennessee and western Kentucky to connect at Cairo with the Illinois Central line to Chicago. The two companies were generously supported by land grants from the federal government. The M&O selected in scattered areas the best of the public lands that it could find, including extensive acreage in the counties of the Upper Tombigbee Valley. The company raised money for construction in Mobile and in northeastern Mississippi, and it also received state aid from both Alabama and Mississippi. While it intended to serve many interests, the dominating force and power lay in Mobile, the commercial interests of which city the company faithfully supported for a century.

The main line was intended to have several feeder branches, which would tap valuable tributary areas for the benefit of the company and of Mobile. The line projected to connect Aberdeen with New Orleans was expected to cross the M&O, so no branch was planned to Aberdeen. The M&O line, which roughly paralleled the Tombigbee River, pushed northward from Mobile through the piney woods and across the Mississippi line in the direction of Macon, which was reached in 1856 in time to handle the season's cotton crop (see table 5). It was also in 1856, at the northern end of the Black Prairie, that the first train of the Memphis and Charleston Railroad reached the projected M&O crossing at Corinth.

On Christmas Day in 1857 M&O trains reached West Point. By this time Columbus, which had shown little interest in the railroad, realized that it was being bypassed and took steps to secure the construction of a branch line from Artesia, 13.5 miles away. In 1859 the tracks of the M&O reached Okolona, and the company was busy laying track in Tennessee and Kentucky. The whole line, from Mobile to Columbus, Kentucky, with steamboat connections to Cairo, was opened in April 1861 just as the Civil War began.

The building of the M&O through the prairie country parallel to the Tombigbee had a terrific impact not only on the country through which it passed but also on the river towns and on the function of the river in the life of the area. A string of commercial towns, mostly new, quickly developed on the railroad line. At West Point there were initially no warehouses, and cotton bales for shipment had to be piled along the track. Yet, between September and November 1858, 17,215 bales of cotton were shipped from that place. Soon West Point had a newspaper, the *Southern Broad-Axe*, in the early columns of which we are informed of the following services and institutions

Table 5. Principal Articles Carried by the Mobile and Ohio Railroad in 1856

Southbound Freight

74,885	bales of cotton	303	barrels of tar
2,193,000	bricks	1,063	livestock
10,950	cords of wood	5,154	dozen poultry
1,306	barrels of turpentine	24,050	dozen eggs
507	barrels of rosin		

Northbound Freight

298	bales of hay	2,066	sacks of bacon
3,448	sacks of meal and bran	1,437	casks of bacon
4,088	sacks of corn and oats	5,532	kegs of nails
2,069	barrels of molasses	2,765	boxes of tobacco
3,663	barrels of whiskey	6,981	pieces of bagging
1,088	barrels of pork and beef	7,333	coils of rope
6,344	barrels of flour	516	barrels of rice
4,847	sacks of coffee	1,150	boxes of candles
3,109	barrels of sugar	1,162	boxes of cheese
13,184	sacks of salt	330	carriages and wagons

Source: Mobile and Ohio Railroad Company, Annual Report, 1856.

serving West Point: daily passenger and freight trains, a male and female academy, an Ambrotype gallery, a church, a tin shop, street improvements, a post office, various mercantile establishments, a blacksmith business, a retail lumber establishment selling machine-dressed flooring and weatherboarding, a drug store, a hotel with a restaurant serving fresh oysters, schools, a dancing academy, and a livery stable.

In November 1859 the railroad was having so much trouble hauling off all the cotton offered to it at West Point that some was sent by wagon to the river landing at Waverly. The M&O was getting the expected rich business of the prairie country. Columbus was hurt, but it still had the river, and in 1859 the opening of the Columbus branch of the M&O gave it a railroad connection. Aberdeen was hardest hit. In 1859 and 1860 this formerly thriving place saw its cotton trade melt away to the railroad towns. While there was reason to hope that the legal tangles preventing the construction of its railroad might soon be straightened out and the road completed, the Civil War intervened. Aberdeen headed into a steep decline. With the opening of a new bridge across the Buttahatchie River, even its trade with the country east of the Tombigbee was siphoned off by Columbus.

The railroad and the river had entered into competition of a complex economic nature. The river was a seasonal transportation route, available to all on equal terms without cost. Transportation by steamboat and barge was relatively cheap when it was available. While the wooden boats deteriorated rapidly, they could be laid up and their crews discharged when they were not needed. They could go only where the river went, however, the navigation of the tributary branches being generally unsatisfactory. The boats competed with each other, but they could withdraw from the business and go

Map 12. Mobile and Ohio Railroad, 1861

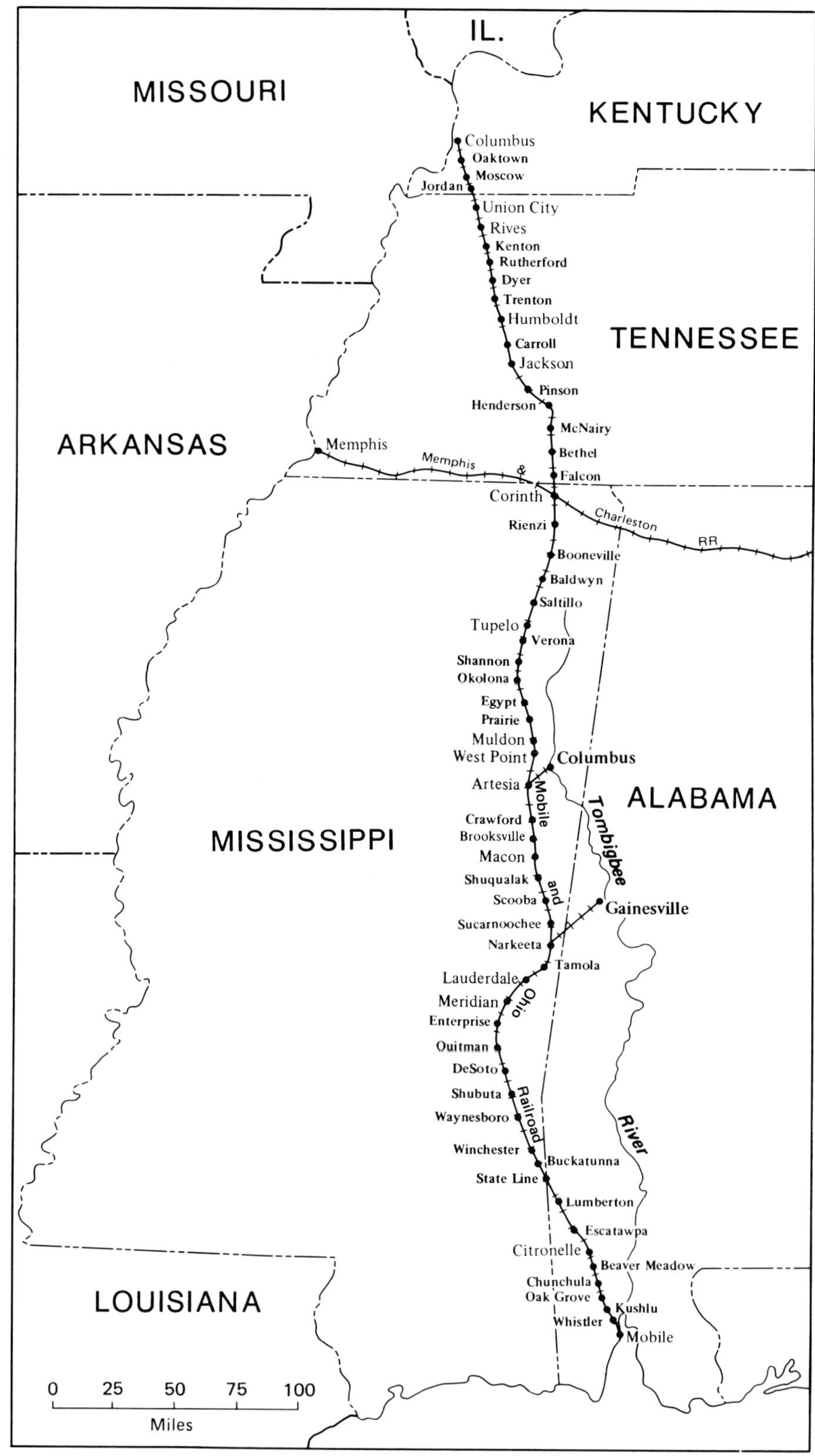

somewhere else when operations became unprofitable, there being no fixed investment in immovable facilities and improvements. The boats were highly flexible in the rates which they could charge. Their business was risky, but it usually carried a high profit margin.

The economics of railway operation were poorly understood in the 1850s. There was a very heavy fixed investment and a high maintenance cost that was largely independent of the volume of the business. Any additional business which might be taken from another carrier, or which could be created where it did not exist before, could contribute something to the payment of the fixed expenses, even if the rates charged were only a little more than sufficient to pay the immediate operating expenses involved. It was desirable to attract business that paid anything at all above operating expenses, so there was a great margin for rate cutting when competition required it. Nevertheless, the total business would have to be sufficient to cover all of the fixed expenses as well as operating expenses if the enterprise were to remain solvent. Railroad companies commonly charged passengers at a flat rate per mile, and the freight was charged for on the basis of a mileage scale not directly proportional to distance. For example, in September 1858 cotton rates to Mobile from Macon (197.5 miles) were $2.35 per bale, and from Okolona (261 miles) $2.70 per bale. The rate to Mobile from Gainesville Junction (163 miles) was $2.15. The rates, of course, covered terminal costs, which were about equal in each instance.

During much of the year the railroad had no competition from the river, except that shipments might be withheld to await a rise of the river and the arrival of the steamboats. The railroad was a dependable, all-season, all-weather carrier, quick and with reliable schedules and financially responsible owners; and the riverboats were generally deficient in these features. Some people who lived near the river, however, found transport by water more practical than by the more distant railroad.

In April 1861 the railroad's branches reached the Tombigbee River at Gainesville and Columbus but not Aberdeen. It crossed the Memphis and Charleston at Corinth and other railroad lines in Tennessee and Kentucky, at each of which the transfer of traffic was possible. Its terminus at Columbus, Kentucky, was connected by river ferry with railroads under construction west of the Mississippi and by steamboat with the Illinois Central at Cairo, twenty miles upstream. The impact of railroad transportation and that of the Civil War struck the Upper Tombigbee at about the same time.

6

Antebellum Homes of the Wealthy

Top: The Cedars at Columbus, expanded from a three-room log cabin which may have been built as early as 1810, is one of the oldest structures in the Tenn-Tom country. Photo: David C. Weaver.

Above: Sipsey, the William B. Willis house at Eutaw, is a one-story, "L"-shaped, clapboarded building in the Greek Revival style on a high brick foundation. Originally built at Pleasant Ridge in 1831, it was moved to Eutaw and was restored in the late 1970s. Photo: Roy Swayze.

As cotton wealth accumulated in the Upper Tombigbee Valley from the mid-1830s through the 1850s, the affluent developed a major interest in the construction of buildings indicative of their social and economic status. By 1860 the dullness of frontier housing had been relieved by large houses, among which there was a rich diversity of sophisticated design. Architectural traditions were widely borrowed from both Europe and the American seaboard, as design concepts rapidly flowered and faded. The town became the main focus of impressive buildings, but large houses were also built in the country by people of means. They were to be seen in plantation areas but were largely absent where small landholdings and low cash-crop production prevailed.

In design some big houses were simply adaptations and refinements of the smaller local forms. Numerous log houses were expanded and subsumed in larger structures. A few of these survive today, such as Hickory Sticks and The Cedars in Columbus. The log cabin of The Cedars may date from as early as 1810. The forms of others were derived from distant centers of design and fashion. Generally, the larger homes were designed by professional architects or were built with the help of published drawings. Their construction required skilled artisans and imported materials. These houses have been characterized as "academic" or "polite" by architectural historians. While variations in detail produced a great variety in appearances, most of the big houses can be categorized on the basis of structural forms or layouts and architectural styles or decorative designs.

Structural Forms

The most important structural forms represented a continuation of traditional practices. All incorporated folk and vernacular precedents. Rooms continued to be few but were made more spacious, and ceilings were raised to enhance air circulation in the summers.

Above, left: The Daniel Wright house at Eutaw, late 1840s; *top:* the Pratt-Thomas house, 1853 at Columbus; *above:* Carrington, 1855 at Aberdeen are outstanding restored examples of the "raised cottage." Photos: Jan Weaver.

Five basic structural forms can be discerned: one-story four-room houses, raised cottages, story-and-a-half houses, two-story four-room houses, and two-story eight-room mansions.

Large, one-story houses were normally design expansions of early central-hall structures of two rooms. One or more rooms, including bedroom and kitchen, were added to the traditional plan to give a square or "L" shape to the house. In the beginning the added back rooms were usually smaller than the original rooms, but later additions grew in size. Gable roofs conformed to the shape of the floor plan. Lean-to porches were frequently tacked to one or more sides. Surviving examples include Dunlee in Aberdeen (1853) and the Willis (1830s) and Gowdy (1850s) houses in Eutaw.

Raised cottages were similar to one-story houses but were raised high off the ground. Their origin is uncertain, but as they were extensively used by early French and Spanish settlers along the lower Mississippi River, they have commonly been referred to as "Raised Creole" houses or cottages. The form probably evolved originally from attempts to deter rotting of timber in damp areas and to catch summer breezes in a hot country. Although less common than houses in the other categories, the raised cottage was not scarce, and five specimens survive in Columbus. They usually had a square or "L" shape, with three, four, or five rooms and connecting halls. The two largest rooms faced the main approach. Pyramidal roofs and front and side porches were common elements. Examples include the Wright (1847), Vaughan (1841), and Littleberry-Pippen (1840s) houses in Eutaw, the Pratt-Thomas House (1833) in Columbus, and Carrington (1855) in Aberdeen. Because of the elevation of the first floor these houses sometimes had elaborate decorative staircases on the front exterior. The Pratt-Thomas house provides a particularly good example.

Story-and-a-half houses were common. They combined four ground-floor rooms and a hall with two large bedrooms centered over the four lower rooms. All six rooms fitted compactly under a

Top: The Stephen F. Hale house, built in the 1840s at Eutaw; *above:* The Burr W. Head house, built in the 1850s at Eutaw; and *above, right:* Twelve Gables, 1840s at Columbus, are surviving examples of the once common story-and-one-half house forms. Photos: Roy Swayze (Hale and Head houses); Jan Weaver (Twelve Gables).

Glennville, the J. P. Glenn home at Eutaw (1840s), was originally an "I" house with two stories, four rooms, a center stairway, and two end chimneys. It was later expanded with the addition of four rooms at the back and the colossal Doric portico on the front. Photo: Roy Swayze.

simple gable roof. They could accommodate a large family and frequently stood among smaller outbuildings such as kitchens, servant quarters, stables, carriage houses, and smokehouses. Sometimes extra rear bedrooms or storage rooms were added. Antebellum survivors include Twelve Gables (1840s) and Lemquen (1840s) in Columbus, the Lenoir Plantation House (1847) north of West Point, and the Samuel Murphy (1850s), Stephen F. Hale (1842), Gardner Elliott (1840s), and Burr W. Head (1850s) homes in Eutaw.

The most widespread big-house form in the region was the two-story residence of two rooms upstairs and two down, with a central hall on each floor connected by a stairway. There was an external chimney on each end providing a fireplace in each room. This building is recognizable as the "I" house described in chapter 4. As a house form this standard plantation house of the Upper Tombigbee Valley had long-standing antecedents in Virginia, Georgia, and the Carolinas. Front and rear porches and room extensions, sometimes omitted at first, were generally added. Some fine examples survive, such as Franklin Square (1835) in Columbus and the J. P. Glenn (1840s) and Herndon-Webb (1840s) homes in Eutaw.

The last major form, two stories with four rooms up and four down, was by far the largest in floor space and the furthest removed from the frontier folk house. Most specimens were basically rectangular, but some assumed "L" and "T" shapes. A broad central hall was standard, upstairs and down, sometimes transversely divided, with stairways in both front and rear sections. From 1830 to 1850 most had a long gable roof with the ridge line parallel to the front. In the 1850s the "Temple" form with a very low-pitched, pyramidal roof became common.

The eight-room (minimum) mansion represented the apogee of the cultured lifestyle in the Upper Tombigbee Valley, as in other parts of the South in the antebellum period, and it has come to epitomize the plantation economy in the popular mind. In reality most such homes were in the towns. While many owners were masters of

Figure 2. Regional form of an eight-room mansion of the mid-nineteenth century.

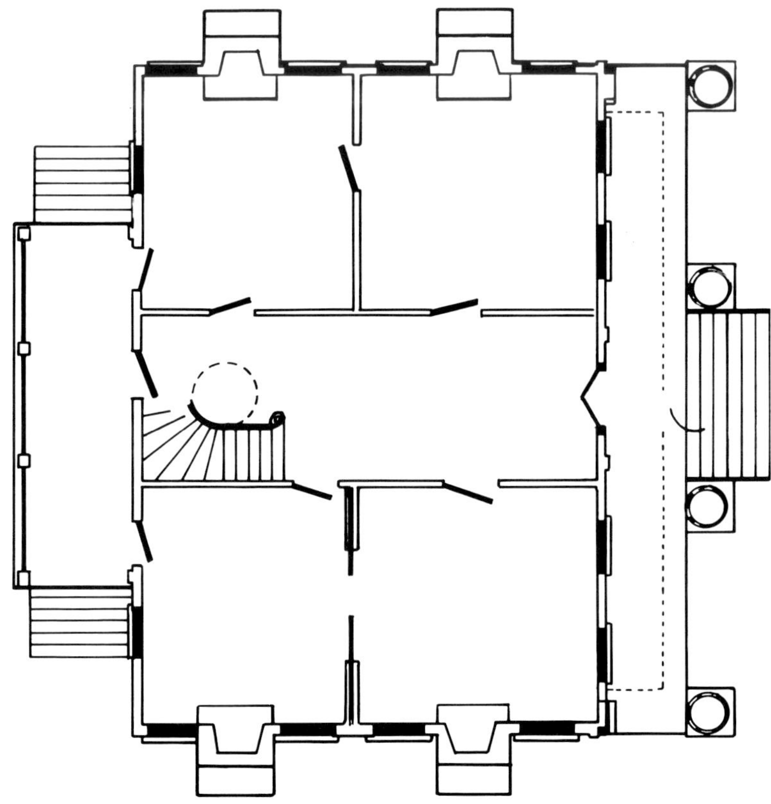

Above: The Herndon-Webb house at Eutaw was originally built at Finche's ferry (old Erie) as an "I" house. It was moved to Eutaw in the mid-1840s and was given a front portico and a raised, extended roof. Photo: Jan Weaver.

Top, right: Side view of Rosemount near Forkland in Greene County in 1934, when the mansion was run-down. The house, which had begun in the 1830s as a simple two-story structure, was later expanded toward the front to produce the grandiose mansion pictured elsewhere in this book. Photo: Library of Congress.

Right: The Magnolias at Gainesville is an elegant Greek Revival mansion begun in the early 1830s. The house has massive fluted Ionic columns supporting a two-storied gabled portico. An unusually high brick wall runs across the front of the house. Photo: Jan Weaver.

plantations, some were also doctors, lawyers, and merchants. Among the best known and most impressive of the surviving great houses are Kirkwood (1850s) at Eutaw; Waverly (1852) on the Tombigbee in Clay County; Colonnade (1860), Shadowlawn (1860), and Homewood (1840s) in Columbus; Sunset Hill (1847) and The Magnolias (1850) in Aberdeen; The Magnolias (1852) in Gainesville; Belle Oaks (1844) in Macon; Gaineswood (1859) in Demopolis; and Thornhill (1833) and Rosemount (1832) near Forkland in Greene County.

Architectural Styles

Variations in the structural forms of the big houses were accompanied by differences in their interior and exterior detail. Decorative concepts reflected periodic and transitory architectural fashions, often briefly dominant but always operating in an environment of mixed tastes and preferences, where design elements from one mode could be adopted and incorporated with another. There were six main architectural styles represented in the homes of the wealthy of the Upper Tombigbee between 1830 and 1850: the colonial, or Georgian; the postcolonial, or Federal; the Greek Revival; the Gothic Revival; the Romanesque Revival; and the Italianate. Two of these were legacies of fashions common in the South before the Tombigbee area was settled. The others were introduced to the region at the time of their greatest national prominence. The affluence of the Black Belt resulted in the construction there during these years of some of the most outstanding representations of the then-current residential design fashions to be found anywhere in the country.

The American colonial style, which flourished in the eighteenth century as the dominant form in Virginia and the Carolinas, has commonly been called Georgian because of its similarity to eighteenth-century English styles. Fronting on the street, the entrance opened into a central hall, where an elaborate stairway was the primary decoration, with turned spindles and delicately carved tread brackets. Chimneys were at each end of the building, and fireplaces with prominent mantels were emphasized. Window trim was simple, although true cornices or even pediments were occasionally used over the window heads in framed houses. There was little other exterior ornament. Some of the last survivors in the Upper Tombigbee region are in Eutaw and date from its earliest years. They include Grassdale (late 1820s) and the Richard G. Steele House (late 1830s).

Postcolonial buildings (1790–1830) are essentially modifications of earlier Georgian forms. The style is frequently called Federal because it has been considered to represent a rejection of English styles after the American Revolution. The most noticeable changes are exterior. The portico (a porch with a roof supported by pillars) came into its own in the Deep South, where the practical and aesthetic advantages of the "front porch" were appreciated. Early postcolonial porticos were generally one story high, with many decorative variations involving numbers and types of columns, roof shapes, and friezes. In the early nineteenth century, two-story porticos became common but were generally confined to the front-door surrounds. Front doors were often topped with fanlights in contrast to the heavy colonial doorway pediments. Windows and window panes became larger. Postcolonial interiors maintained fireplaces, door casings, and cornices in an earlier style. As the Upper Tombigbee settlement was not under way until the 1820s, only a few direct survivors of the postcolonial style remain. Two of the best examples are the restored

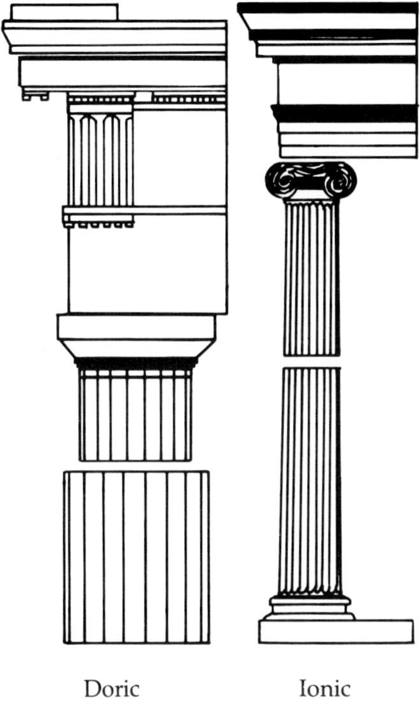

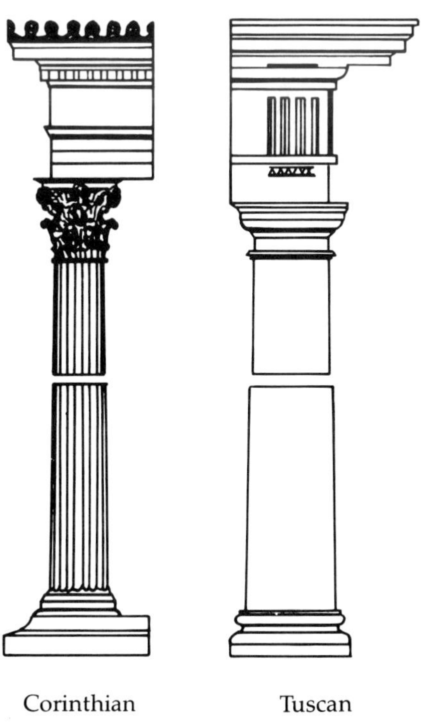

Figure 3. Columns and capitals.

Above: The G. W. Shawver house, Eutaw (late 1840s), presents an early example of the Greek Revival front-span, colossal-order portico. Photo: Jan Weaver.

Right: The William P. Webb home, Eutaw (1840s), is a modified "I" house with a two-story square portico. The single-story extension to the central portico was added in 1914. Photo: Jan Weaver.

Foster-Herndon house (1840s) and the William P. Webb house (1840s), in Eutaw.

After 1820 there was a transition from Federal to classical Roman and Greek orders, but Roman elements were quickly overshadowed by Greek styles. Certain features were common to most Greek

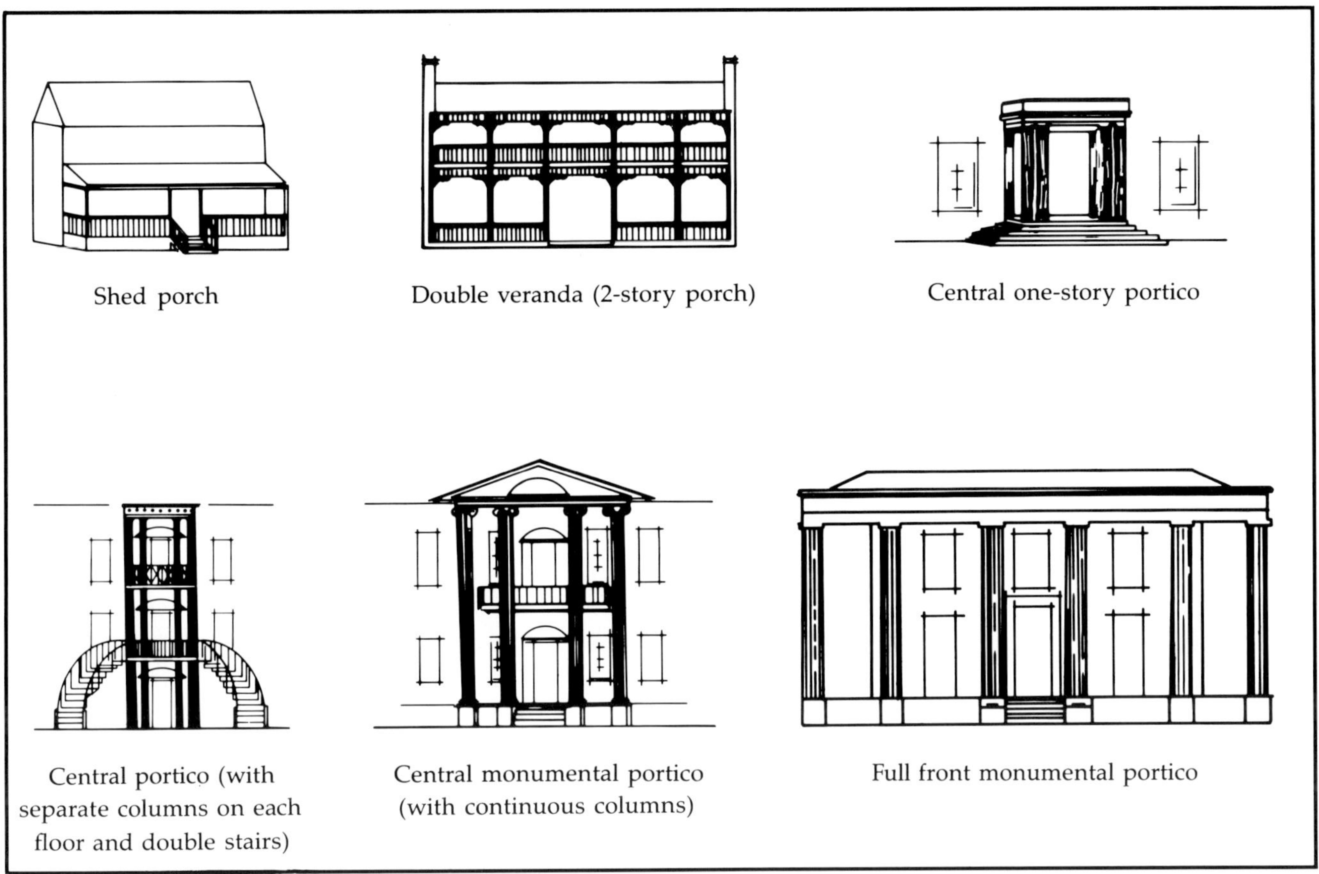

Figure 4. Porches.

Revival houses, the most impressive being the pillared porticos. These ranged from the relatively modest one-story front porch to the huge, two-story, full-front portico in the proportions of classical colossal order. The dominating feature was the main roof overhang, typically a full Greek architrave, frieze, and cornice. Columns were massive rather than delicate. Back porches were as important in Greek Revival design as the front, both in function and in detail.

Double front doors became common. Entrances were given sidelights and straight-top transoms instead of Federal fanlights, because the Greeks rarely used arches. Windows had a sliding sash as in the Georgian style but had larger panes. They frequently came down to the floor, particularly under porches or balconies where they could be used as doors. Some house exteriors were of brick; others had a plaster finish over brick, but the greatest number by far were clapboarded. In the wooden houses flush wallboards were laid for a smooth surface. Wooden porch floors were usually supported by brick piers with the between-pier spaces frequently filled by brick or wood lattices. Exteriors were almost universally painted white, perhaps intended to represent ancient Greek marble. Inside and outside, symmetry was the hallmark of the Greek Revival.

In the largest mansions, ceilings were high, with plaster entablatures around them. Plaster cornices were common, and rosettes

Above: Colonnade at Columbus (late 1850s), of Greek Revival style, has extensive outside decoration, including a jigsaw balcony balustrade and many roof brackets. Photo: Jan Weaver.

Right: Riverview, Columbus (1852), perhaps the largest antebellum house surviving in north Mississippi, has an unusual combination of rooms three deep. Built of brick, it has five levels and includes a basement, six rooms and two hallways on the ground floor, bedrooms and ballrooms on the second, storage space on the third, and a view of Columbus and the Tombigbee River from the cupola. Photo: Jan Weaver.

The great central hall at Waverly mansion extends to the full height of the building and provides a natural updraft for summer ventilation. Its cantilevered octagonal balconies are reached by curving stairways. Photo: Jan Weaver.

surrounded hanging chandeliers. Main rooms opened into each other and into hallways, and free-standing, classical-order columns were often used for interior decoration. Staircases were simple and somewhat plain, with square or round spindles. The fireplace was less prominent, and the overmantel was often discarded in favor of a large mirror. The fireplace was usually of marble and was often elaborately carved. Imported mirrors and ceramics from Europe became popular in the interior of the Greek Revival home. Two of the most lavish, pretentious, and magnificent examples of these palatial residences are found in the valley. Waverly, in Clay County, introduced in chapter 1, has a great central hall sixty feet high, filling the entire area between the front and back porches, and twin curved stairs leading to a second-floor balcony area. Rosemount at Forkland, built in 1832, unusually early for its type, also has a superb hall.

The Gothic Revival style might have either flat roofs with crenelated parapets or steep roofs with wide eaves and gables with carved or fancifully sawn barge boards. There were turrets, bay windows, pointed-arch doors, porches with carved or sawn wooden tracing between the columns, and elaborate chimneys often with separate top flues and chimney pots. Columns, slender and frequently octagonal, were sometimes used in clusters. Gothic attained no great popularity for residences in the Upper Tombigbee, although there are a few remaining traces such as in the Azmi Love and Elias Fort houses in Columbus and the Old Homestead in Aberdeen (1852). Gothic design was primarily reserved for churches, such as St. John's Episcopal Church in Aberdeen (1853), St. Paul's Episcopal Church in Columbus (1858), and St. John's Episcopal Church at Forkland (1859).

The Romanesque revival was based on English Romanesque, frequently called Norman. It relied on bold masonry and powerful arches. It was better suited to brick and stone than to wood, which may have reduced its popular appeal in the region. Houses were occasionally built in the Romanesque style in the Upper Tombigbee,

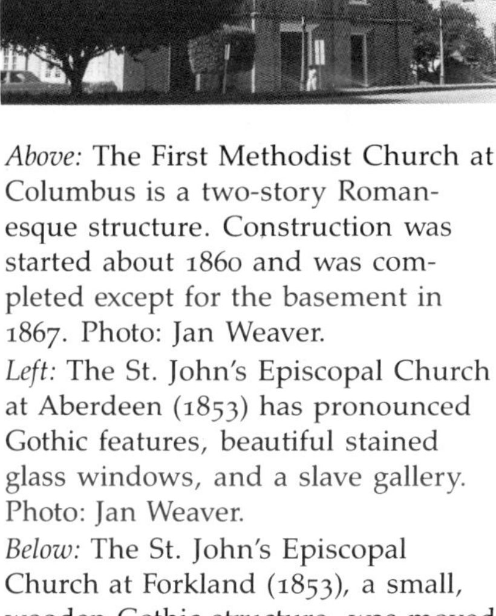

Above: The First Methodist Church at Columbus is a two-story Roman-esque structure. Construction was started about 1860 and was completed except for the basement in 1867. Photo: Jan Weaver.
Left: The St. John's Episcopal Church at Aberdeen (1853) has pronounced Gothic features, beautiful stained glass windows, and a slave gallery. Photo: Jan Weaver.
Below: The St. John's Episcopal Church at Forkland (1853), a small, wooden Gothic structure, was moved from a site near Greensboro in 1878. Photo: Jan Weaver.

but the best examples are to be found in industrial and commercial buildings and in churches. Perhaps the best surviving example in the region is the First Methodist Church (1860) in Columbus.

Italianate style, somewhat similar to Romanesque, was more decorative. It was introduced in the decade before the Civil War. With this style the word "villa" came into fashion as a common designation for the big house. Buildings with irregular plans and a projecting tower in front were called Italian villas; those which were symmetrical, with a middle tower in the roof, were called Tuscan. Italianate style had low-sloping roofs, verandas, arches, and Renaissance detail. Porch columns were smaller than those of the Greek Revival style and were often only one story high. Roof brackets supported wide eaves, and arches on doors, windows, and porches were integral

Above: Rosedale at Columbus (1855) is an excellent example of Italianate design, incorporating rounded arches, a flat roof, a tower, canopies supported by curved rafters, and balconies with iron grillwork. Photo: Library of Congress.

Right: The Duncan Dew house at Eutaw (1830s) was originally a plain "L"-shaped two-story residence, with a two-story front portico. The house has been altered a number of times, most recently in the 1930s, when it was given a full-front Greek Revival portico from a house in Pleasant Ridge. Photo: Jan Weaver.

Themerlaine at Columbus (1844) is an exotic mixture of classical styles in design. Photo: David C. Weaver.

elements. Interiors were ornate. Some Italianate-style residences survive, including White Arches (1857), Rosedale (1855), and Shadowlawn (1860) in Columbus.

Relatively few examples of any pure architectural style appeared. Changes in architectural fashion infused new concepts into established patterns, and many an addition to an existing structure was of a style different from the original. Many buildings became composites of form and style as they were extended and modernized, compounding the variety and complicating questions of cultural and architectural pedigree.

Notable examples may be found in Columbus, where several houses, such as Themerlaine (1844), Errolton (1850), and Shadowlawn (1860), combine Greek Revival concepts with Gothic, Romanesque, and Italianate detail. The Harrison house in Macon has Italianate details on a Greek Revival base, as does the Pierce house in Eutaw. The Duncan Dew house in Eutaw has a main body of the Federal style, with a Greek Revival front which was added in 1934 from a house at Pleasant Ridge. The style mixing may reflect both selective preferences for the parts of buildings and progressive adaptations to changing popular tastes by a series of owners.

7 *Civil War and Readjustment, 1860–1870*

Reuben Davis of Aberdeen was a lawyer, soldier, judge, congressman, author, and leading citizen. Photo: Evans Memorial Library, Aberdeen.

In the Civil War, which began in April 1861 and lasted until the late spring of 1865, the Tenn-Tom country was a main center of conflict only at its northern end. The direct military actions in the rest of the area were associated with cavalry raids and the battles resulting from them. Columbus was fortified but not attacked, and military activities in the Alabama counties were minimal. Nevertheless, the war had a far-reaching destructive influence upon the valley and its people. The Reconstruction era which followed was, except for the absence of killing, perhaps worse than the war itself. Powerful disruptive influences, accentuated but not all caused by the war, were at work.

In December 1860, there were various attitudes toward secession in the Upper Tombigbee Valley. There was opposition among the great planters, who had much to lose in war, and also among the small farmers and herdsmen, who had no stake in slavery. The general feeling was that some adjustment would be made without war if the South would but stand firm.

Congressman Reuben Davis of Aberdeen made a last-minute effort to secure a compromise, then prepared to go home. He later reminisced:

> On the 5th of January, 1861, I left Washington for home. [I] crossed the Potomac, and, looking back at the Capitol, saw the Stars and Stripes. Around that flag the whole South had rallied, not many years before, with passionate pride and devotion. It was with a fierce pang of renunciation that we left it.
>
> At Corinth I met the tidings that the ordinance of secession had been adopted by the convention. Mississippi was now a separate nationality, and expected soon to become a coordinate power in a Southern republic.
>
> Most of us knew that war would follow, but we had all the confidence of stout hearts and small experience.[1]

1. The Davis quotations are from Reuben Davis, *Recollections of Mississippi and Mississippians* (Boston and New York: Houghton Mifflin, 1899), pp. 401–402. The quotations are abridged.

Sunset Hill at Aberdeen built in 1847, for some twenty years the home of Reuben Davis, is a typical eight-room, central hallway house, with added rooms that give it a "T" shape. Photo: Jan Weaver.

Military preparations were widespread. For example, a cavalry company was organized in Noxubee County in November 1860. It was said to be an aggregation of citizens of every class and condition, inspired with patriotic fervor. Carbines, pistols, and sabers were ordered, and drills were held weekly. At Camp Goodwin, near Macon, ladies presented the troops with a silk banner. One ecstatic cavalryman observed, "All know that a beautiful woman is the prettiest thing on earth, and a fine horse is next."[2] The military preparations were pursued earnestly but with little knowledge of what lay ahead.

In April 1861 Thomas D. Duncan of Corinth, a mere boy, enlisted in the Corinth Rifles. His father gave him a good horse and had him transferred to a cavalry unit. As Duncan later told it:

> None knew, except those who lived during those stirring times, the atmosphere of excitement that pervaded this Southern country.
>
> At Columbus the companies stationed there were lined up along the principal thoroughfares to receive us. In new uniforms and well mounted, these troops seemed the very spirit of war.
>
> I looked upon the great and tragic issue as depending upon tinsel trappings and martial splendor. But in the hard school of experience I was soon to learn a different lesson.[3]

Military activities did not directly touch the Tenn-Tom country during 1861. After Confederate forts Henry and Donelson in northern Tennessee had fallen to the Federal forces in February 1862, however, invasion of the lower South came quickly—by steamboats moving up the Tennessee River.

2. J. G. Deupree, "The Noxubee Squadron of the First Mississippi Cavalry, C.S.A., 1861–1865," in *Publications of the Mississippi Historical Society*, Centenary Series, vol. 2 (Jackson: n.p., 1918), p. 18.

3. The quotations, here abridged, are from Thomas D. Duncan, *Recollections of Thomas D. Duncan, a Confederate Soldier* (Nashville: McQuiddy, 1922), pp. 12, 15–16, 193.

Map 13. The Tenn-Tom country
during the Civil War

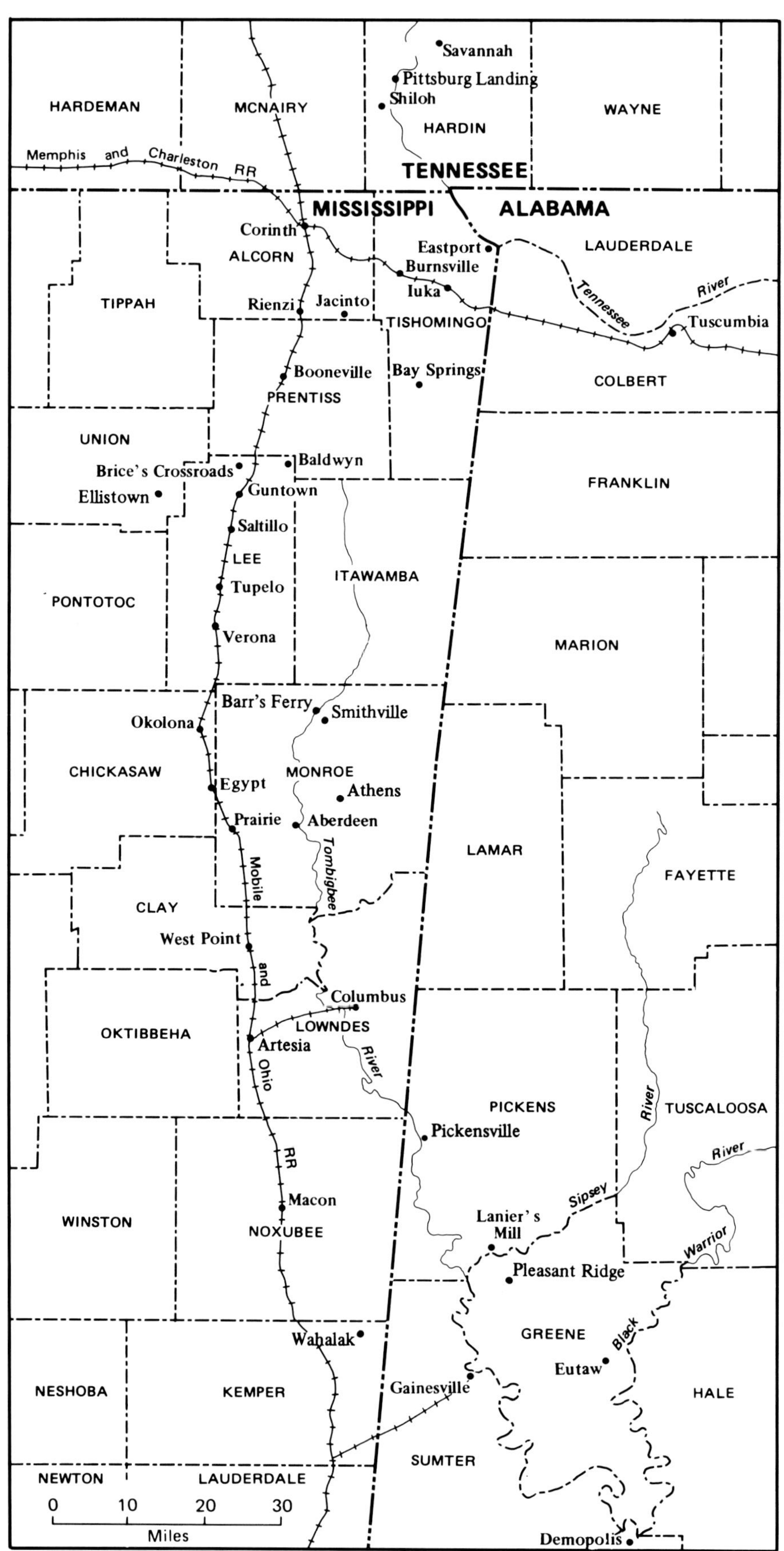

The gunboat *Lexington* on the Tennessee River gave very effective support to the Federal armies and contributed to the Confederate defeat at Shiloh. Photo: Naval Audio-Visual Center.

Federal transports on the Tennessee River in 1862. River steamboats gave powerful support to federal forces invading the South. Photo: Library of Congress.

The rails of the Mobile and Ohio and the Memphis and Charleston railroads crossed at Corinth, giving that point a special strategic importance and making it an object of Union attack. As early as March 14, after armored gunboats had probed Confederate defenses as far up the Tennessee River as Eastport, General William Tecumseh Sherman took a whole division of Federal troops on nineteen steamboats to the mouth of Yellow Creek, where he sent out a large cavalry force, equipped with axes, crowbars, and picks, to cut the Memphis and Charleston line at Burnsville. Because of heavy rains and the presence of large Confederate forces at Iuka and Burnsville, however, the troops were withdrawn and the mission failed.

The Federals under General Ulysses S. Grant, however, proceeded to occupy Pittsburg Landing on the Tennessee River. At Corinth, twenty-five miles to the southwest, the Confederate armies were consolidated under General Albert Sidney Johnston, with P. G. T. Beauregard second in command and with corps under Leonidas Polk, Braxton Bragg, William J. Hardee, and John C. Breckinridge.

General P. G. T. Beauregard took command of the Confederate forces at Shiloh after the death of General Albert Sidney Johnston on the first day of the battle. Photo: Library of Congress.

On April 6 the Confederates surprised the Federal army at Shiloh Church, near Pittsburg Landing, and carried the day, but their commander was killed. Armies each having more than forty thousand men faced each other. Next day, with General Beauregard in command, the Confederate force met defeat and retired to Corinth. This was one of the great battles of the war, and the losses on both sides were heavy. Wounded men were brought in and crowded into public buildings, which served as hospitals. Those who could be moved were sent south by rail as rapidly as possible, to be cared for in public buildings and private homes all the way from Rienzi to Mobile.

Drinking water and sanitation in the camps around Corinth were so bad that disease spread rapidly. Soldiers made holes in the mud and drank the water that accumulated in them, from which their horses sometimes turned away. The army became debilitated and many soldiers died. Beauregard prepared elaborate defenses in an arc several miles long around Corinth, while the Federal commander gathered more than a hundred thousand men and moved methodically toward the town. Beauregard, with now perhaps two-thirds that number, decided to retreat. He ordered the railroads to make a great noise to suggest defense preparations; then at dark on May 29 he began to move his force down the M&O line toward Tupelo, where he established his headquarters. Federal troops occupied Corinth on May 30 and cut the Memphis and Charleston Railroad, rendering Memphis and the upper Mississippi River posts indefensible by the Confederacy. The Federal force at Corinth had the same problems with drinking water, sanitation, and disease that had formerly beset the Confederates.

Many women performed heroic services during the war. Some had to flee from their homes before the invaders and find refuge wherever they could. Their privations and tribulations were many. Some saved the lives of their sons and husbands by nursing them back to health. Many homes were opened to shelter, feed, and nurse strangers. In the Tenn-Tom country the northern counties had the greatest need for such services.

While the Battle of Shiloh was being fought, a body of gentlewomen of Mobile prepared to go to Corinth to perform nursing services. Leaving Mobile on April 7, the second day of the battle, was Kate Cumming, who later wrote in her journal:

April 8.—Arrived at Okolona this morning. Citizens of the place opened their houses for our reception. The cars at 11 A.M. were filled with wounded on their way to Mobile and other points. About midnight a train came down to get negroes to build fortifications.

April 11.—Arrived at Corinth today. When within a few miles of the place, we could realize the condition of an army immediately after a battle. As it had been raining for days, water and mud abounded. Here and there were wagons hopelessly left to their fate, and men on horseback trying to wade through it. As far as the eye could reach, in the midst of all this slop and mud, the white tents of our brave men

The Tishomingo Hotel, shown in this 1862 etching, served as a hospital where Kate Cumming and other women performed heroic services. Railroad trains stopped in front of it. At different times both Confederate and Union encampments occupied the foreground. Photo: National Archives.

could be seen through the trees, making a picture suggestive of any thing but comfort.

We are at the Tishomingo Hotel, which, like every other large building, has been taken for a hospital. Nothing that I had ever heard or read had given me the faintest idea of the horrors witnessed here. Gray-haired men, beardless boys, Federals and all, mutilated in every imaginable way, lying on the floor, just as they were taken from the battle-field, so close together that it was almost impossible to walk without stepping on them. There was work to do, so I went at it. The Federal prisoners are receiving the same attention as our own men; they are lying side by side.[4]

Kate Cumming's observations are supported by other nurses, in particular Susan E. D. Smith and Ella K. Newsom, both of whom served in a number of Confederate war hospitals. Mrs. Smith, of Memphis, was briefly in Corinth after the Battle of Shiloh and then became matron (head nurse) at the Newsom Hospital in Columbus while her husband and son convalesced there from typhoid fever. Mrs. Newsom, who played a major role in organizing Confederate hospitals, also worked in Corinth after Shiloh and graphically described conditions in and around the Tishomingo Hotel in the days before Beauregard's retreat.[5]

At Tupelo on June 17, General Braxton Bragg succeeded the ailing Beauregard as commander of the Confederate western department. The federal forces were planning an invasion of East Tennessee, so Bragg decided to move into Tennessee first, and on July 27 he began shifting his army by railroad from Tupelo to Mobile and then to Chattanooga.

4. Kate Cumming, *Kate: The Journal of a Confederate Nurse*, ed. Richard Barksdale Harwell (Baton Rouge: Louisiana State University Press, 1959). The quotations are greatly abridged.

5. Mrs. Susan E. D. Smith, *The Soldier's Friend; Being a Thrilling Narrative of Grandma Smith's Four Years' Experience and Observation, as Matron, in the Hospitals of the South, During the Late Disastrous Conflict in America* (Memphis: Bulletin Publishing, 1867); J. Fraise Richard, comp., *The Florence Nightingale of the Southern Army: Experiences of Mrs. Ella K. Newsom, Confederate Nurse in the Great War of 1861–1865* (New York: Broadway, 1914).

General Sterling Price commanded the Confederate forces in the Battle of Iuka, September 19, 1862. He served under Van Dorn in the subsequent Battle of Corinth. Photo: Library of Congress.

General Earl Van Dorn commanded the Confederate army in the Battle of Corinth, October 3–4, 1862. Photo: National Archives.

Between Tupelo and Corinth there was a sort of no-man's-land, subject to cavalry patrols, sometimes in considerable force, where skirmishes were frequent. Neither side firmly held any place in the area for long. Many inhabitants continued to cultivate their fields, and the corn crop was good in 1862, but the insecurity of life and property caused others to flee southward for safety. Those having slaves were particularly anxious to take them to a secure place. In August, a Federal force struck the textile mill at Bay Springs, and a good deal of other property was put to the torch. By 1863 Unionists in some areas were pillaging the countryside.

Kate Cumming left Corinth just before it was evacuated and moved down the railroad line. Her journal continues:

> *May 28*—Arrived at Okolona yesterday. I am staying at Judge Thornton's. It is filled with refugees, and sick and wounded soldiers. Mrs. Thornton has every corner of her house filled with the latter. I am informed that all private dwellings in the place are in the same condition.
>
> *May 29.*—I am told that there are no less than two thousand patients in the place. Quite a number of new buildings have been erected—large wooden sheds, well ventilated, and capable of holding from twenty-five to thirty patients each.
>
> *June 4.*—This place is filled with strangers; the rear of the army being here—quartermasters, commissaries, etc. Mrs. Thornton's house is like a hotel; the men walk into it without asking any questions, sit down at the table, take what they want, and some times they pay. Mrs. Thornton has not the heart to prevent it, as the men seem to be so hungry.
>
> *June 10.*—As soon as her patients are well enough to be moved, some kind friends from the country take them to their homes.
>
> *June 16.*—A few days ago Mrs. Thornton received news that her son had been wounded in the late battle near Richmond. She is very hopeful as to his being cared for, and is certain that some good woman is administering to his wounds in Virginia.

Kate Cumming's career as a Confederate nurse had only begun, but the rest of it was to be in distant places.

On September 19, Confederate General Sterling Price, who had occupied Iuka a few days before, was attacked and defeated by a Federal force from Corinth under General William S. Rosecrans. Some 17,000 Federals were opposed by 14,000 Confederates, but the actual fighting involved much smaller numbers. After the battle, Price retired to Bay Springs and then to Baldwyn on the M&O Railroad.

A battle occurred at Corinth on October 3–4, 1862, when Confederate troops under Generals Earl Van Dorn and Sterling Price attacked from the northwest. After severe fighting on the first day the Federals retreated closer to the town. On the second day the fighting was again severe, but Corinth was not taken. Some 22,000 Confederate troops confronted about 23,000 Federals. On December 9 a Federal reconnaissance expedition moved from Corinth toward Tuscumbia, which movement was accompanied by considerable skirmishing.

Soldiers of the Ninth Mississippi Regiment, which fought in the Battle of Corinth on October 3–4, 1862, in camp. Photo: Library of Congress.

On December 14–19, 1862, the M&O Railroad below Corinth was hit by a double raid. A Federal force under Union General Grenville M. Dodge struck south from Corinth and, against some opposition, reached Tupelo, doing as much damage as possible to the railroad. At the same time Colonel Theophilus Lyle Dickey struck the railroad from the west and destroyed trestlework and bridges from Saltillo to Okolona, thirty-four miles away, and a large bridge south of Okolona over a branch of the Tombigbee. Federal troops took some two hundred prisoners. The Confederates went promptly to work to restore the operation of the railroad.

Moving from both north and south on the Mississippi River, the Federals sought in 1862–1863 to cut the Confederacy in two, but they found a difficult obstacle at Vicksburg, which was the main focus of military activity in central and western Mississippi until early July 1863. During the spring the activities of Federal troops at Corinth were directed toward the Tennessee Valley in Alabama. After the fall of Vicksburg and the concurrent Confederate defeat at Gettysburg on July 3–4, 1863, the fortunes of the Confederacy gradually declined. There was skirmishing near Corinth in November. On January 25, 1864, Union troops evacuated Corinth in a move to consolidate their forces elsewhere.

In the plantation country black slaves greatly outnumbered the white population. This made it possible for a large part of the white men to be away on military duty, leaving plantation management in the less firm hands of women, boys, and old men. There was ever present a fear of slave insurrection. While such did not occur, agricultural production lagged, and many slaves ran away to, or were taken away by, the Federal armies. A great number of the runaways returned or were recaptured, however. Many of the slaves, particularly house servants, were quite loyal to their beleaguered masters and their families. Many a soldier took a personal servant with him to perform camp duties, look after his clothing, horse, and other possessions, nurse him in sickness, and search for him wounded or dead on the battlefield. There was often a close personal bond between master and slave as they shared hardships. In the late years of the war most of the servants had to be sent home.

The main contribution of the slaves was in performing agricultural labor, but they were employed by the Confederacy in building fortifications at Corinth, Columbus, and elsewhere and in doing other military fatigue duty. They were also used in work on the Gainesville Branch railroad. Slaveowners received payment, but they were generally reluctant to have their slaves taken away from their own management. The slaves might be overworked and poorly fed or otherwise mistreated, and their health might be damaged. They might run away, be retained beyond the agreed time, or be arbitrarily transferred to work elsewhere.

Plantation overseers were difficult to keep. Inflation pinched them, and they demanded higher wages, often more than plantation owners in straitened circumstances could pay. An Alabama physician tending the wounded at Corinth had left his young wife on a plantation with more than a hundred slaves and no white man but the overseer. In some instances slaves were actually given the supervision of their masters' plantations. These slaves had presumably been drivers or foremen before the war.

At Aberdeen in 1861 a gin factory and foundry were converted into a cannon and gun factory. The owner's son later wrote:

> All the sporting rifles, for miles around, were brought there, and the older ones restocked. Hammers and percussion cap tubes were put on old "flint and steel" guns and all the rifles bored out to a uniform size to carry Minie balls. They were distributed, first to State troops, and the overplus to the regular army, and were used at Vicksburg and in the Mississippi campaigns. A few cannon, six pounders, had been cast, when a number of cannon and a large quantity of the small arms were destroyed by the burning of the factory by incindiaries about March 1, 1862.[6]

Columbus had a hat factory, and there were various small factories scattered about, and the only active textile mill in Mississippi late in the war was one established in Columbus in 1864. The household industry necessarily assumed greater importance. Clothes were made at home for the soldiers. Old clothes were patched and made over. Women, rich and poor, learned to sew and knit. Old spinning wheels and looms were put to work, but there was a scarcity of cards. Buttons were used over and over. Items of practical use were made in great variety on plantations and farms. Wax candles, ink, and dyes were made from unaccustomed materials. Butchering and preserva-

---

6. R. C. Beckett, "Antebellum Times in Monroe County," in *Publications: The Mississippi Historical Society*, vol. 11 (University, Miss.: Mississippi Historical Society, 1910), p. 100.

tion of meat were widely practiced as before. New cornmeal and flour mills were established.

Substitutes had to be found for supplies that were cut off. Mary J. Welsh of Wahalak in northeast Kemper County described the deprivations and improvisations associated with the exigencies of the times. Coffee, she said, was replaced by parched corn, then burnt molasses, then sweet potatoes cut into small squares and parched and ground, and finally okra seeds. Real coffee was saved for very special occasions. For chocolate, the substitute was groundpeas, or goobers (peanuts). For tea, sassafras roots or raspberry leaves did fairly well. Sugar was missing, but molasses and honey were used in creative ways. There was plenty of fruit which could be preserved with honey. Figs could be boiled for a few minutes with molasses, then dried and packed away for winter use. "In every emergency," she says, "there was one unfailing resource—if we could not find a substitute for any article we could do without it." The hardest thing to do without was salt, but by salvaging it from smokehouse floors, shaking it off dry pork, and similar expedients the scant supply was made to go twice as far. The constant inventiveness and constant work that were required helped keep minds from dwelling on the dangers and privations of the men away in the Confederate army. The Welsh family's slaves were loyal and strongly supportive, although they were much confused by the war. Most white families did not own slaves, however, and the absence of their men created worse hardships for them.[7]

The principal economic function of the Upper Tombigbee Valley in support of the Confederacy was in providing food, for it was an area of high food-producing capacity. Great numbers of cattle and hogs were bought up or driven off, until the number remaining declined to a mere fraction of what it had been in 1860.

While General Grant was rampaging through central Mississippi and the fall of Vicksburg was imminent in 1863, the governing officials of Columbus pointed out the importance of protecting their city and its surrounding area against attack. Their rich valley, they said, had been so planted in grain and other subsistence crops that it had become one vast cornfield capable of sustaining the entire army of the West if protected from the enemy. Extensive fortifications had been erected at Columbus, but the local government urged larger forces for its defense and pointed out a need for a defensive arc extending from New Albany to the northeast corner of the state. Their thinking is clearly reflected in the subsequent military policies of the Confederate government, and the actions of the Federal forces suggest similar concepts.

Food for soldiers and horses was provided by commissary agents who searched the countryside. They bought or seized the property they wanted. Usually they went through the formality of paying for

---

7. Mary J. Welsh, "Makeshifts of the War between the States," in *Publications of the Mississippi Historical Society,* vol. 7 (Oxford: Mississippi Historical Society, 1903), pp. 101–113.

what they seized, but the currency was often paper of questionable value. When necessity required, and sometimes when it did not, soldiers went on their own foraging expeditions and tended to grab what they wanted, furtively or openly. However it was done—by commercial bargaining, seizure with payment, or theft—military foraging stripped the country of necessary supplies. The northern counties suffered heavily in 1862, as did all areas later subject to the movement of large military forces.

The Mobile and Ohio Railroad was the backbone of the Tenn-Tom country during the war, and the towns along it were centers of strength as foci of social and economic life. The importance of the railroad in moving supplies, equipment, and people made it an object of attack and destruction. But permanently destroying a railroad was easier said than done. Burned-out rolling stock could be rebuilt, if the metal parts survived, as they usually did. Bridges could be rebuilt, and so could the tracks, and the work could be done quickly if enough men were at hand to do it. The M&O was repeatedly destroyed and rebuilt during the war.

Travel by train, however, was often unpleasant. Kate Cumming, returning from Okolona to Mobile on June 18, 1862, wrote:

> The train was crowded. I scarcely know how I managed to get on it, as the guard tried to prevent us; my friends threw me on, minus half of my baggage. I stood on the steps of the car for a while, when one of the soldiers inside, with true southern gallantry, insisted on my taking his seat. As the car was filled with sick and wounded men, I was unwilling to do so; but from his importunity I was compelled to accept. The intention was a good one, and I received it in the spirit with which it was given, but I did not relish the change. The car was so close and crowded that I could scarcely breathe. I had to hold my head out of the window to get fresh air. To add to all, we had no water.
>
> General B[eauregard] was on the train. He and his *staff* had the ladies' car and the baggage-car next, which was the cause of our being so crowded. The sight of them ought to have consoled me; but alas! for poor, weak *humanity*, I could not help envying them their comfortable seats. [Beauregard, exhausted and ill, had just been relieved of command.]

Criminal courts in Mississippi during the war were generally inoperative, and local jails were easily broken into. Vigilantes moved in to provide summary justice. Committees conducted trials and executions. They were particularly active against Negroes considered dangerous and persons suspected of disloyalty. The Confederate court for the northern district of Mississippi moved to Columbus for safety and that for the southern district to Macon, but most cases had to be postponed. The Alabama counties suffered less from disruption.

The most important problem of the Confederate court in northern Mississippi was the trial of persons charged with illegal trading with the enemy, but the court's efforts were largely ineffective. A great deal of cotton moved north through the lines and was paid for in money, and there was some other trade. Both sides permitted trade by judiciously looking the other way. Northern Mississippi was an important area for this trade, much of which went through Memphis.

There were many people in the Confederacy of strong Unionist sentiments, some of whom fought in the Union army. In the hill country of Tishomingo County (then including present Alcorn and Prentiss counties) and in Itawamba there was considerable opposition to secession in 1861. Although these counties contributed a great many men to the Confederate army, there remained some diehard Unionists, who were emboldened in 1862 by the close proximity of the victorious Union army. A few clergymen harbored Unionist or antislavery sentiments. Most notable was a Presbyterian evangelist named John H. Aughey, who led an active body of men resisting the draft and conspiring to aid the Federal troops while Corinth was under attack. He engaged in contraband trade and landed in a Confederate military prison, but he was soon out again. Another Presbyterian minister with strong Unionist sentiments was John A. Lyon of Columbus, a prominent man with strong personal friends. He suffered persecution but managed to remain in Columbus. At one time in 1862, it was reported, there were in a military prison in Columbus a Methodist minister, a Presbyterian, and a United Brother.

While it was hard to bring public authority effectively to bear against Unionists, vigilance committees, supported by public opinion and not restrained by legal niceties, were effective in suppressing most vocal dissent as well as overt acts of disloyalty. Terrorism enforced conformity rather effectively. Discontent and even violent public denunciation of civil and military officials, however, did not necessarily mean Unionist sentiment, and bitter complaint did not usually mean disloyalty or indicate a disposition to join the enemy.

Desertion from the military forces constituted a serious problem. Early in the war it was difficult in the face of adverse public opinion to enforce capital punishment for desertion. After the Battle of Shiloh most of the twelve-month enlistees present wanted to go home, and some did so, despite a new draft law, the enforcement of which they considered a breach of faith. General Bragg resorted to extreme measures to check the movement and to enforce discipline. In February 1864, General Forrest was confronted with a problem of absence without leave and desertion by new troops. He gave the order for nineteen deserters to be shot while sitting on their coffins; after nearly scaring the life out of them, he relented at the last minute on their promise to do their proper duty in the future. Desertion did not necessarily mean disloyalty; more often if reflected deep concern about families back home. Many who deserted returned subsequently of their own will to service. Efforts to round up deserters were sometimes effective, but only in the case of men who were inherently loyal.

So many clergymen departed to join the army that organized religion at home was partially disrupted. Many accounts of the war, however, indicate a general interest of both civilians and soldiers in

Lieutenant General Nathan Bedford Forrest commanded cavalry forces defending the Tenn-Tom country from Northern invaders. Photo: Agee Collection, University of Alabama Library.

Marker at Brice's Crossroads, scene of the battle on June 10, 1864. Photo: Jan Weaver.

attending religious services. Improvisation was sometimes necessary. When all the churches at Okolona were being used as hospitals, Kate Cumming wrote: "This morning I went to church. A Mrs. Chute and I raised the tunes. The services were held under a large oak-tree."

A Federal expedition from Vicksburg in February 1864 under General William T. Sherman was directed against Meridian and the M&O Railroad. Sherman was to destroy the railroads in the Meridian area, and an associated cavalry expedition from Memphis under General William Sooy Smith was to effect destruction on the M&O to the northward. The two forces were then to unite and, if the situation was favorable, to raid Selma and even attack Mobile. Sherman wreaked heavy damage on Meridian and its associated railroads and fell back to wait for Smith. The latter, after much delay, left a point on the Memphis and Charleston Railroad near Memphis with some seven thousand cavalry and moved southeastward to Okolona, then on down the M&O line past West Point. He was opposed by a smaller but ably led cavalry force under General Nathan Bedford Forrest, who harassed him and fell back until Smith was deep in hostile territory, then attacked and defeated him in a running battle from West Point to Okolona. Unable to reach Sherman, Smith fell back in haste to Memphis, but he had extensively destroyed railroad facilities, as well as homesteads, cotton gins, cotton, and corn. He carried away hundreds of Negroes, of whom many were later recovered by the Confederates. These raids were particularly damaging to the M&O, but repair work began as soon as the hostile forces were gone.

After the Meridian expedition, General Sherman was sent to Chattanooga to command a large military campaign against Atlanta, and for many months federal military activities in northeast Mississippi had the object of keeping General Forrest out of Tennessee, where he might cut Sherman's supply lines to Chattanooga. General Samuel D. Sturgis and some eight thousand men left Memphis in early June 1864 with orders to strike the M&O line at Corinth, capture any force there, and move southward, destroying the railroad to Tupelo, Okolona, and as far south as he could get. He was also to destroy Forrest's cavalry and to ravage the prairie country. Learning that the Confederates had evacuated Corinth and moved south, he sent Colonel Joseph Kargé to destroy the railroad southward from Rienzi, but Forrest's men drove Kargé off. Sturgis proceeded toward the M&O Railroad at Guntown, but Forrest, with a much smaller force, met and defeated him at Brice's Cross Roads. Sturgis's force, hotly pursued, fled toward Memphis.

A new expedition under General A. J. Smith left the Memphis area in early July 1864 with 14,700 men, with the repeated object of striking the M&O railroad at Tupelo, wreaking destruction on the prairie country, and destroying Forrest. On July 14–15, there was a bloody battle near Tupelo. The result was indecisive, but Smith had to retire to Memphis without destroying Forrest, and he succeeded only in tearing up about four miles of the M&O track at Tupelo. He did not penetrate deeply into the prairie region. The Confederate

A Civil War cemetery at Okolona. Photo: David C. Weaver.

army this time was commanded by General Stephen D. Lee, under whom Forrest served. General Smith was sent again into Mississippi in August 1864, but Forrest upset his plans this time by raiding Memphis.

On December 21, 1864, a cavalry expedition under Brigadier General Benjamin H. Grierson left Memphis to threaten Corinth, then in Confederate hands, and proceeded down the Mobile and Ohio Railroad spreading destruction. The railroad was being used to send supplies to Confederate General John B. Hood's beleaguered army in Tennessee. The expedition's success reflects the waning fortunes of the Confederacy. Among other things, the invaders destroyed bridges between Booneville and Guntown, surprised and captured Tupelo, surprised and dispersed Forrest's force at Verona on Christmas night, burned 300 wagons (most of which had been taken by Forrest from Sturgis), seized 4,000 new English carbines and other guns intended for Forrest's forces, thoroughly wrecked the railroad between Egypt and Prairie Station, and intercepted Confederate telegraphic dispatches. Fourteen railroad locomotives and 100 cars were destroyed, along with a pile driver and its engine, 700 hogs, and large amounts of corn and wheat. In addition the expedition took some five hundred prisoners and continued to ravage the country as it moved west toward Vicksburg.

Cotton production was greatly diminished during the war, as emphasis was placed upon food crops. Social pressure was brought to bear to reduce the attention given to cotton, but it was the great money crop, and few were willing to abandon it entirely. To be sure of getting food for its armies, the Confederacy imposed a tax in kind. A commissary station was established at Gainesville in 1864 for its collection, and Foster M. Kirksey of Eutaw was appointed deputy commissary agent, with the responsibility of buying supplies and assessing and collecting the tax in Greene County. The crops taxed were corn, buckwheat, rice, Irish potatoes, cured fodder, sugar cane

Lieutenant General Stephen D. Lee, under whom General Forrest served, was in general command of the Confederate forces in the Battle of Tupelo, July 14–15, 1864. Photo: Library of Congress.

molasses, sorghum molasses, cotton, peas, beans, groundpeas (peanuts), wheat, oats, rye, cured hay, and wool. Ten percent of the production was collected in tax. The principal productions were corn and cured fodder. There was a substantial amount of wheat and some rice and a good deal of sorghum molasses. Peas and groundpeas were produced generally but in modest quantities. Kirksey's records for 1864 show that a great many farmers produced no cotton in that year. The crops collected were sent in sacks by wagon to Gainesville, where transportation by railroad and steamboat was available to Mobile, then under siege. Crops for feeding hogs were exempt from the tax, but meat animals were taxed at 10 percent, payable in kind, and an additional 6 percent tax on pork had to be paid in bacon.[8]

Kirksey was instructed to make engagements wherever possible with families to care for cattle, and get every family to promise to fatten one or more beeves for government to be delivered in the fall or winter. On one occasion anonymous donors put 214 sacks of corn on a steamboat for Mobile.

Columbus, the principal town of the Tenn-Tom area, had a well-developed social and economic life and was spared the direct effects of the enemy's incursions. It saw considerable military traffic and for a brief time was the headquarters of General Forrest. To soldiers in training or fresh from combat it looked wonderful. A pontoon bridge connected military camps west of the Tombigbee with the town. Soldiers tell of boundless hospitality, stately homes, and attentive ladies. Many officers were comfortably quartered in citizens' homes.

Thomas J. Key, retreating with General Hood's army after its disastrous campaign in Tennessee, came to Columbus on January 5, 1865. As he saw it:

> There were many magnificent palaces and residences as we approached the business section of the town, and the handiwork of beautiful women was displayed in the tastily arranged gardens that furnished indubitable evidence of her cultivated mind. The streets of Columbus were wide and well arranged, and the buildings looked new and in good repair.
>
> There were a number of mercantile houses open but the supply of goods was not large. The official in charge of the Newsome [Newsom] Hospital carried me through the spacious buildings, showing me the conveniences provided for the sick and wounded soldiery. In one parlor today I met three generals on crutches.[9]

Columbus dwellers, however, suffered from numerous privations from the scarcity of supplies during the war, as did other people of the region. Innovative substitutions and doing without were common. As the only large town in Mississippi escaping raids, Columbus became a center of government late in the war.

8. The Kirksey Papers in the University of Alabama Library provide the records relied upon here.

9. Wirt Armistead Cate, ed., *Two Soldiers: The Campaign Diaries of Thomas J. Key . . . and Robert J. Campbell* (Chapel Hill: University of North Carolina Press, 1938), p. 178. The quotation is abridged.

Home of General Stephen D. Lee in Columbus. After the war Lee wrote historical accounts of the battles of northeast Mississippi. Photo: Library of Congress.

W. O. Hart, born in 1857, whose mother moved her family to Gainesville in 1863 to be near her soldier husband, later wrote about Gainesville as he remembered it.

When it was expected that Mobile was about to fall [in 1865], in our house a newspaper was published by the owners of some paper in Mobile. After the supply of paper they had brought with them was exhausted, and the small amount that was in the town, they began to publish their newspaper on wall paper and kept it up until the end of the war.

Gainesville before and during the war was a flourishing town and a great shipping point. The boat trade on the Tombigbee river to Mobile and Columbus was very large, and I saw many boats on its waters. There were many large stores there, and a short railroad connected the town with the Mobile and Ohio. The place was frequently visited by large bodies of Confederate troops, and many times prisoners were brought in to be taken to other points for exchange or confinement.

I remember the cloud of dust as the [Federal] cavalry came into town [probably in late December 1864]. They burned the telegraph office, tore up part of the railroad tracks, and carried off all the horses they could find. As far as I can remember, no damage was done to private property. But several times afterwards, when it was reported that the raiders were coming back, we buried all our silverware in the yard.[10]

As late as January 9, 1865, the Federals carried out a reconnaissance from Eastport toward Iuka, and on January 19 there was a skirmish at Corinth. After four years of war, however, the strength of the Southern armies was worn thin. Collapse came in April. General John T. Croxton's cavalry force burned the University of Alabama at Tuscaloosa and moved through Pickens County into northern Greene, burned Lanier's Mill on the Sipsey River on April 7, skir-

10. W. O. Hart, "A Boy's Recollection of the War," in *Publications: Mississippi Historical Society*, vol. 12 (University, Miss.: Mississippi Historical Society, 1912), p. 151.

mished with a Confederate contingent, then retreated northward. The Confederates evacuated Mobile on the eleventh, and Federal troops entered the city the next day. The capture came too late to have any effect upon the war, for General Robert E. Lee had surrendered at Appomattox Court House in Virginia on April 9. General Forrest's force, recently defeated by General James H. Wilson's cavalry in Alabama, was disbanded at Gainesville on May 9, 1865. The war was over.

Returning home to Corinth, after serving through the war with General Forrest, Thomas D. Duncan, that eager young cavalryman of 1861 (previously quoted), observed: "The whole prospect was a picture of desolation, as this town and vicinity had been under the very heel of war for four long, weary years; but nature had not forsaken the landscape entirely, for it was carpeted with grass and clover and wild flowers—a beautiful winding sheet for the dead hopes and prospects of the buoyant boys who had marched away from this place under the Southern battle flag."

By good fortune Columbus, Aberdeen, Macon, Eutaw, and Gainesville had largely escaped war destruction, and Lowndes, Noxubee, Pickens, Greene, and Sumter counties had seen little military activity. These counties had been the great growers of cotton. But now by the freeing of the slaves the labor system which had produced most of the surplus for export had been destroyed. Liquid capital was gone, and buildings and fields suffered from neglect.

Of the Confederate soldiers who returned home after the war, a large part came back too late to engage in the planting of a new crop. Many were wounded and in generally poor health. Their homes and farms were usually in dilapidated condition, and their livestock was largely gone, as were stores of food. For a time resources had to be devoted primarily to the problem of staying alive. Many families, both white and black, struggled against starvation.

In the summer of 1865 large numbers of the freed slaves roamed about, living off the country. Many freedmen moved into centers of population such as Columbus, Aberdeen, and Eutaw. Even the Black Belt villages saw the addition of an idle black population, which lived in wretched poverty with the aid of meager rations from the federal government. Hundreds died when their settlements were ravaged by epidemics of cholera and typhoid fever. All economic groups suffered heavily from the war, but planter-lawyers, who had provided the leadership for business and society before the war, had the most to lose. They were generally unable to meet their debts in 1865. The merchants were in an equally bad predicament. Unconditional Unionists were hit as hard as the rest.

At the end of the war, local and state governmental authority disintegrated. Many men, demoralized and faced with poverty, turned to plundering their neighbors. Violent crimes were very numerous, but they were not generally against the freedmen. When felons were apprehended, there was no way to punish them except through the summary action of vigilantes. Military government was inadequate to the systematic maintenance of law and order.

During the summer of 1865 new state provisional governments sought vainly to cope with the problem of civil disturbances. When local governments were reestablished, they were very weak and could not cope with the situation without military assistance. Yet mass substitution of Negro troops for whites when the northern men went home created severe racial tensions and inhibited cooperation between local civil authorities and the military.

Repudiation of the huge Confederate debts and currency issues had devastating effects on the credit standing of their holders. U.S. currency was so scarce that the payments to soldiers quartered in the area became very important to the local economy. Merchants and planters needed credit to get started again. Cotton was a tangible thing of value, and during the war it had been used as a source of ready cash when traded through the lines. The Confederate government had acquired title to a great deal of it to secure foreign loans, and individual farmers and planters in the Upper Tombigbee Valley continued to grow and store it for postwar rehabilitation. Selling at a high price in 1865, it was an important marketable asset that might provide for the payment of debts and lay a basis for economic revival.

People who held cotton, however, were confronted with a heavy federal tax. Treasury agents were responsible for collecting the tax and for locating and seizing Confederate cotton. Their operations, laced with corruption, were accompanied by those of bandits, unscrupulous military officers, merchants, and others who took advantage of the breakdown in the rule of law. The outcome was that the federal government received very little Confederate cotton, and a large part of that which was privately owned was stolen also. Since some of the thieves were local people, it may be presumed that a portion of the proceeds remained in the area and contributed to its rehabilitation. The situation created much bitterness, however.

At the end of the war there was a general assumption in both North and South that prewar prosperity and stability would soon return. Slavery had been abolished, and the general Northern assumption was that the former slaves, inspired by freedom, would turn into prosperous farmers and would greatly increase output. Black Belt planters, on the other hand, were fearful that free Negro labor would never be productive. Under severe economic pressure, the planters tried hard to make accommodations. The freedmen, associating work with slavery, were reluctant to work unless driven by compelling necessity, and even then their reliability as laborers left much to be desired. Investment in a growing crop could be completely lost unless the crop was carried through to harvest, and some means was required to prevent the workers from quitting in the middle of the season. Various devices were tried, then abandoned or revised. Some kind of enforceable labor contract providing for payment after the crop had been sold was a possible answer, but it required the advance of supplies on credit.

The rapid decline in the price of cotton and the serious crop failures in 1865, 1866, and 1867 complicated matters by draining away meager resources and further damaging the credit of planters and merchants. The people became slaves to cotton, but they could not restore its production to the levels of 1860. They were thrust, without money, into a money and market economy, where, black or white, they lived at the mercy of creditors.

Although conditions noticeably improved in 1868 and 1869, destitution continued to be widespread among people of both races through the rest of the decade. It is to be remembered that most of the white people in the Tenn-Tom country had never been slave-owners, and most of them did not employ Negro labor after the war. Those in the northern counties, where the white population predominated, suffered heavily with the rest.

In the 1860s and for long afterward the demand for railroads was universal. The Upper Tombigbee Valley obtained a few additions in the 1860s. A branch of the M&O had been opened to Gainesville, but it was soon abandoned. The Selma and Meridian line, which ran through Demopolis and crossed southern Sumter County, was completed in 1865. The Aberdeen branch from the M&O line was opened in 1869. The Alabama and Chattanooga Railroad, begun before the war, was actively under construction at the end of the 1860s. It ran from Meridian through Tuscaloosa to Chattanooga and passed through Sumter and Greene counties. Yet the Mobile and Ohio remained the transportation backbone of the Upper Tombigbee Valley.

Despite the war damage, the M&O at the end of the war was in fair running condition from Mobile to Okolona and was passable for trains to Corinth. Yet there remained vast damage to be repaired. While the company had suffered heavy financial losses because of the war, particularly from the repudiation of Confederate debts, its principal loss came from the deterioration of the productive capacity of the region which it served. It converted a large part of its liquid assets into cotton. Although some of this was burned, stolen, or confiscated, what remained was important for rehabilitation.

The federal government had accumulated at Nashville large numbers of new locomotives and cars, built to the southern railroad gauge, for an expected military campaign in 1865. The M&O was able in time to buy some of this equipment, at a high price but on credit, for renewed operations.

The Memphis and Charleston Railroad was very heavily damaged; yet at the end of the war, trains were being run by the federal military between Memphis and Corinth. Sam Tate, the company's president, had invested part of its funds in prewar Tennessee state bonds and had hoarded some cotton, assets which were converted into cash after the war to aid in restoration.

Restored to operation after the war ended, the Mobile and Ohio Railroad moved large quantities of cotton from the Upper Tombigbee counties to both Mobile and Memphis (via Corinth). Initially, however, a combination of cotton agents, cotton factors, Memphis agents, and military officers, taking advantage of the company's shortage of rolling stock, sent trains down the M&O line to take cotton and haul it to Memphis without the company's consent. Not including these movements, from June 1, 1865, to April 1, 1866, 100,549 bales were shipped to Mobile on the M&O and 17,179 to Corinth for Memphis. Macon shipped 15,886, Columbus 12,215. There were 6,120 from Prairie, most of which had probably come from Aberdeen by wagon.

Steamboat activity on the Upper Tombigbee underwent a marked decline during the war. The cause appears to have been not so much the war as competition with the Mobile and Ohio Railroad and a decline in cotton production. When Mobile was threatened by the enemy in the spring of 1865, steamboats left that city hastily to hide in a secure place up the Tombigbee River, but by May 11 they had returned. During the 1865–1866 boating season, some of them were back on the Upper Tombigbee to supplement the M&O Railroad in the movement of traffic. Twenty-five visits by the boats to Columbus are recorded and nine to Aberdeen, but traffic on both river and railroad fell off considerably the next year.

In 1869 Columbus was receiving some cotton by rail from neighboring towns. It shipped out 14,142 bales by rail. Of this only 3,684 went to Mobile; the rest went east through railroad junction points to the north, particularly Humboldt, Tennessee, and Columbus, Kentucky. This last traffic was much reduced in the 1870s. The largest part of the Columbus cotton sent to Mobile in 1869, perhaps ten thousand bales, went by steamboat.

By the end of 1869 Aberdeen was getting the full benefit of its new railroad connection with Mobile. Most of its previous business had gone to steamboats. The rest had gone out by wagon to nearby stations on the M&O. With the direct rail connection, however, Aberdeen entered a new commercial era. At the end of the 1860s Memphis, Tennessee, was supplying some of the distributive trade of the Upper Tombigbee Valley through the railroad junction at Corinth, although the Mobile and Ohio was taking strong measures to favor Mobile. Other traffic was still tending to follow the same routes as cotton, but the trade pattern was undergoing rapid change.

Despite the survival of some of the little river ports, the shift of commerce away from the river to towns along the line of the M&O is clearly indicated by the traffic figures of that railroad for 1869. Cotton, the principal item carried, was at that time being shipped from a host of small towns along the railroad. These competed with Aberdeen and Columbus, which had no special rate advantages except when steamboats were in port. All were concerned almost exclusively with local trade. Railroad traffic figures from 1869 through 1873 show only a very unimpressive wholesale trade at Columbus and Aberdeen with the neighboring towns.

Politically, Alabama and Mississippi were under outside control in the Reconstruction era. That control, although dominant where exercised, did not extend to all matters, and local interests had an opportunity to engage in local politics and to battle over local issues within the new rules, the main one of which provided, beginning in 1867, the voting franchise for freedmen. Alabama was under direct military rule in 1865 and again from 1867 to 1868, Mississippi in 1865 and then from 1867 to 1870. There was really no room for a liberal political party, for there was scant wealth to be redistributed, and indeed there was no such party. Republicans, supported by federal troops and the Negro vote, predominated. The Negro vote might decide elections, but it could do little for the great body of freedmen. White factions contested with each other for control of the Negro vote. While Alabama was readmitted to the Union in 1868 and Mississippi in 1870, federal troops remained to support the puppet regimes. Local governments were weak, and disorders were common. This was a ready-made situation for vigilantes or private law enforcers, most notably the Ku Klux Klan. As generally happens with vigilantes, the more responsible men soon dropped out, leaving extremists in control, and the Klan itself became a leading source of the lawlessness that it was supposed to suppress. Its life, however, was short, the Klan of the twentieth century being a later creation.

Reconstruction under outside control eventually produced among local elements a unity that led to the formation of the Democratic and Conservative party, which in the 1870s redeemed the states from Radical rule. When military occupation was ended, the redeemers established a new system of order and control, but they could not bring prosperity.

The New Economy, 1870–1890 8

Change without Prosperity

The generation following the Civil War saw a vibrant economic expansion in the nation, a widespread exploitation of natural resources, and a rapid accumulation of capital, but the Upper Tombigbee Valley did not share in this good fortune. It had reached its peak of prosperity just before the Civil War. The damage from the war itself was formidable, and the years of the Reconstruction era did not bring revival.

In the post-Reconstruction years, there was a continuing decline in the production of corn, wheat, potatoes, peas, beans, and orchard products as well as a steady further reduction in the number of cattle, sheep, and swine. The number of hogs per person, a measure of self-sufficiency, which had gone from 2.4 in 1850 to 2.0 in 1860 as farmers concentrated on cotton, dropped to 0.9 in 1890 and continued to contract further (see table 6; county figures appear in the appendix). The region lost not only its self-sufficiency but also much of its ability to produce cotton, the market crop on which its prewar prosperity had been founded. The average of 1.8 bales of cotton produced per person in 1860 fell to 0.7 in 1890. Furthermore, the market price of cotton continued to move down.

The dynamics of economic development and decline are full of subtleties that are difficult to grasp or to measure, but several important elements in the Upper Tombigbee picture can be readily described. Self-sufficiency plus bountiful commercial crops from virgin soils tilled with slave labor had brought prosperity in 1860. Now, however, there were ominous signs of soil exhaustion, and the slave labor was gone. Time was required to rebuild livestock herds; yet the surviving animals were needed for food. Furthermore, the accumulated capital necessary to support new initiatives and developments was gone. The size of farms underwent a steady reduction, as did production per farm. The destructive effect of all this is reflected in the declining proportion of farms operated by owners, which had by 1890 sunk to a level of 23.5 percent in Greene County and 26.9

Table 6. Statistics for Ten Tenn-Tom Counties, 1850–1960

Item	1850	1860	1880	1890	1910	1930	1960
Population	161,236	184,629	204,771	212,462	235,582	235,096	218,792
Whites (%)	45.6	41.8	35.6	36.1	40.4	49.6	58.2
Farms	8,411	7,624	19,689	24,818	39,085	38,630	17,902
Cotton bales							
Total	107,011	328,340	154,444	143,957	138,883	164,492	91,693
Av. bales per farm	12.7	43.1	7.8	5.8	3.6	4.3	5.1
Av. bales per person	0.7	1.8	0.8	0.7	0.6	0.7	0.4
Corn bushels							
Total	6,860,664	8,793,436	4,973,426	4,887,719	3,705,025	5,075,333	3,025,009
Av. bushels per farm	815.7	1,153.4	252.6	196.9	94.8	131.4	169.0
Av. bushels per person	42.6	47.6	24.3	23.0	15.7	21.6	13.8
Hogs							
Total	380,694	370,950	185,173	189,324	147,699	83,369	71,254
Av. hogs per farm	45.3	48.7	9.4	7.6	3.8	2.2	4.0
Av. hogs per person	2.4	2.0	0.9	0.9	0.6	0.4	0.3
Beef cattle							
Total	81,782	73,349	55,435	77,281	70,817	81,529	206,631
Av. cattle per farm	9.7	9.6	2.8	3.1	1.8	2.1	11.5
Av. cattle per person	0.5	0.4	0.3	0.4	0.3	0.3	0.9
Milk cows							
Total	41,746	40,067	43,913	50,022	59,957	67,425	41,757
Av. cows per farm	5.0	5.3	2.2	2.0	1.5	1.7	2.3
Av. cows per person	0.3	0.2	0.2	0.2	0.3	0.3	0.2
Sheep							
Total	72,903	79,062	42,206	—	13,270	6,933	17,100
Av. sheep per farm	8.7	10.4	2.1	—	0.3	0.2	0.9
Av. sheep per person	0.5	0.4	0.2	—	0.1	0.0	0.1
Value of livestock ($)							
Total	4,735,201	10,346,295	4,334,451	5,503,930	10,430,030	12,208,212	48,590,780[a]
Av. value per farm	563	1,357	220	222	267	316	2,714
Av. value per person	29	56	21	26	44	52	222
Farms operated							
by owners (%)	ca. 80.0[b]	ca. 80.0[b]	48.3	38.9	30.4	23.7	44.5
Value of mfd. goods ($)	633,002	2,227,852	1,113,646	843,928	—	11,793,681	64,721,000[c]
Wage earners	852	1,437	759	942	—	4,437	14,815
Wages ($)	307,039	449,700	129,033	179,873	—	2,843,638	36,757,000[c]
Av. wage per worker ($)	360	313	170	191	—	641	2,481
Av. value of mfd. goods							
per worker ($)	743	1,550	1,467	896	—	2,658	4,369

Note: The counties are Greene, Pickens, Sumter, Clay, Itawamba, Lowndes, Monroe, Noxubee, Prentiss, and Tishomingo, the first three being in Alabama and the last seven in Mississippi. Significant changes in counties and county boundaries between 1860 and 1880 mean that totals are not always strictly comparable.

[a]Value of sales of livestock and its products.

[b]See Frank L. Owsley, *Plain Folk of the Old South* (Baton Rouge: Louisiana State University Press, 1949), p. 182; Herbert Weaver, *Mississippi Farmers, 1850–1860* (Nashville: Vanderbilt University Press, 1945), p. 65.

[c]Amount for Tishomingo County withheld to avoid disclosing figures for individual companies.

Source: U.S. Decennial Census.

Table 7. Occupations in Pleasant Ridge in 1880

		Heads of household	
Occupation	Total Population	White	Black
None	674	8	13
Laborer	565	5	78
Farmer	400	81	231
Home	139	11	0
School	88	0	0
Cook	74	1	18
Teacher	11	3	1
Servant	11	0	0
Wash woman	6	0	0
Mechanic	5	3	2
Merchant	5	3	1
Blacksmith	4	2	0
Nurse	4	0	1
Carpenter	3	1	2
Physician	3	1	0
Store clerk	3	1	0
Fireman	2	0	1
Lawyer	2	0	1
Miller	2	2	0
Minister	1	1	0
Total	2,002	124	348

Source: Manuscript returns, U.S. Census, 1880.

percent in Noxubee, although in the northern counties it was much higher, running to 77.2 percent in Tishomingo. By that time most of the tenants were sharecroppers. Over the next forty years there was a great further reduction in the percentage of owners. The average value of farms, which had reached rather high levels in several of the prairie counties in 1860, had fallen very low by 1890. Figures representing black and white farmers show that, although the condition of both was bad, that of the blacks was worse, and black-operated farms were less productive.

The counties differed markedly in the proportion of white to black population. In general there was a steady decline in the white percentage down to 1890. In that year Greene County was only 14.7 percent white and Noxubee County 17.2 percent. Yet the white portion of Itawamba County was 91.6 percent and that of Tishomingo 89.3 percent. Where blacks were few their economic characteristics seem to have been more like those of the whites than in counties where the black population was proportionately higher. In the Pleasant Ridge community of Greene County the population grew from 1,300 to 2,002 between 1860 and 1880 (see table 7). In 1880 there were 210 farms in Pleasant Ridge, but only 85 farmers owned their land; 26 farmers rented land on a fixed-rent basis (as cash tenants), and 99 farmed on shares. Tenantry had taken the place of slavery.

Livestock producers who depended on the open range were coming to the end of an era. A growing population was occupying the lands and building fences, and worst of all, the spread of "stock law" required stock growers to fence their stock in. It became impractical to drive animals to market over long distances as ranges to feed them on the road became more difficult to secure. Furthermore, the railroads began to pour in packed pork and beef from the western and northern corn, hog, and cattle farms, where production was more bountiful than in the Tombigbee area.

Producing a commercial crop required financing, for people must live while they grow a crop. With money gone, the region could not restore commercial production until it could acquire a surplus to sustain life while the market crop was being produced—that is, for one year. The surplus might be accumulated a little at a time, a long-drawn-out process, or credit might be sought to support the farmer during the year while the crop was being produced. Under the gradually evolving new credit system, merchants having direct contact with individual crop producers located themselves along the railroad lines. Little settlements grew into larger ones, and an increasing number of people came to live in commercial centers of sizes varying from the crossroads to a town as large as Columbus.

A merchant furnished supplies to the farmer and sometimes a little cash, and for security he commonly demanded a lien (mortgage) on the future crop. The application of fertilizer did not compensate for the exhaustion of the upland soils of the Black Prairie, and yields per acre sharply declined. As merchants demanded planting of more cotton to cover their liens, production of meat and bread fell off. Fatback pork from the North replaced the earlier lean meat. Concentration on this and on wheat flour produced an ill-balanced diet, causing widespread dietary deficiencies and a disease called pellagra.

The year 1873 was particularly disastrous. The ledger of the general store of J. C. H. Jones of Fairfield for that year provides a sample of local conditions. Randomly picking a group of fifteen men and three women from that ledger, we find a total expenditure of $203.18 for whiskey during the year at prices of $0.50 to $0.60 per quart. At an average of $0.55, 20.5 quarts of whiskey were consumed per customer. One bought none, but another spent $61.40. Presumably nonpurchasers aided in the consumption. The group spent $227.79 for smoking tobacco, snuff, and chewing plugs, an average of $12.60 per customer. The store sold many classes of items, including food, dry goods, hardware, and even livestock. John Buck bought a mule for $170, and Dick Nash bought two mules and a horse for $500. Purchases averaged $197.13 per customer, ranging from $1.75 in one case to $998.74 in another. Of particular interest is the item of bacon. Seven of the group bought none, but one traded bacon as a credit to his account. The other eleven bought $908.91 worth at $0.18 to $0.20 per pound. At an average of $0.19 per pound, this represents 435 pounds for each of the eleven who bought bacon on credit. This figure reflects the postbellum lack of self-sufficiency. A more extensive analysis of 109 of the ledger accounts reveals an overall debit balance at the beginning of 1873 of $2,717.27, but a year later the amount had increased to $10,386.01. Individual debts at the latter date range from $0.85 to $1,296.27. The year had been a disastrous one for Jones's customers.[1]

The retail merchant's business was usually small and his markups were large. He might charge interest on open accounts. Jones charged 10 percent. The merchant's business was risky, however, for he made advances on the security of a crop not yet produced, with a market price which was hard to predict. As cotton prices declined over the years, the farmer was increasingly unable in bad years to pay out at the end of the season. The merchant had to be careful not to advance too much. He was himself a debtor, receiving his stock on credit from wholesale merchants, who expected to be paid off at the end of the season.

The farmer did not have the freedom to change from one furnishing merchant to another until he had paid his debt to the first. Nor could the merchant rid himself of a customer who could not pay off his debt at the end of the year, unless he was willing either to sacrifice the debt or to advance supplies to the farmer for another year to make a crop which might or might not pay off the debt. Pressure of circumstances forced the merchant to make advances with caution and in installments. Many a farmer, particularly among the freedmen, would be wasteful and improvident with supplies advanced too early and in too-large quantities, and the crop might be neglected. The merchant needed to know his man and keep up with his progress in cultivation. As conditions gradually worsened, more and more people became enmeshed and ensnared in the crop-lien system. Merchants obtained an increasing control over their lives, and the economic position of many degenerated into a state of peonage. Some slipped off to Texas, leaving their debts behind.

Some of the people operating on credit were tenants and some were landowners. In decade after decade, however, we see the growth of tenantry. Some tenants rented land for a cash payment to be made after the crop had been harvested. More and more, however, the system of sharecrop tenantry spread. According to varying contracts, the landlord might furnish a dwelling, land, tools, and work stock, and the tenant and his family would provide the labor. At the end of the season the cotton crop would be divided, the tenant's share being one-third to one-half, depending on the time and place and on who furnished what. The corn crop, too, would be divided, the proportions depending on who furnished the work stock and perhaps on other factors. The sharecrop system was unsuited to livestock production.

A landowner might advance various supplies to his tenant, these becoming a charge against the tenant's share of the crop. If the landowner lacked the necessary resources, he had to resort to a merchant and perhaps agree to a lien on both land and crop. The tenant was responsible for the lien, but so was the landlord. Conflicts developed between landowners and merchants over their respective

---

1. There is a copy of the Jones ledger in the University of Alabama Library.

This tenant farmhouse at Cotton Gin Port is pictured in the 1890s. The farm specialized in cotton production and was representative of a type well known from 1870 to 1940. Photo: Amory Regional Museum.

A Columbus blacksmith shop photographed late in the nineteenth century. Photo: Lowndes County Public Library.

legal rights of control over both tenants and crops, conflicts which the state legislatures were unable to resolve conclusively. Merchants tended to become landowners and planters and vice versa.

The declining productivity of the soils gave rise to various efforts to find solutions to the agricultural problems. Some enterprising farmers worked to develop more efficient methods, experimenting with new crops, with commercial livestock production and dairying, and with increased use of fertilizers, but they found the technical and economic problems far from easy to solve—and very few farmers could afford to experiment. The establishment of land-grant agricultural schools and experiment stations at Auburn in Alabama and Starkville in Mississippi brought attention to agricultural problems but little immediate practical improvement on the farm. A boy at-

The sawmill at Amory soon after the town was founded in 1887. Photo: Amory Regional Museum.

tending one of these institutions of enlightenment soon learned that the farm was no place of opportunity for him.

Manufacturing operations in the Upper Tombigbee Valley were few, and the successful ones were almost entirely connected either with agriculture or with the exploitation of the forests. High transportation costs had protected local handicraft manufacturing, but the situation changed with the construction of the Mobile and Ohio Railroad in the 1850s. Local producers found it difficult to compete with large and well-organized northern industries in local markets as transportation became cheap and reliable. At the same time, the people's disposable income for the purchase of anything beyond necessities was not such as to provide an encouraging market for new products. Extreme scarcity of capital and inexperience in industrial production militated against the development of manufacturing industries, except when the factors were exceedingly favorable. The local economy was oriented toward agricultural production, and neither planters nor merchants wished to lose either their labor supply or their social position to industry and industrial developers.

Yet there were opportunities in the processing of local raw materials and in selling them in distant markets. Cotton and cottonseed were in abundant supply, and both hardwood and pine timber were plentiful in various parts of the area. Local labor was cheap, and the railroads and waterways provided low-cost transportation for heavy raw materials and products. The manufacture of cotton products at Bay Springs and at the unsuccessful Cibolo Mills at Artesia amounted to very little. The lumber industry, however, developed on a commercial scale rather quickly after the end of the depression of the 1870s. The Upper Tombigbee River and its tributaries proved useful in floating logs downstream from the woods to lumber mills along the river, and the construction of new railroads tapped additional timber resources. Competition in the distant markets, however, lim-

The Columbus Woolen Mill was one of the few in the South in the late nineteenth century. It used a raw material of declining production in the Upper Tombigbee Valley. Photo: Lowndes County Public Library.

This cotton gin at Amory is representative of a great many found in the Upper Tombigbee Valley in the late nineteenth century. Photo: Amory Regional Museum.

ited the financial potential of the lumber business. Manufacture of staves became a specialty of some of the mills of the Upper Tombigbee. Steam compresses to reduce the size of cotton bales and increase the carrying capacity of ships and railroad cars required heavy equipment and employed people in such commercial centers as Columbus, Aberdeen, and West Point.

In the 1880s cottonseed oil mills were established at numerous points in the cotton country where transportation costs were favorable. The mills would commonly re-gin cottonseeds twice with very sharp saws to remove the short fibers called "linters," which had a commercial value, then crush the hulls to separate the yellow "meats," the oily interiors, which were squeezed in presses to produce cottonseed oil and cottonseed meal, both valuable products.

In 1885 the industries of Columbus included a woolen mill, an ice factory, cotton gins, gristmills, a cotton compress, a wooden ware manufacturing plant, a gasworks, a cottonseed oil mill, a flour mill, sawmills, and a stave mill. There were hotels, livery stables, cotton sheds, and cotton yards. Aberdeen industries in 1885 included a cotton compress, an oil mill, saw and planing mills, cotton gins, a gristmill, and a stave mill. There were also hotels, livery stables, cotton sheds, and cotton yards.

Traffic, Trade, and the River in the 1870s

Transportation influences had much to do with the changing economic structure in the 1870s and 1880s. The Mobile and Ohio Railroad Company went to great lengths to favor Mobile as a trade center and to keep Mobile's freight rates equalized with those of New Orleans. This policy required extreme long-and-short-haul discriminations in rates. Traffic figures show that by the early 1870s nearly all cotton was moving southward to Mobile.

Foodstuffs brought from the West, known as "western freight," produced a heavy tonnage of low value per ton. A large element in the value of the foodstuffs was "place value," in which transportation cost was a prime factor. A difference of a couple of cents per hundred pounds in the freight rate would build up one trade center at the expense of others, so such rates were an extremely sensitive matter. Under the basing point system, rates on western freight from Cairo to Columbus direct were the sum of those from Cairo to Mobile and back from Mobile to Columbus. The important thing to Columbus, however, was the relationship between its own rates and those of competing trade centers.

The distribution of manufactured goods, which came mainly from eastern manufacturers and suppliers, was another element of traffic. Eastern goods could be obtained from New York and the East either directly by rail or through Mobile jobbers, as credit and convenience might dictate. Transportation costs on such goods were a relatively small part of their value, so the freight rates on them were less restrictive and controlling of the routes of trade than the rates on cotton or western freight.

In Greene County the railroad from Meridian through Tuscaloosa to Chattanooga, construction on which had been under way in the 1850s, was revived after the war, and by 1871 Eutaw had a rather unreliable railroad connection with Meridian and thereby with Mobile. It was several years before this troubled line, the Alabama and Chattanooga, was in reliable and complete operation. While Eutaw was not on the Tombigbee River, it was the dominant trade center of Greene County and of a considerable agricultural area.

The situation of the little river ports continued to be mildly favorable for serving limited areas adjacent to the Tombigbee River and occasionally taking traffic away from the Mobile and Ohio Railroad to the West. They were not favorably situated for the handling of western freight (foodstuffs), however, on a competitive basis. Minimal facilities included a warehouse or cotton shed and some means of getting to the riverboats, perhaps a tramway and cotton slide from a platform at the top of the bluff. The warehouse did not have to be immediately adjacent to the river. If it was too close, sooner or later it would be flooded. The operation of such facilities was seasonal, depending on the stage of the river and the condition of the wagon roads.

Pickensville was one such little river port. It was fairly well equipped and had more than one warehouse. The manuscript records of the 1880 census show a population of 214. Besides 2 retail grocers there were 7 men listed as merchants and 8 as clerks in stores. There were 2 blacksmiths, a barber, 2 carpenters, 3 music teachers, 2 attorneys, 4 schoolteachers, 1 art teacher, 1 warehouse keeper, 1 physician, 1 jeweler, 1 post office clerk, and 9 females from twelve to twenty years of age listed as "at school." Pickensville was on high ground nearly a half a mile from the river.

Vienna, another of the little river ports, was described by the Carrollton *West Alabamian*, January 27, 1875, as "a flourishing little village with two stores." Henry C. Connerly and Company and M. F. Crooks and Company had their names on the stores. W. B. Peebles was also mentioned as a merchant, and Mrs. Haynes as the operator of a boardinghouse. Small flatboats were bringing cotton down the Sipsey River to Vienna. Fairfield, Memphis, and Warsaw continued their prewar functions.

Merchants of towns aspiring to grow as wholesale centers gave their attention to securing differential advantages in freight rates, especially those on western freight. Competition between routes could force rates down at the points of competition, so more railroads were avidly sought. The capital-starved, destitute Upper Tombigbee Valley lacked resources to do much on its own in railroad building, and the area saw little railroad development until the depression of the seventies was over.

Having access to the river, Columbus and Aberdeen were favorably situated for getting reduced rates, but Mobile and Ohio Railroad traffic figures for the early 1870s show only a very unimpressive wholesale trade at Columbus and Aberdeen with the nearby railroad towns, which were at that time more competitors of the river trade centers than tributary to them. Columbus sought to use the river as leverage in getting rate concessions, and the M&O resisted.

In the depression years following the panic of 1873, the M&O was desperately trying to survive on the traffic of an impoverished country by charging all it could where it could. Meanwhile trade centers and merchants struggled in equal desperation for commercial advantage in their competition with each other, burdened as they were with diminished trade and uncollectible debts.

Rate reductions which were compelled at some points by competition made people at other points think they were being overcharged and discriminated against. They also fueled the fire of public antagonism to the railroad companies and stirred the hostility of juries in damage suits. Anger at the Mobile and Ohio rose in Columbus, and

The steamboat *Hard Cash* served the Upper Tombigbee trade for many years in the 1880s and 1890s. Beside it is a barge that could be loaded with cotton bales. Photo: Lowndes County Public Library.

the merchants at that place schemed to use the river as leverage in getting rate concessions. Against river competition the railroad could fight back by cutting the rates to Mobile when a steamboat appeared around the bend, then raising them after the boat had departed empty. Railroad rates might be raised whenever the level of the river was too low for steamboats, which was most of the year, and there were other railroad devices for fighting competition. The Mobile and Ohio completed and opened its Starkville branch in 1874. The company fell into receivership the next year, but the fight by Columbus interests to beat the rates down continued.

In November 1875, the *W. S. Holt*, a 225-ton steamboat with a draft of only sixteen inches, appeared at Columbus. It was partly owned by Columbus mercantile interests and partly by the Central Railroad and Banking Company of Georgia. Its purpose was to serve the commercial interests of Columbus and Savannah and not those of Mobile, with the aid of a railroad connection at Demopolis on the Tombigbee River.

The boating season began early and was very good in 1875–1876. On December 15 a Pickens County newspaper reported six boats running on the river, some going as high as Cotton Gin Port and all going to Mobile with full loads of cotton, much of which had formerly traveled by rail. This was not the usual river traffic but an organized attack on the M&O. It succeeded, and the *W. S. Holt* soon moved elsewhere.

Aberdeen, which had suffered for a decade from the lack of a rail connection, began its commercial regeneration when a spur line to the M&O was opened late in 1869. The town government in April 1870 pledged financial support to the Selma, Marion, and Memphis Railroad, which was to build its main line through Aberdeen. While Reconstruction politics and other troubles prevented the portion of the line through Aberdeen from being constructed, the carpetbag government did manage to get a bridge built across the Tombigbee nearby. Aberdeen was not as well situated as Columbus for down-river water traffic, but its merchants actively pursued measures to draw in the trade of the surrounding cotton country. In 1878 they built the little steamboat *Lillie Lou* and the barge *Maggie Virginia* and sent them out to tap the trade of the east and west branches of the Upper Tombigbee and other seasonally navigable streams. In the following season Aberdeen handled more than eighteen thousand bales of cotton. Columbus and Demopolis also from time to time followed the practice of sending out small steamboats to bring in business.

Macon, on the main line of the M&O, complained in 1872 that its cotton rate to Mobile was five dollars per bale, compared with two dollars and a half at Meridian and Corinth and three dollars and a half at Columbus. Macon wanted lower rates. It was located far up the crooked little Noxubee River, but no steamboat had reached it since the railroad arrived in 1856. It was located in a region of heavy cotton production, but in transportation rates it was hardly to be distinguished from the other stations in the area along the M&O. Discontent with the railroad at Macon was great.

Gainesville merchants often sent barges a few miles up the Noxu-bee River to pick up cotton. Gainesville relied so much on water transportation that the M&O Railroad's Gainesville branch was un-profitable. The cash-starved company sold it for $19,000 to a private buyer in April 1879, and he apparently took up the track for salvage. Eutaw, the principal trade center for Greene County, was well located on the Alabama and Chattanooga Railroad, which came into reliable and full operation in the late 1870s, and Eutaw was less than three miles from good landings on the Warrior River and in a position to control the trade of its limited area, which was essentially Greene County.

The reliable, all-year, all-weather transportation of the railroads was much superior to the seasonal and erratic movements of freight and passengers by steamboat, although the latter could be more convenient for people who lived close to the river and who might be willing to await the boating season. While their limited needs did help to keep steamboats in operation, the principal role of the river in the economic affairs of the region was as an instrument of potential competition in a power struggle over the railroad rate structure. It was a struggle for commercial advantage or commercial survival. It was not river traffic but the credible threat of river competition that was important.

By an act of July 11, 1870, Congress directed the secretary of war to make a survey of the Tombigbee River from its mouth to the head of navigation. At the same time, steamboat captains were strongly complaining of the hazard to navigation caused by the drawbridge of the Alabama and Chattanooga Railroad across the Upper Tombigbee at Jones Bluff (Epes). The survey, hastily made in the winter of 1870–1871 by a representative of the Corps of Engineers when the waters were at flood stage, led to a report that from Columbus, called the head of navigation, to the mouth, the Tombigbee River was not susceptible to permanent improvement by the use of locks and dams. An act of Congress of June 10, 1872, however, appropriated $10,000 for snag removal on the Tombigbee below Demopolis, part of which sum was subsequently transferred to the Upper Tombigbee. A portion of the chalk bluff at Epes was removed to eliminate the hazard caused by the railroad bridge.

Under the same act engineer Powhatan Robinson made a survey with the purpose of ascertaining the cost of establishing all-year navigation from Columbus north to Fulton. He cut through heavy canebrakes to carry in his instruments, measured the flow of water at various points, and calculated the amount of earth that had to be removed by dredging to secure a channel sixty feet wide and two and a half feet deep from Columbus to Waverly, but he found the cost of improvement by this method to be prohibitive. Then he considered a plan for building locks and dams for slack-water navigation. Ten dams raising the water level by six feet each, he said, would be required between Columbus and Aberdeen, to provide all-year navigation. He found the cost excessive when compared with the expected benefits. Then he descended the river in a skiff from Fulton to Columbus and carefully recorded his observations. His conclusion was that the probable benefit would not justify an attempt to secure low-water navigation. He did, however, recommend the removal of snags, logs, drifts, fish traps, and overhanging trees to ensure good navigation at high water.

Robinson observed that navigation was practicable but not good below Aberdeen and that above Aberdeen the planters had no railroad and were subject to heavy costs in getting their cotton to market, so a small sum then available was expended above Aberdeen. Thousands of trees were cut and many logs were removed. Islands were cleared of small growth so as not to obstruct the passage of boats at high water. Late in 1874 the work was completed as far up as Barr's Ferry, near Smithville.

By an act of June 23, 1874, Congress authorized the Army Corps of Engineers to survey the route for a canal to connect the Upper Tombigbee with the Tennessee River. The scheme appears to have originated not with the special interests of Columbus and Aberdeen but with a broad scheme of the Granger movement outlined in the Senate's Windom Report of 1874 to reduce transportation costs for American farmers.

It was again engineer Powhatan Robinson who made the survey, and he did quite a thorough job. He reported in 1875 that slack-water navigation, which involved the use of dams to slow the current and deepen the channel, was possible over the divide between the Tennessee and Tombigbee rivers. With Big Bear and Crippled Deer creeks providing access on the Tennessee side, a canal would carry boats over the dividing ridge to Spring and Mackey's creeks on the Tombigbee side. The water supply at the divide would come from a feeder canal eight miles long from a reservoir to be constructed at a place on Big Bear Creek called The Gorge.

Leaving Mackey's Creek at Bay Springs, the canal would move

clear of the stream, to avoid flooding the lowlands, and would proceed thirty-three miles to Fulton's Ferry on the East Fork of the Tombigbee. The canal system could be operated only at high water on both the Tombigbee and the Tennessee rivers, probably four months of the year. It would be navigated not by steamboats but by canal boats seventy feet long and nineteen feet wide with a draft of four feet. A boat of such dimensions could carry about 100 tons. The cost estimate for the proposed development was $1,705,312. The cost of making the canal usable by Tombigbee steamboats and improving the Upper Tombigbee to match would be prohibitive when measured against expected benefits.

One of the problems was that before the full benefits of such a canal could be realized, the Tennessee River needed improvement. The matter was quietly laid to rest, and no more was to be heard of the building of a Tennessee-Tombigbee canal until 1913. In the Muscle Shoals area of the Tennessee River, however, construction of a new lateral canal was started by the Corps of Engineers in 1875. After coping with many physical problems and with erratic appropriations by Congress, the Corps opened the canal to traffic on November 10, 1890.

Congress appropriated $12,000 in 1878 for the removal of snags, sunken logs, and overhanging trees in the Upper Tombigbee and for the improvement of the worst bars above Columbus. Then an act of 1879 required the Corps of Engineers to survey the Sipsey and the Noxubee rivers and added another $10,000 for work above Columbus. Meanwhile, considerable improvements were being made on the Warrior River and the lower Tombigbee.

Railroad Building and River Improvements in the 1880s

On January 1, 1879, the United States returned to the gold standard, and almost immediately there was a revival of confidence. A new availability of capital stirred economic development in the nation. In its own way the Upper Tombigbee Valley felt the effects, and a period of intense economic activity brought change without prosperity to the area. In the fierce competition between the centers of trade, efforts were focused on improvements in transportation. Congress responded to demands for waterway improvement with increasingly generous appropriations. The new object was to secure uninterrupted, all-season navigation on the Tombigbee from Columbus to Mobile. The Corps of Engineers in 1879 decided that this aim could be accomplished by cutting channels through bars, snagging, cutting overhanging timber, blasting, scraping, building wing dams, and providing shore protection.

In 1879 work was earnestly undertaken to improve the Upper Tombigbee between Demopolis and Columbus, with crews working from both ends. With the prospect of all-season navigation, Columbus interests employed the *Billy Collins*, a sixty-ton side-wheel steamboat, to run to Miller's landing (near Epes). There a connection was made with the Alabama Great Southern Railroad, which ran between Meridian and Chattanooga, thus subjecting the M&O to increased competition. In four and a half months the boat carried 8,000 bales of cotton from Columbus to Epes, 804 bales from way landings to Columbus, 3,032 sacks of cottonseed from way landings to Columbus, and 250,000 pounds of meat from Epes to Columbus. The through rate on compressed cotton from Columbus to Mobile by railroad was forced down to two dollars per bale, and reductions were also secured on return freight. The outlook of Columbus as a trade center was thus brightened.

The effort to secure a year-round navigable depth for the river between Columbus and Demopolis ran into problems at Ten Mile Shoals below Columbus, where the river was obstructed by bars and badly choked with logs for some ten miles. The project depth for the Tombigbee from Mobile to Demopolis was four feet at ordinary low water and from Demopolis to Columbus three feet. All that had been accomplished by 1886 was the following: from Mobile to Demopolis three feet at ordinary low water and from Demopolis to Columbus three feet on a two-foot rise above ordinary low water (this translates into one foot at ordinary low water). The engineers appear to have been very slow to realize that cutting a bar had the effect of draining the pool above and reducing the depth of water, so there was a limit to the benefits of bar cutting in deepening channels. The effort to secure all-season navigation was a dismal failure.

Work on improvements north of Aberdeen was sufficiently completed by late 1879 to permit light-draft steamboats to reach Fulton during the high-water season which followed. The *Lillie Lou*, Aberdeen's little steamboat, made several trips to Fulton during the high-water season of 1880–1881, and in 1886 the river was reported still navigable to Fulton for small boats on a stage of four feet above low water.

Old Town Creek (the West Fork of the Tombigbee) had been navigated at high water as far up as Camargo, sixteen miles from its mouth, prior to the construction of the M&O Railroad. Completion of a project for the removal of snags, logs, and overhanging trees, permitted it to be opened again in 1884 to that point.

With the East Fork open as far as Fulton, engineer Horace Harding was sent in 1881 to examine the possibility of extending navigation as high as Warren's Mill, on Mackey's Creek, five miles above the point where the creek joined Brown's Creek to form the East Fork. The engineer concluded that above the mouth of Brown's Creek steamboat navigation was not practicable, because Mackey's Creek was only twenty-five feet wide and had abrupt bends. Below Walker's Bridge, a county bridge that crossed the East Fork immediately below the junction of the creeks, however, he found the stream as well adapted to high-water navigation as it was below Fulton. Navigation might be facilitated, he said, by cutting overhanging trees and removing logs, stumps, and snags. The benefit to be derived would be a freight saving of $2.50 per bale on about 4,000 bales of cotton annually and a further saving on return supplies. All of these were

The little steamboat *Aberdeen* at work on the Tombigbee River above Aberdeen. Photo: Evans Memorial Library, Aberdeen.

then being hauled over bad roads twenty to thirty-five miles to the Mobile and Ohio and the Memphis and Charleston railroads. So the project of extending high-water navigation to Walker's Bridge was adopted. A project it remained until bypassed by the Tennessee-Tombigbee Waterway. Walker's Bridge has never seen a steamboat.

In 1880 an engineer of the Corps made an examination of the Sipsey River, which flows into the Tombigbee below Vienna, to determine the feasibility of improving it for navigation. He found it to traverse areas from which produce could not be taken to a railroad without a wagon trip of fifty to sixty miles. There were coal seams in the upper areas, which might be reached by barges. At great expense, he said, it might be made navigable for several months of the year. The district engineer described the river as "narrow, crooked, shallow, and very much obstructed by snags, logs, overhanging trees, bridges, fish traps, and mill dams." No recommendation was made, and the matter died quietly.

Ambitious interests at Macon hoped that by opening navigation on the Noxubee they could force the M&O Railroad to reduce its cotton rates to such an extent that they might be able to compete with Columbus and Meridian merchants in buying cotton. No steamboat had gone to Macon since the arrival of the railroad there in 1856, although flatboats or barges from Gainesville had continued to ply the lower part of the Noxubee to move cotton. A report of the Corps of Engineers on a survey of the Noxubee from its mouth to Macon, dated March 6, 1880, was very detailed and comprehensive. Except for a few shoals, the principal obstructions to navigation were described as snags, drift logs, mill dams, fish traps, and overhanging trees. The shoals were found to be of white lime rock, easily removed. Improvement of the river was declared to be practicable and comparatively inexpensive.

The Corps of Engineers adopted a project of creating a channel on the Noxubee navigable during nine months of the year, from the river's mouth to Macon, and started to work on it in August 1880. After several seasons of work by the Corps with limited funds, the steamboat *Dove* arrived at Macon from Mobile in late January 1883. In February the *Dove* was back at Macon again, followed by Aberdeen's little *Lillie Lou*, but neither boat seems to have gotten much cotton. The *Lillie Lou* struck a snag and sank before reaching the Tombigbee; the vessel was soon refloated, however. That year the average rate of freight on cotton from Macon to Mobile by railroad was said to be $3.75 per bale and that by river steamer about $2.50 per bale, including insurance.

Except for barges operating on the lower part of the Noxubee there was not much traffic on that river in later years. Gainesville merchants continued to tap it for trade, however. Early in 1887 they leased the little steamboat *Viola* to run on the Noxubee. It finally reached Macon in February 1887 and offered to take cotton to Mobile for $1.50 a bale. It obtained little, but the M&O Railroad was soon hauling cotton to Mobile for $1.60 a bale.

While it was still in the hands of receivers the Mobile and Ohio Railroad Company opened an extension from Columbus, Kentucky, to the Ohio River opposite Cairo on December 1, 1881, from which it could ferry its cars across the river. The company's property was returned to the stockholders in January 1883. After changing its own track to the standard gauge, the company became the lessee of a narrow-gauge line from Cairo to St. Louis, which it proceeded to convert also to the standard gauge.

There was a great growth of railroads in the Upper Tombigbee Valley in the 1880s. The new lines consisted of feeder branches extended into the area and transit lines built across it to connect distant points. In 1884 the Illinois Central opened a branch from Durant, on its main north-south line in western Mississippi, to West Point and Aberdeen. The new branch introduced competition at these points and gave them a good connection with New Orleans. Soon the completion of the New Orleans and Northeastern provided a rival connection with the same place via the M&O and Meridian. In the early 1880s the Georgia Pacific Railway Company, a subsidiary of the Richmond and Danville, projected a line from Atlanta to the Mississippi River at Greenville, via Birmingham and Columbus. The panic of 1884 caught the company before it could complete its line and left it with three unconnected divisions. One of these reached seventy-six miles from Columbus eastward to the coalfields in Alabama, providing an important supply of coal to the Upper Tombigbee Valley. The line was subsequently built westward from Columbus, crossing the Tombigbee at Waverly and passing through West Point, and it was put through to Greenville in 1888.

In 1887 the Kansas City, Memphis, and Birmingham opened a line across northeast Mississippi from Memphis to Birmingham. Its construction bypassed Cotton Gin Port by two miles, quickly killing that little river port but at the same time giving rise to the town of Amory nearby. In January of the following year the company opened a

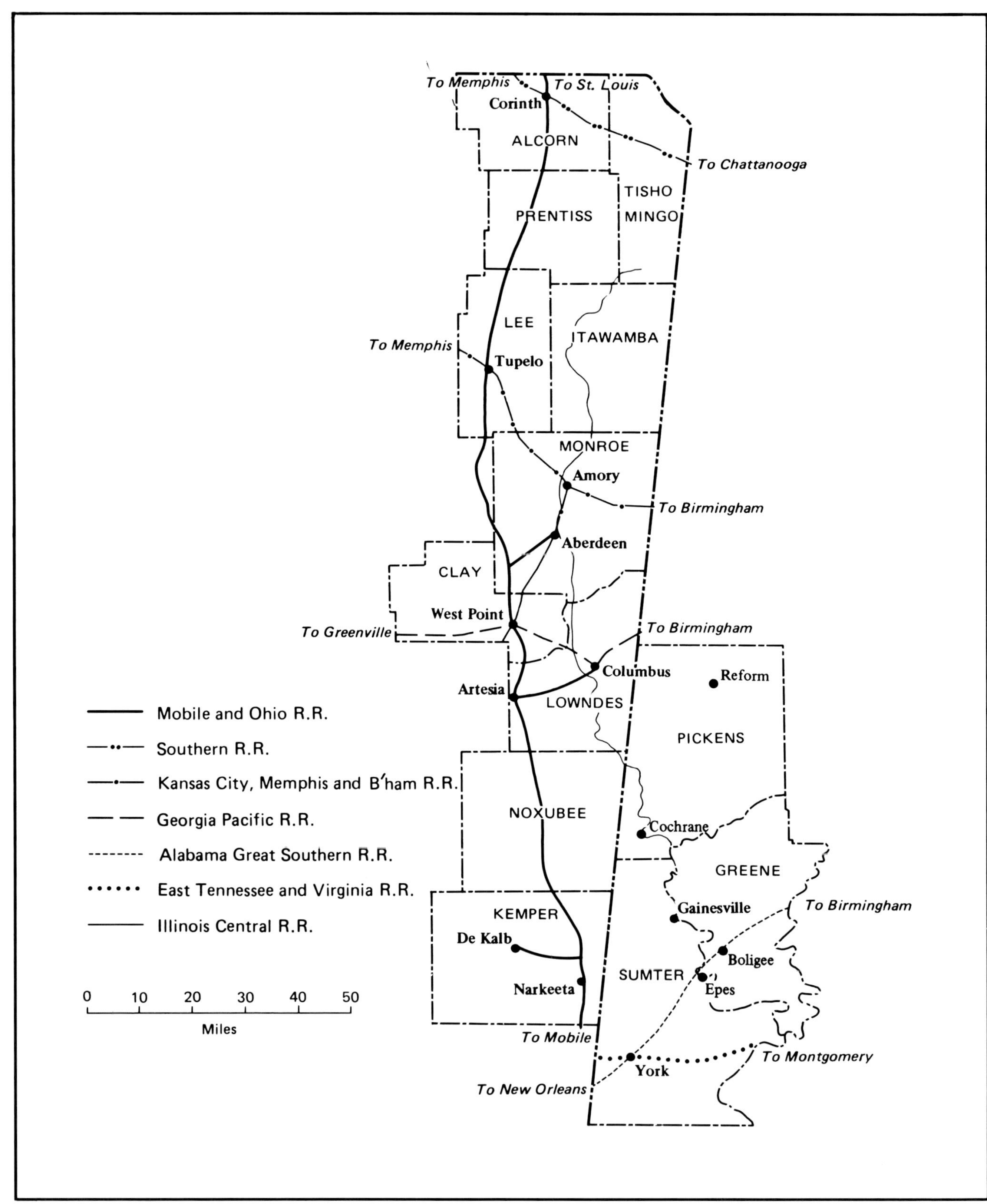

Map 14. Railroads in the Tenn-Tom country in the 1880s

branch from Amory to Aberdeen. As a result of the new construction Aberdeen became the terminus of three branch lines. Three railroads passed through West Point, two through Tupelo. With the opening of the New Orleans and Northeastern, Eutaw, as well as the towns on the M&O main line, secured a new connection with New Orleans. The resources of local people were too slender to exert much influence upon these developments, which were mainly instituted for the benefit of outsiders. Nevertheless, merchants of the local trade centers were deeply affected.

Railroad competition meant not only lower rates but also sharper discriminations in rates, which gave one place an advantage or disadvantage with respect to another. There was a strong tendency for favored centers to grow and for others to decline. Yet general growth was stunted by the basic poverty of the region. Railroad construction and competition of the 1880s firmly established Columbus, Aberdeen, and West Point as the principal distribution centers of the Upper Tombigbee Valley, Macon and Eutaw being places of local importance, as were Tupelo and Corinth to the northwest. West Point, not on a river, was the most interesting beneficiary of new railroad construction. It happened to be in the right place. Other business centers within the area were confined to a local trade. Columbus and Aberdeen overshadowed everything else on the river.

Under the new conditions of competition, Gainesville and the little river ports suffered heavily and tended to dry up, but at some of them there remained a continuing local business.

9

Doldrum Days, 1890–1940

The Life of the People

In the 1880s the new economic scheme of things was firmly established, and the basic pattern then set continued to dominate the scene until 1940. There was a tendency through this period to economic degeneration rather than development. Little change occurred in the character of industrial operations. Traces of improvement did appear between 1900 and 1930, but the economic and social bondage of sharecrop tenantry and peonage seemed at the same time to be extending its hold. Money was scarce. The region was in the suppressive grip of a colonial economy, and there was little hope for improvement.

The common recreations for men and boys were fishing and hunting. Bream, bass, perch, trout, and catfish were waiting to be caught in the Tombigbee and its tributary streams. Hook-and-line fishermen abounded. Fish were an important element of food for many people. Weirs and fish traps were common and were often complained of for interfering with navigation.

Both rich and poor engaged in hunting with the aid of dogs. The poorer a family was, it seemed, the more dogs it had. There were pointers, setters, coon hounds, fox hounds, deer hounds, and other specialists. Rabbits, raccoons, opossums, and partridges (quail) were standard quarry; ducks were sometimes hunted too. Deer and wild turkeys could also be found. For boys with slingshots and guns, any kind of a bird was a likely target.

Fox hunting, a popular sport, was commonly practiced in the early part of the night. In the late afternoon the hunters would set out on horseback, accompanied by a pack of hounds on leash—and often a fox in a box. As the entourage came down the road a hunter would blow his horn. The dogs got into the spirit of the thing and exuded excitement. While the fox did not register his sentiments orally, at a suitable place he would be released and would "light a shuck" for the woods. After an interval the dogs would be unleashed to pursue. The hunters would rest until they heard the dogs pick up the trail and would then follow on horseback at their leisure. When the dogs treed the prey, the fox was rescued and was taken home to be kept for the next hunt.

Women generally stayed busy with chores at home, but sometimes they shared in the fishing. When they went visiting, they often did needlework while they chatted. Farm people were neighborly. They shared the produce of their gardens. They helped each other, minded each other's business, and shared each other's secrets. The last was greatly facilitated by the advent of the rural party-line telephone.

Religion was dominated by the Protestant sects, particularly Methodist and Baptist. It deeply influenced the lives and education of the people. The Baptists exerted a discipline over their members and frequently brought sinners to trial before the congregation. Those who failed to mend their ways were put on probation or were expelled from the fellowship of the church. While some of the "sins" look mild in retrospect, the process provided an important instrument of social control. Baptist preachers were often part time and rather short on book learning, but they had a message to convey, and they delivered it in the language of their people. Methodists had an episcopal system of control that was efficient, and ministers were given rotating assignments by their bishops. The population was so scattered and the churches were so poorly supported that lay preachers had to conduct many of the services, with the ordained minister, who had to serve several churches, appearing at each of them only once or twice a month at best. Camp meetings and revivals were held, as in earlier times, in the late summer, after the crops had been laid by, and they were attended as much for social purposes as for religious inspiration. Other Protestant denominations also had their churches in the area, and there was a substantial Catholic congregation in Columbus. Black churches, which had split off on their own in the Reconstruction days, served the religious and social needs of the black community.

Columbus far exceeded the other towns in size and in the complexity of its life and institutions. It was a commercial center and was dominated socially and economically by a mercantile class. Its people, like those in the smaller places, were local-minded, and there was a strong community spirit. Great wealth was conspicuously absent, but merchants, bankers, and lawyers were influential people. While social prominence depended partly on wealth, many highly respected people had scant financial means. There were fine antebellum homes and some substantial new ones, but many of the people living in them were of distinctly modest means. Food was cheap, and so was domestic labor. The considerable black population contained few families of even modest means. Many blacks, particularly women, served as house servants for the whites. There were systems of sanitary and storm sewers, sidewalks, curbs, and gutters, but few streets were paved. There was a municipal water supply system, and an electric power system provided lighting. These improvements, usually financed with borrowed money, were paid for gradually from tax revenues and special assessments as well as by

The main street in Aberdeen, in 1890 shows the downtown characteristics of towns of the era. Photo: Evans Memorial Library, Aberdeen.

Feet could get muddy on this business street in Amory on a rainy day in the 1890s. The draymen stand ready for delivery service. Photo: Amory Regional Museum.

service charges. Other towns in the area, all smaller, had most of the same characteristics.

In education the academies were gradually replaced by a public school system, which was plagued by a lack of revenues and had poorly trained teachers, but there was a gradual improvement and a movement toward universal education. Schools for blacks and for whites were kept separate. Eagerness for education was not notably strong, for its benefits seemed elusive. How would book learning help a boy to become a better plowhand? And why teach girls to read and write, when these skills would only make them more troublesome to their husbands and more demanding? Yet there was a school for girls (now a state university) at Livingston, a college for women (now a state university) in Columbus, and the Mississippi Agri-

cultural and Mechanical College (now a state university) at Starkville. The black population, which paid little in taxes to support
schools, showed scant interest in school education.

The scarcity of property and of income to be taxed made extensive
governmental services difficult. Land values were very low, and
landowners both large and small found taxes burdensome, for the
income with which to pay them was small. The resistance to efforts
to impose taxes to expand public services was intense. The doctrine
that better education would lead to better jobs and to a more abundant life did not go over well. Taxation was primarily ad valorem on
real and personal property, and owners sought vigorously to keep
the assessed values as low as possible.

The systems of crop liens and of share and cash tenantry that had
appeared after the Civil War and spread gradually in the 1880s and
1890s became even more prevalent in the twentieth century, as farmers continued to face difficult conditions. The 1890s were an especially bad period, but from 1898 to 1914 the farmer's lot generally
improved. Then came the worsening of conditions in 1914, followed
by an unprecedented boom in the late years of World War I. In 1921
there was a collapse of farm prices, followed by surpluses and
depression during the rest of the decade. As the Great Depression
struck the nation in the 1930s, farmers in the Upper Tombigbee Valley
were already suffering from a prolonged depression.

The black population of the Upper Tombigbee Valley was concentrated in the more southerly parts and tapered off gradually to the
north. While incomes were almost universally low, averages for
the black part of the population were much below those of the white
except in the northern area, where there were few blacks. A large
part of the black population consisted of tenant farmers, who were
controlled by both landlords and merchants. They operated on
credit, produced little, and lived on little. They generally accepted
their lot, for there was little else they could do. They were kept under

Scientist Roland Harper of the Alabama Museum snapped this picture
of a tenant farmstead in Sumter
County in the 1920s. Photo: Roland
Harper Collection, University of Alabama Library.

tight control, but landlords and merchants were also tightly controlled by the system, which had been shaped by economic forces. The landowners were described as "land poor." They were owners of great areas that produced little revenue and could be sold for very little, and their monetary assets were notoriously small.

The blacks were no more caught in the system than were other people, but they were at the bottom of it. In social life they followed their own traditions, with which the whites had little to do and which they generally disdained. There was a fixed caste system. Personal relations between the races were generally friendly and cooperative. Blacks and whites knew each other well and often laughed and joked about relationships. But this camaraderie lasted only as long as the rigid requirements of the caste system were observed. Weak law enforcement and memories of Reconstruction days encouraged vigilante actions and permitted the notorious excesses of lynch mobs, but by the 1930s public opinion and state authority had effectively curbed such practices.

While the social distinctions perhaps made no theoretical sense, they were a practical modus vivendi, a way of getting along that worked. Violent friction tended to occur chiefly in places where the black and white populations were nearly equal. In the Black Prairie–Black Belt areas, open racial friction was rare. The white people had preponderant power, and it was unquestioned. Furthermore, blacks were vitally dependent upon whites in many ways. Courtly social manners and mannerisms were cultivated by the Black Belters, and they still prevail among both black and white, but prejudices and resentments against outsiders who intruded manifested themselves quickly in unattractive ways. While today there are open conflicts between black and white interests, there is still a unity of Black Belters against all others. They seem to know how to join forces when they need to.

In the 1880s the lumber industry in the South started supplying northern parts of the country with construction material. Cheap transportation rates were essential, and the railroads were eager for the business. The raw materials were plentiful, and there was competition with sources of supply closer to the markets, so prices of lumber and wages in the lumber industry were kept very low. These were fine stands of hardwoods in the swamps, and pines were plentiful in the Fall Line Hills of the Upper Tombigbee Valley and in Pickens County and southern Sumter. These were extensively exploited between 1880 and 1930, by the end of which time a large part of the timberlands had been cut over. The building of the Mississippian Railroad from Amory to Fulton in the 1920s improved access to the forest resources in Itawamba County and eventually had some impact on industrial development there. Staves were made in mills along the Tombigbee north of Cotton Gin Port and Amory. The wood products industries employed a great many people and brought in needed revenues where remunerative work was scarce.

Most industries in the towns were small and were focused on supplying the local wants. Such industries included blacksmithing, cabinetmaking, millwork (making ornamental elements of wood for buildings), iron founding, and manufacturing simple furniture. Associated particularly with agriculture were cotton ginning, baling, warehousing, and compressing. There were cottonseed oil mills, and there was some cotton textile manufacturing. In general, however, it may be said that, except for wood products industries, agriculture and agricultural thinking dominated the area.

There was little opportunity to bring basic social and economic improvements to the area by governmental action, although the Populists actively tried. In 1890 Mississippi disfranchised the blacks and most of the whites, leaving a very limited electorate. Alabama did the same in 1901. Stock law, control over tenants, regulation of railroads, and regulation of elections were state political issues. Control was in the hands of the Democratic and Conservative party, a highly flexible and adaptable institution, within which policies were thrashed out. Lawyers were particularly influential locally, and control tended to center in the courthouse officeholders. The stakes were low, but the intensity of the election struggles was great. Where property interests were concerned, conservative policies generally prevailed.

The Folk House in the Postbellum Era

After the Civil War, the character of new buildings in the region reflected the dramatic readjustments in other aspects of life. Economic hardships diminished the penchant for the status-indicative and decorative excesses of the prewar era. While some large homes were constructed in the region after 1870, they were almost entirely built for individuals employed in the industrial, transportation, and service sectors of the economy. Very few large farmhouses were built between 1870 and 1940, as farm income remained at a low level. Most

A board and batten saddlebag house with a wood shingle roof in Itawamba County. Photo: Eugene M. Wilson.

Above: Servant's quarters at the Smith House, Eutaw, in 1935, showing single-pen floor plan with board and batten wall construction. Photo: Library of Congress.

Right: Preparing to ship watermelons on the line of the Mobile and Ohio Railroad in the mid-1890s. Photo: T. E. Armistead/Museum of the City of Mobile Collection, University of South Alabama Photographic Archives.

of the substantial buildings erected during these years were utilitarian, including railroad bridges and depots, retail stores, and industrial facilities. Nearly always function and cost rather than aesthetics determined the form and features of construction.

Most of the residential building between 1870 and 1940 was of simple folk or vernacular character, produced by or for the area's small landowners and tenants. This construction perpetuated the long-standing frontier building forms first brought to the region in the early nineteenth century and discussed in chapter 4. Dogtrot, single-pen, double-pen, and saddlebag houses continued to be built long after the Civil War, most with only minor modifications of form from earlier times. The main structural changes occurred with the advent of balloon framing, which appeared in the late nineteenth century and provided somewhat greater flexibility of form than was possible in the early folk houses built of logs. Clapboard and board-and-batten exteriors were common, sometimes as a veneer for log walls. While house forms introduced during the early part of the nineteenth century, such as the dogtrot and saddlebag types, remained dominant until World War II, there were some new introductions. The most noteworthy include the shotgun house, the pyramidal-roof house, and the bungalow.

The shotgun house form is of obscure origin but is thought by some students of architecture to have come from West Africa, to have been adapted in the Caribbean, and then to have been transferred to the Gulf Coast. The shotgun consists of a single row of rooms, arranged with one room at the front of the house, one room at the rear, and another sandwiched between them. Roofs are gable end, with the gables in the front and rear. Such roofs are entirely opposite

Two generations of the dogtrot, central-hall house form owned by a single family, the Butlers of Bay Springs, Tishomingo County. The log house (*top*), built about 1870, was located about thirty feet from the frame house (*above*), which was constructed in 1913. The latter had a two-room ell at the rear and a back porch continuing from the central hall. Photos: Library of Congress.

Left: Urban shotgun houses adjacent to the M&O Railroad at Columbus. Photo: Jan Weaver.

in orientation to those of the early Georgian house forms, where the roof ridge runs parallel to the front. Many shotgun houses were built for rental in urban areas of high population density, and the style spread to rural areas, where they were built for tenants. The type was ideally suited to the narrow, long-lot subdivision of the large blocks frequently found in southern cities, and it was much more popular as a residential structure in the towns than in the country. There were also double shotguns under a single roof. Shotgun houses may still be found scattered through the Upper Tombigbee Valley.

The pyramidal-roof house, which became extremely popular during the last three decades of the nineteenth century across the upland South, was a variation from earlier Georgian architectural

A rural shotgun house built in the 1930s at Carmen Church in Lowndes County, seen from the front and side. Photos: Library of Congress.

A Pickensville house with a pyramidal roof. Photo: Eugene M. Wilson.

design. It was to some extent a postwar successor to the popular "I" house as the residence of the more-affluent farmer, but in contrast to the "I" house it was constructed with only one floor. The basic plan was roughly square, with a central hallway and with two rooms on each side, two side chimneys, and a front porch. Occasionally porches were incorporated on the back and sides of a pyramidal-roof house. Several specimens from the late nineteenth and early twentieth centuries can still be seen in the Tombigbee region.

The bungalow was a house form of external origin introduced into the South in the early twentieth century. In west Alabama and east Mississippi the first examples can be traced to the World War I period. According to Eugene M. Wilson, a cultural geographer at the University of South Alabama, "The most popular version was a fairly simple front-facing gable house with an attached gable porch supported by two pillars, the lower portion of which was often bricks. One or two front entrances and one or two central or side chimneys were usually present. Rooms, varying in size, were usually in two rows, separated by a center wall."[1]

Similar in form to the "double shotgun," the bungalow had a single floor and was notable for the absence of a central hallway. The popularity of bungalows reached a peak in the 1920s. In the 1930s they were sometimes called "depression" houses. Sets of working drawings could be bought for as little as five dollars, and the thin interior walls reduced construction costs to a minimum. As a result, the house form became a favorite in poorer areas. Bungalows were particularly common in the extreme northern counties of the region.

Transportation and the River

From the middle 1880s, work on the Upper Tombigbee River and its branches by the Corps of Engineers was largely confined to the maintenance of existing improvements. An elaborate engineering report of 1890, however, recommended a system of improvements for the Warrior and lower Tombigbee rivers to provide a channel with a depth of six feet at low water, maintained by a system of locks and dams. Considering the rivers as one system, a further recommendation was made to extend the six-foot depth up the Tombigbee as far as Columbus by the installation of dams with pneumatic gates.

Some work was done from time to time on the Noxubee, but the navigation season for that river was found to be much shorter than previously supposed. The district engineer in 1889 remarked that the proposed completely improved channel from the mouth of the Noxubee up to Macon had substantially been attained. He added that no

1. Wilson has extensively studied rural housing structures in Alabama and northeastern Mississippi. The quotation is from *Alabama Folk Houses* (Montgomery: Alabama Historical Commission, 1975), p. 20. Among his other publications are *An Analysis of Rural Buildings in the Tombigbee River Multi-Resource District, Alabama and Mississippi* (Philadelphia: National Park Service, 1981) and *A Sketch of the Upper Tombigbee Valley* (Philadelphia: National Park Service, 1983).

further improvement should be considered until the Tombigbee River below Gainesville had been completely improved. Only an occasional steamboat appeared at Macon, and none did so after 1889. The railroads had lowered freight rates sufficiently to keep business away from that river, but the river was cleared of obstructions again in 1894. There was some navigation of the lower part of the Noxubee in 1899, and in that year further work was done in removing obstructions, but fish traps were soon reported in the channel again, and no further work was done on the Noxubee.

Forest industries developed along the entire Upper Tombigbee, from its mouth to the upper reaches of Mackey's Creek and the other tributary streams. Logs, heavy timbers, lumber, and staves were heavy commodities, in the production and marketing of which cheap transportation was a vital factor. The streams served with the railroads in providing the transportation, and forest products gradually came to be the principal commodities transported on the river. In the 1880s the production of lumber and staves was an important industry from Aberdeen northward. The *Lillie Lou* was joined in 1885 by the fifty-seven-ton *Hattie Belle*, giving Aberdeen two homemade steamboats to ply the upper river.

Between Fulton and Walker's Bridge the channel was originally precariously navigable for small timber rafts at high water. By mid-1891, clearing of the river in that area was sufficiently complete to permit rafts eighty-eight feet long by twenty-two feet wide at high water. After the building of the Kansas City, Memphis, and Birmingham Railroad bridge across the Tombigbee at Amory, two large lumber mills were located at that point on the river. Clearing of the river above encouraged lumbermen to open up tributary creeks to float logs down to these mills. In 1895 the log traffic amounted to 30,000 tons.

The log traffic above Amory remained important well into the twentieth century, for Itawamba County had no railroad, and none was convenient to the forested areas on the upper tributaries of the Tombigbee. Construction of the Mississippian Railroad, a logging road, was started northward from Amory in 1921, running close to the East Fork, and it was completed to Fulton in 1925. The population of that little center increased from 200 in 1920 to 800 in 1930.

The rapid improvement of the railroad connections of Columbus in the 1880s diminished the importance of river traffic there just as the plan to provide all-season navigation by bar cutting was proving a failure. By 1889 few steamboats were venturing above Vienna, but the area below that point continued to be served by them in the handling of cotton, grain, iron, lumber, and general merchandise. Construction of locks and dams for slack-water navigation on the river lacked economic justification.

Columbus interests built and put into operation the little steamboat *City of Columbus*, of fifty-six tons, for local trade. Small steamboats also operated out of Demopolis, in the interest of that place, and larger boats from Mobile continued to traverse the river regularly as far up as Vienna. Removal of obstructions was continued each year

A bungalow at Carmen Church near Nashville ferry in Lowndes County, front and back views. Photos: Library of Congress.

Above: A logging scene in the piney woods on the line of the Mobile and Ohio Railroad in the 1890s. Photo: T. E. Armistead/Museum of the City of Mobile Collection, University of South Alabama Photographic Archives.

Right: The steamboat *Vienna*, built and operated by Columbus interests, at the Columbus landing. The *Vienna* was wrecked in 1907 at Ten Mile Shoals. Photo: Lowndes County Public Library.

by snag boats between Demopolis and Columbus, although the channel was not really well maintained. The packet boat *Vienna*, a vessel of 176 tons, was built at Columbus by Columbus interests in 1898 and remained in operation until it struck a hidden obstruction at Ten Mile Shoals in 1907 and sank.

Commercial vessels, however, continued to perform in a limited way their old functions of gathering freight for the local trade centers, moving cotton from the little river ports to railroad connections or to Mobile, and serving to some extent as a club over the heads of the railroads in rate matters. By far the largest tonnage came to be that of logs, lumber, and other forest products. Below Columbus the mode of floating logs and timber in the river was gradually abandoned, until practically all were carried on barges.

In 1898 the Mobile and Ohio Railroad opened an important branch eastward from Columbus to Tuscaloosa and Montgomery, Alabama. Then the Alabama, Tennessee, and Northern Railroad, constructed during the first decade of the twentieth century, reached northward from Mobile and up the western side of Sumter County to Stone's Ferry near Fairfield, crossed the Tombigbee, and went on to Aliceville and a connection at Reform with the new branch of the M&O. The St. Louis and San Francisco Line (Frisco) from Columbus to Pickensville, Aliceville, Boligee, Demopolis, and Pensacola was not built until 1927.

After 1890 the Warrior River and the Tombigbee below Demopolis underwent a rapid canalization. After the first three locks and dams had been completed at Tuscaloosa in the middle 1890s, others were gradually constructed, both above and below that place, until in 1916 the last of seventeen dams and eighteen locks was opened for business, giving an all-season six-foot-deep channel from Mobile to the coalfields above Birmingham. Tow boats could move heavy coal barges over the full distance, passing through the locks. At high water the steamboats could move upstream or downstream, right over all the dams except the uppermost. The actual development of traffic was rather slow, but the new competition had its effect on the rates of the railroads, particularly after the establishment at Demopolis, Tuscaloosa, and Birmingport of terminal facilities for general cargo, with railroad connections. The effects were accentuated by the establishment of the subsidized Federal Barge Lines. All these developments, however, bypassed the Upper Tombigbee. In 1897 the chief of engineers recommended a six-foot channel from Demopolis to Columbus, with ten locks and dams like those under construction on the lower Tombigbee and the Warrior, but nothing came of the proposal.

Construction began on a canal around Colbert Shoals and Bee Tree Shoals in the Tennessee River below Florence in 1891, but the canal was not fully opened until 1911. Perhaps the best that can be said of it is that its design and construction gave important experience to Colonel George W. Goethals and the Corps of Engineers, which they used soon afterward in the building of the Panama Canal. The Muscle Shoals canal continued to operate until 1918, but it never carried much traffic. In that year Congress authorized the construction of the mile-long Wilson Dam across the Tennessee at Florence. Lateral canals had become outmoded.

The Columbus and Greenville Railroad, originally a part of the Georgia Pacific line from Atlanta to Greenville, never prospered. Yet it was probably a more important part of the competition at Columbus than was the Tombigbee River, for it introduced an alternative route, via the Mississippi River, for the heavy-tonnage traffic in foodstuffs from the Midwest. The circuitous route might not haul

A passenger train on the Columbus and Greenville Railroad passes the railroad water tank at Columbus. Photo: Mississippi Department of Archives and History.

much, but it could maintain cut rates on a traffic which might not come to it at all at fully remunerative rates. It served West Point in a similar fashion.

With the opening of new transportation routes, Columbus, Aberdeen, West Point, and Starkville were successful in securing standing as basing points for freight rates, thus assuring their preeminence as wholesale centers. They might have been expected to grow large enough to become industrial and commercial centers of considerable local importance, and to an extent they did just that. Their growth was stunted by the economic weakness of their tributary territory, however.

Improvement of the lower Tombigbee and Warrior rivers led to several investigations of the Upper Tombigbee in response to Congressional prodding. In 1905 the Corps of Engineers made a study of the river from Demopolis to Columbus and concluded that although improvement by locks and dams was physically feasible, the small benefit to be derived did not justify the work. In 1911, all work of improvement above Aberdeen was suspended.

In response to an act of Congress, the chief of engineers in 1913 reported a plan for joining the Tennessee River with the Tombigbee River by means of a canal, following essentially the same route as that proposed in 1875, utilizing Big Bear and Crippled Deer creeks. To provide a six-foot channel with locks to match those below Demopolis and provide all-season slack-water navigation from Demopolis to the Tennessee River, it was reported, would require sixty-five or more locks with a large feeder canal and would probably cost more than $10 million. A special board concluded that the cost of the project exceeded any benefits that might be derived from it.

While the 1913 survey was being made, E. N. Lowe, the state geologist of Mississippi, proposed a scheme to divert the floodwaters of the Tennessee by way of Yellow Creek and cut through the divide

to Mackey's Creek, with the purpose of relieving damaging floods on
the lower Mississippi River. The engineers concluded, however, that
such a channel would cost $11 million, would flood the lowlands
along the Tombigbee, and would give little relief from the Mississippi
floods, for it could not divert enough water. Besides, high-water
stages commonly occurred on the Tennessee and Tombigbee rivers at
the same time.

A further study was made of the old project to provide slack-water
navigation from Demopolis to Columbus, but the report, rendered in
1916, recommended only snag removal to permit high-water navigation. The Corps of Engineers reported in 1921 that there were no
terminals along the river except for log landings, where floating
derricks were brought along with each tow to lift the heavy logs.
There was no interchange of traffic between railroads and riverboats.
The existing facilities were considered ample for current and prospective commerce. The Rivers and Harbors Act of 1922 required a
reexamination of the Tennessee-Tombigbee canal proposal. The report, rendered late in 1923 but never published, discussed a waterway of six-foot depth with sixty-two locks and dams to be built at an
estimated cost of $44 million. The report was adverse and recom-
mended only such snagging operations as might be justified by the
small existing commerce.

The completion of the Wilson Dam on the Tennessee River at
Florence in 1925 and the creation of the Tennessee Valley Authority
in 1933 led to the construction in the 1930s and 1940s of dams
providing a nine-foot channel on the Tennessee River from its mouth
to points well up its major tributaries in eastern Tennessee. In 1932,
an extensive report of the chief of engineers contemplated a nine-foot
channel from Columbus, Mississippi, to the mouth of Bear Creek on
the Tennessee River, to be provided by seventeen locks and dams, a
summit-level canal over the divide, and a reservoir, at an estimated
cost of $43 million. The report concluded, however, that the benefit
to be derived did not warrant construction. After that time, snag removal and river improvement were kept to a minimum.

On April 17, 1936, the chief of engineers ordered detailed surveys
of two routes for a canal, one to connect the Tennessee River with the
Tombigbee and the other to connect the Tennessee with the Warrior,
the chief tributary of the Tombigbee, after the adequacy of the water
supply of each route had been affirmatively determined. The Ten-
nessee-Warrior route for the canal proved impractical primarily, it
seems, because of the great amount of expensive rock cutting that
would be required. The report on the Tombigbee route, made in
1939, proposed a divide cut from the Tennessee, by way of Yellow
Creek to Mackey's Creek. The cut would be twenty-seven miles long
and deep enough to divert water to the Tombigbee from the pool
behind the planned Pickwick Dam in sufficient quantity to operate
the locks of a Tennessee-Tombigbee waterway. The channel would
have a minimum bottom width of 170 feet in river and canal sections
and 115 feet in the divide cut, with locks 75 by 400 feet (clear inside
dimensions). The estimated cost of construction of the waterway was

$66 million. A combination of canals, cutoffs, and locks and dams would provide a channel nine feet in depth from Demopolis to the Tennessee River. The waterway was intended to permit modern barge line operation between the Tennessee River and Demopolis. Standards applied to the Tennessee River required locks 110 by 600 feet and a navigable channel with a minimum width of 300 feet.

In a report submitted about the same time as that discussed above, the chief of engineers recommended the construction of a new dam at Demopolis 40 feet high, which would back water up the Warrior to replace four existing locks and dams, and up the Upper Tombigbee as far as Gainesville, with a lock chamber 75 feet wide by 600 feet long.[2]

Other Developments

Meanwhile other works of hydraulic engineering were under way. In the Black Prairie areas there were extensive bottomlands with poor drainage. If these could be drained, they might replace exhausted upland soils. In the 1880s there had been experimentation in Mississippi with drainage on individual farms and in small areas, but not until 1910 were extensive drainage districts organized under state law with the power to levy charges against the landowners who would benefit. For the next twenty years in several of the counties extensive works of drainage were in progress. The drained lands with heavy bottom soils became the most productive areas of the prairie. The course of creeks was changed, so that some ran almost in straight lines for miles. Rainwater no longer flooded the adjacent lowlands, so new alluvial deposits largely ceased. The silt was carried off in the rapid-running water and settled in the floodplains of the Tombigbee and its major upper branches. Better drainage solved some problems, but it also created new ones. Man-caused environmental change in the valley did not start with the Tennessee-Tombigbee Waterway.

In the depression years, under authority of the Flood Control Act of June 22, 1936, a project was authorized for the alleviation of floods in Itawamba County for a distance of fifty-three miles along the East Fork of the Tombigbee from Walker's Bridge to the Monroe County line. There was to be a clearing of trees and underbrush from the banks and a removal of drift jams. Excavation of thirteen cutoff channels was to protect people and valuable agricultural property

2. The Demopolis lock, when actually constructed after World War II, measured 110 by 600 feet. By that time the Oliver lock on the Warrior River at Tuscaloosa, measuring 75 by 450 feet, had already been built, leading to a traffic bottleneck at that place in recent years. The locks built later on the Warrior were 110 by 600 feet. An expensive replacement of the Oliver lock and dam is now being planned. The decision by the Corps of Engineers to adopt the Tennessee River channel width and lock dimensions for the Tennessee-Tombigbee Waterway became a subject of subsequent litigation. Locks 110 by 600 feet are now standard on the Black Warrior–Tombigbee System and the Tennessee-Tombigbee Waterway.

This old covered bridge near Steens in Lowndes County was still in use when it was photographed in 1936. Photo: Library of Congress.

from the overflow waters of the river. The work was done by the Corps of Engineers in 1938 and 1939. The further concerns of the federal government with the Upper Tombigbee were associated with plans for the Tennessee-Tombigbee Waterway, as will appear later.

Roads in the Upper Tombigbee Valley were not notably improved between 1860 and World War I. The Federal Highway Act of 1916, however, established a plan of grants-in-aid to the states for the construction of a national system of public roads. The grants were apportioned among the states according to area and population, not wealth or tax revenues. To receive a grant, however, a state had to set up a highway department, provide matching funds, and submit to the supervision of the U.S. Bureau of Public Roads. The general plan was to interconnect county seats by all-weather thoroughfares. The planned system was essentially complete by the early 1930s, except for paving, which proceeded slowly in the Tenn-Tom areas of Alabama and Mississippi.

One might think that agricultural conditions could not get worse, but in the 1930s they did. Prices for produce fell nationwide about 50 percent below those of 1929. In the Upper Tombigbee Valley, agricultural income, already at the bare subsistence level, also fell about 50 percent as the markets collapsed. In 1933 the federal government moved to the rescue of people threatened with starvation and helped to keep many thousands in the valley alive, but recovery did not come. In 1940 survival remained the prime object of life.

Since Mississippi was overall the poorest state in the Union, and Alabama was not much better off, the principle of distributing federal funds where the people were rather than where the money was had startling potential, even on a token basis. The devastating effect of the depression in the early 1930s was felt nationwide, and the failure of other approaches quickly led to the distribution of huge relief funds. First came the Federal Emergency Relief Administration, then the Civilian Conservation Corps and the Civil Works Administration.

Right: Tenants at Strawberry Hill plantation near Forkland in Greene County were still occupying an old slave cabin in 1936. The fireplace (*below, right*) of the old log house still served its original purpose. Photos: Library of Congress.

A tenant farmer and members of his family hoeing cotton in a field near Eutaw in July 1936. Photo: Library of Congress.

A tenant farmer with a mule in Lee County in August 1935. Photo: Library of Congress.

This view near Tupelo shows the tragic effects of soil erosion, March 1936. Photo: Library of Congress.

Cultivating a field near Tupelo in March 1936. Photo: Library of Congress.

This farm scene, photographed in the 1930s near Nashville Ferry in Lowndes County, might actually have occurred almost anywhere in the Tenn-Tom country. Photo: Library of Congress.

Children of a tenant family pose at the old wash place at Thornhill plantation, Watsonia, Greene County, in 1934. Photo: Library of Congress.

The Public Works Administration finally got under way. Biggest of all, the Works Progress Administration operated from 1935 to 1943. Relief money was spent where the people in need were, and both Mississippi and Alabama received more than they paid in taxes. The result beyond immediate objectives was rather limited, but new thinking was going on and new concepts were being developed and accepted which were to bring lasting changes within a few years. Their effect, however, was hardly noticeable before the end of the terrible decade of the 1930s.

The extension of cheap electric power to farms and small communities was stimulated by the creation of the Rural Electrification Administration in the New Deal days, with access to the federal treasury. By the 1950s nearly all Mississippi and Alabama farmers had electric power. The Tennessee Valley Authority was also helpful. Its construction of locks and dams on the Tennessee River prepared a northern connection for the later Tennessee-Tombigbee Waterway.

When the federal government moved to provide relief from the depression in the 1930s, the intervention was thought to be a temporary, emergency phenomenon, but it actually marked the beginning of a new departure. When years passed and no strong revival appeared, more and more radical legislation was adopted by Congress. Recovery had not really come when a new collapse arrived in 1938. Southern representatives in Congress, dissatisfied with President Roosevelt's wages-and-hours bill, blocked the measure for several months and asked that special attention be paid to the problems of their region. The president responded by appointing a large committee of representative Southerners, who, in a fact-filled booklet called *Report on Economic Conditions of the South*, tersely told him what he needed to know.

The Great Awakening: The Transformation since 1940

10

The patterns of life in the Upper Tombigbee Valley that had been set by 1885 remained in effect to 1940. While the construction of several branch-line railroads, the draining of bottomlands, the building of all-weather gravel roads, and the relief measures of the federal government in the depression years were developments of some significance, agricultural production, trade patterns, and industry saw little basic change. The valley remained a poor agricultural area, with a few low-wage industries but without much local capital.

World War II and Its Impact

Congress in 1938 created the Temporary National Economic Committee and began to study the nation's economic problems intensively. The result of its efforts, however, will never be known, for World War II, which broke out in Europe in 1939, soon overshadowed everything else. The war gave rise to economic demand, which stimulated a rapid increase in employment in the United States. As the country prepared to participate in the war, a broad economic stimulus was felt but with little immediate effect on the Upper Tombigbee Valley.

The Columbus Air Force Base was opened in 1941 for a school of aviation. From 1952 until 1969 the Strategic Air Command used it as a base for B-52 bombers. It has since been used for training American and Allied officers to fly jet-powered aircraft. Here a jet trainer prepares for takeoff. Photo: Air Force.

After the United States entered the war in December 1941, an effort was made to mobilize national resources of every kind. More than 10 million people were employed in the armed services at one time, and great numbers of others were required for war-supporting industry.

War work was available outside the area, so many people left to seek employment where the jobs were. As labor became scarce, industries were established where the people were, at the expense of the federal government. The Upper Tombigbee Valley perhaps got less than its proportionate share, but it obtained the great air base north of Columbus, which continues in operation to this day. Existing industries found a ready market for all they could produce. In 1943 the last of the relief programs was abandoned, and in 1944 the nation reached full employment, with more jobs than there were people to fill them.

Persons entering the armed services, and their dependents, were paid at a uniform rate nationwide, to the great advantage of regions with low incomes. There was work for the uneducated, the unskilled, and the "unemployable," all of whom had previously had trouble competing for jobs. Training became widely available. Opportunities were open to black as well as white people. Furthermore, there was an increased demand for agricultural products as farmers moved into war work and as accumulated surpluses disappeared. With farm labor scarce and farm income improved, tractors and other farm machinery came increasingly into use, and output per man hour rose. As the slack in the national economy disappeared, the nation was able to fight the greatest war in history and greatly raise its standard of living at the same time. The depression was over.

Postwar Federal Policies

The pent-up needs of the depression years emerged as new demand when people had the money with which to buy. Expansionary economic policies, new credit institutions designed to promote the free flow of capital into regions where it was scarce, and a host of federal programs were put to work to reconvert the economy to a peacetime basis. The G.I. Bill of Rights, giving opportunities to war veterans, helped formerly disadvantaged people and disadvantaged regions. Farm price supports and quotas gave a boost to an area which depended primarily upon agriculture for support. Keeping national demand at a high level brought opportunity to poorly educated and inexperienced people and to entrepreneurs in all parts of the country. There seemed to be a market for everything, including farm products, and the prices were good.

Agricultural Changes and Population Shifts

Technological change finally hit agriculture with terrific force. Within only a few years, the mechanical cotton picker and new cultivation techniques reduced the amount of labor required to produce a bale of cotton to about one-seventh of what it had been in 1930. This development had an extremely serious effect on an area that specialized in cotton production and had a large, poorly educated population not readily adaptable to anything else. Furthermore, the demand for cotton underwent a decline as synthetic fibers made their appearance. One two-row cotton picking machine lumbering across the fields could do the work of a hundred human pickers, who could sometimes be seen in the field desperately trying to meet the competition. The inevitable outcome was that thousands of agricultural workers ceased to be needed. Yet while the number of farmers sharply declined between 1940 and 1960, farm income rose. The size of farms and the productivity of farm workers increased mightily as

A promising-looking bull is auctioned off at West Point. To this sales arena prairie stock growers bring their cattle, hogs, and goats, skinny or fat, young or old, for sale by the auctioneer to the highest bidder. Photo: Jan Weaver.

results of rapidly improving technology and greater capital investment in equipment.

Not all local agricultural communities could easily adapt to the responsibilities of the new agriculture. The improving technology made special demands, such as the greater cost of and maintenance of farm equipment. When sharecropping was no longer feasible, the agricultural basis for making a living was destroyed for a large, uneducated population. There was a strong tendency in the area to turn to beef and dairy cattle, which required large investments in working capital and extensive pasture lands but less labor than row crops. In the 1950s the production of poultry by new methods was rapidly expanded. Many farmers became chicken-factory operators aided by service and processing firms which supplied the baby chicks, mixed the feed, dispensed necessary advice, and processed and marketed the product. The widespread construction of hard-surfaced roads gave access to towns and made practicable the use of large and small trucks everywhere.

By maintaining price supports and quotas for cotton, Congress allowed many of the older sharecroppers to continue operating one-mule farms for some years, after which several kinds of charitable aids from the same source enabled them to remain where they were and continue their lives much as before, while younger members of their families, more adaptable, obtained the benefits of education and training for different kinds of work. Vast numbers emigrated, particularly the young and unattached, in search of economic opportunities.

The heavy exodus of population from the area between 1940 and 1960 was much greater in the black component than in the white. Because the more mobile and the better educated were generally the first to leave, there remained in the region many poorly educated, economically distressed black citizens. Although there was also a heavy exodus of white people, the white percentage of the population in ten Tenn-Tom counties increased from 49.6 in 1930 to 58.2 in 1960 (detailed figures appear in the appendix). The population movement was largely from farm to town, but most of the employment opportunities were outside the Upper Tombigbee Valley. Towns and cities of Mississippi and Alabama rapidly increased in population but were unable to absorb the rural exodus fully. Mississippi had an absolute loss in population, and Alabama's gain was quite small during the twenty-year period, despite a great excess of births over deaths.

The years from 1940 to 1960 saw the growth of a large rural nonfarm population. Some people commuted to work at a considerable distance on newly improved roads. Some lived cheaply on government benefits. They could do without modern conveniences and could produce much of their own food. Some worked part-time at one kind of remunerative activity or another. A large number were underemployed. The more southerly counties of the Tenn-Tom area, where the black population predominated, stagnated economically.

The Growth of Industry

In the postwar years, the expansionary economic policies of the nation gradually stimulated economic demand and produced near-full employment in the nation. The time was ripe for industrial development in the Upper Tombigbee Valley, where the people began a transformation to adapt to new conditions and opportunities.

Experienced outsiders, attracted by the availability of people eager for employment, made vital contributions. They brought in the sewing industries, which are labor intensive and require relatively small investments in equipment, and can be moved close to the labor supply. The work requires dexterity but little school education, and the essential skills are rather easily learned. The wages paid were low, but they provided a ready source of income for a great many people, particularly women, and the federal minimum wage law has protected the workers' pay rates. Such employment served to condition people into the labor force.

Below, left: If you need a thousand dozen pairs of pants, go to Amory, the "pants capital of Mississippi." Shown are pressers performing the final manufacturing operation at an Amory Garment Company plant. Photo: David C. Weaver.

Below, right: The Iuka Shirt Company makes men's shirts. Sewing operations such as this give employment to a great many people, particularly women. Photo: Jan Weaver.

The people's culture was rich and alive, and they had those qualities of heart and mind that can lead to successful accomplishment, but conspicuously absent were capital, a skilled labor force, and an entrepreneurial tradition. Local leadership, starved by the barrenness of past opportunity, needed time to develop, but it soon made appearance in unpredictable places, sprinkled like pepper. The variety of industrial enterprises now thriving in the Upper Tombigbee Valley is such that none is fully representative of the rest, for each case tends to be unique. However, examination of a few can present a more understandable picture than can any attempt at generalization.

An unlikelier enterprise would be hard to find than a large stone monument producer in Columbus. Yet that is just what William L. Jones has in the Columbus Marble Works. Columbus has no special advantage of location. There is no pool of skilled labor except for people trained by the company. The heavy raw material, marble and granite blocks, is brought in by railroad and truck from quarries, partly owned by the company, in Alabama, Georgia, North Carolina, South Carolina, Virginia, and, occasionally, Vermont. Ten-foot diamond-studded circular saw blades slice great blocks of hard granite into smooth slabs of precise dimensions on huge machines imported from Germany. The slabs are further cut, polished, and en-

Bags by Pat is a small manufacturing business owned by Wiley S. Scarbrough (shown here) and his wife, Pat, in Columbus. Photo: Jan Weaver.

At the Columbus Marble Works William L. Jones explains a big polishing machine to author Weaver (back to camera) while a workman looks on. Photo: Jan Weaver.

graved by sand-blasting machinery, operated by skilled workers who require minimal supervision. There is only a tiny local market. The products are shipped by truck line to markets spread from Maine to California.

Jones came to Columbus in December 1926 from Missouri with the building of the Frisco Railroad through the city. Leaving the railroad company, he took a job with a local monument business then owned by the McGahey family but which dated back to 1846. In association with the McGaheys, and with his own son and nephew after they had passed from the scene, Jones worked to build the business.

When monument sales were hard hit by the depression of the 1930s, automobile license plate manufacture was added to the company's business. Jones still produces all the license tags used on automobiles in the state of Mississippi. One of his companies makes marble dust by grinding chips into fine particles for use as filler in paint, vinyl tile, and upholstery. "We recently were declared a kosher institution by a rabbi in Birmingham," he says "at the request of one of the producers of breakfast cereal, which buys calcium to use in the cereal. They said they could not sell it to their kosher customers unless we were kosher. I don't know whether anybody else in the marble business is kosher or not."

As they looked for new fields of business enterprise, Jones and his son were joined a few years ago by a local friend who was experienced in the production of prefabricated steel buildings. Their fabricating business, located at Starkville, employs about three hundred people and is one of the largest local employers. The Jones story is told here to show what local enterprise can do in industrial development, even when the other factors of production look unfavorable. Jones points out that the success of these enterprises has actually come from the joint efforts of the many people associated with him. Now thoroughly assimilated into the local culture, Jones says, "I feel like a native Mississippian. The people tend to assimilate strangers and make them like themselves, and they really have not been overwhelmed by outside influences."

Bob Tiffin's property at Red Bay, Alabama, is so close to the Mississippi line that he can spit across it. He never went to college, but he is a faithful fan of the University of Alabama's football team, on which his son has recently played. He drives up with his Allegro motor home the night before the game and waits another night to go home. It is a good way to take the family out for a weekend and escape from business cares. Tiffin builds his own motor homes, and, if he likes, he can try a new one for each trip.

Tiffin is from a family that came to Red Bay before 1900 and accumulated some capital from local mercantile businesses. The coming of the Illinois Central Railroad in 1907 gave the town a local importance. In 1970 the family owned a cotton gin and a cotton warehouse. "We are also in the house-building business," says Tiffin. "We had a lumberyard here in town, and we built houses for the retail trade." In 1972 the Tiffins built a new 10,000-square-foot cotton warehouse just as the cotton business fell off sharply.

"I had a friend who was in the motor home business down at Tremont, Mississippi," Tiffin says. "He went out of business, and we bought his merchandise and some of his chassis. There was another motor home outfit at Iuka, Mississippi, and they went out of business about the same time. The enterprises at both places were grossly mismanaged, but both had people who knew how to build motor homes. I knew what was going on, and I saw a good opportunity, because at that time the motor home industry was really booming.

We built five motor homes in the warehouse in 1972 and really got off the ground in 1973. We kept improving as the years went by and wound up with a pretty good product. The outfit at Iuka built with aluminum and steel, and we copied their design. It has worked out real well."

Tiffin's master workmen are high school graduates, and some are college graduates, trained on the spot. "People here don't mind working," he says. "We still have people who want to give eight hours' work for eight hours' pay. That is unusual in this country." Some of his workmen are specialists, but he says, "I've got several men out here that can do any job we have." In the plant they work like beavers, with minimal direct supervision.

Bob Tiffin, still youthful and athletic looking, is very much "one of the boys" in the community. He dresses in stylish blue jeans and is thoroughly informal in manner. The door to his "private" office remains open. His secretary calls information in, and he sees visitors and answers the telephone promptly. Through a side door employees pop in with shop problems. He listens carefully, settles matters with dispatch in a friendly voice, and, unruffled, turns to take up an interrupted subject. Despite such casually hectic activities, things appear to be so well organized that the employees could easily run the plant if he took the day off.

One of Tiffin's Allegro motor homes sells at a price between $25,000 and $100,000. "Our market area," he says, "covers the continental United States and some foreign countries. In 1977 we shipped thirty-seven units to Saudi Arabia." During the severe recession of 1982 the plant was running at full capacity.

The power of local enterprise working under unpromising conditions is further demonstrated by the career of Hugh W. King and his heirs at Corinth. In the early 1950s he was in the woodworking business, making screen doors, columns, and other wood products for the local trade. To solve a practical problem he invented the King E-Z Safety Feed. Attached to a ripsaw, jointer, or molding cutter, it feeds the material against the blade safely and produces a smooth cut. This is one of those simple little machines that were widely wanted but which nobody had yet invented. Manufacturing the

Left: Bob Tiffin stands at the door of a motor home, newly built in his plant at Red Bay. *Right:* Allegro motor homes, shown under construction at the Tiffin plant, reach nationwide and foreign markets. Photos: Jan Weaver.

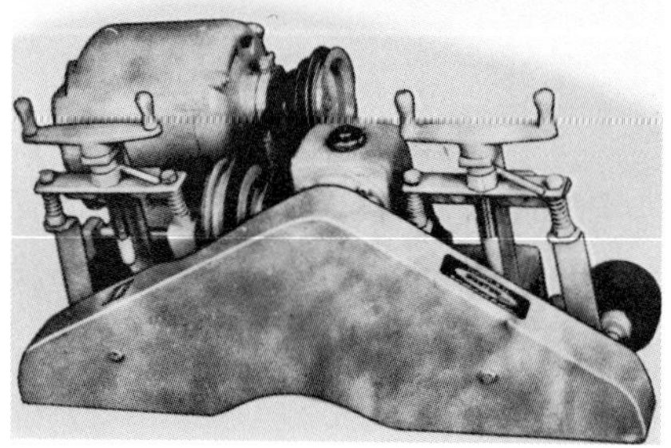

At the locally owned King Manufacturing Company plant in Corinth, Arnold T. King (*top left*) makes metal stampings with a heavy press, and Jim McAfee (*top right*) produces machine parts with a large automatic screw machine. *Above:* the King E-Z Safety Feed, a very useful device invented by Hugh W. King, is produced by King Manufacturing Company at Corinth. Photos: Jan Weaver.

machine put King into the metalworking business, which he learned very rapidly. Metalworking machinery is costly, but King learned that equipment that was obsolescent for low-margin production work but quite suitable for a job shop could be bought at favorable prices and that he had the mechanical ability and the patience to restore defective equipment to reliable operation. His son, Charles Wayne King, now president of the company, has these same abilities. The King company gradually acquired an impressive collection of both light and heavy metalworking equipment and developed a capacity to do tool and die work, plating, and a wide range of other work with metal, while it retained the old woodworking shop as a minor operation. As Corinth and the surrounding area underwent industrial growth, the King company became a profitable contractor for jigs and fixtures and for short-run production jobs, and it still does a thriving business. The enterprise is strictly local, serving a territory with perhaps a 150-mile radius. It expanded with the growth of local industries and has adapted itself to changing needs and opportunities.

Says Thomas E. Robertson, King vice-president: "We produce our own skilled labor. We hire a man, and if he is real good, we train him ourselves and move him around to find out what he is best suited for. The quicker he is to learn, the better the job he will end up with. If a young man at the age of twenty is aggressive and there is a slot open that we think he can handle, we move him up. I would say 50% of our employees have been with us ten years, at least." A machine operator may be trained quickly, but not an all-round machinist. The company tries to keep a thoroughly experienced man as a foreman for each department. When there is a mechanical failure that stops production, Wayne King can usually make repairs himself. Employees and management share a small cafeteria, and easy socialization promotes understanding and cooperation.

While local initiative is vital to industrial development, its most effective influence in the Upper Tombigbee Valley has not been in directly establishing successful enterprises but in attracting industry from the outside and creating a protective umbrella under which industry can thrive. This has been accomplished in an exemplary manner by the initiative of the Community Development Foundation (CDF) at Tupelo. Its objectives and philosophy are broader than those of a chamber of commerce, for it is designed to bring both social and economic betterment to an area reaching out some thirty miles in all directions from Tupelo. Sponsored by merchants, bankers, newspaper publishers, and professional people, the foundation has centered on broad economic developments calculated to increase payrolls, from which secondary developments and services can follow. Led since the mid-1950s by the vibrant and energetic Harry A. Martin, a native Mississippian, it has been outstandingly successful. Although Tupelo, in rural Lee County, has only 24,000 people, the little county now has some one hundred fifty widely diversified industries with 13,000 employees. Let Martin tell the story:

Wurlitzer organs manufactured at Corinth have reached an extensive market. Some are much more elaborate than this specimen. Photo: courtesy of the Wurlitzer Company.

We evolved from rural development initially into an organization that is in everything: rural community development, industrial development, retail trade, tourism, cultural enrichment, and the whole gamut of services.

The only thing we have had is a commitment and leadership. It is all around town. I mean hundreds of young people and middle-aged people and older people. We have pooled their thinking and their resources. We did not have the basis for industry in Mississippi, so we had to attract it. After a research and development group does the research to find out what is needed, I get out and find the company that will fit and bring it here.

We are interested only in primary economic input. We are trying to build not an urban center but a suburban, industrial community with Tupelo as the service center. The services come because the primary economic base is here. We are trying to reinforce the smaller communities and keep our people in their rural neighborhoods, in the native environment that they grew up in.

We don't want any giants in any field. We like an assortment of industries. We have a few dying all the time, and we have a few being born all the time. We are getting to where we can be more selective in what we do, because we have a good reputation and a good community, with a good environment.

The well-equipped North Mississippi Medical Center at Tupelo employs nearly two thousand people. In operation is a profusion machine, used to take over the functions of heart and lungs during surgery. Photo: North Mississippi Medical Center.

Two things that the South is particularly short on are technology and capital. We are still importing both. In the past thirty years we have brought in some 500 families in permanent positions to provide special technology and support. Eventually that fellow from New York retires, and then the Mississippian takes his place. We have moved a lot of fine families into this area. They have had to be assimilated into the cultural life of the community and not separated, with groups polarizing. We have had a good integration of the cultures.

We have had good cooperation from the state agencies, and the federal government has been helpful in providing highways and grants for sewer systems, water systems, housing, in-plant instruction, and vocational training, but the primary job of economic development belongs to the local community and can never be done by an outsider.

Although Tupelo is located in a region of excellent agricultural land, the area has become overbalanced in the direction of industry. There are facilities at Tupelo and West Point for slaughtering 9,000 hogs a day, and live animals are being trucked in from hundreds of miles away. They could be raised locally. To help the farmers of the surrounding counties take advantage of the obvious opportunity, CDF in 1980 brought Greg Giachelli, an enthusiastic young hog specialist, to Tupelo, and his efforts have begun to show results. Pigs fed on locally produced milo (grain sorghum), soybean meal, and wheat, he says, make good pork, and the new diet reduces the need for corn imported from the North. Giachelli produces a newsletter called "Hog Cent$."

Bob Stembridge near Mooreville started out with hogs about 1970. He lost most of his buildings to fire in 1981 and had to rent his fields out while he built a roof over his pigs. In 1982, he was struggling to complete new buildings while he fed his young pigs on Tail Curler, Sr., a prepared feed. He raised them on heavy wire mesh and

Harry A. Martin has been for many years the executive head of Tupelo's Community Development Foundation, which has aggressively followed policies that have transformed the surrounding area economically and socially since World War II. Photo: Community Development Foundation, Tupelo.

plastic-covered steel gratings. His well-designed farrowing house held 120 sows, producing about 10.5 pigs per litter and averaging 2.2 litters per year. He had to buy eight or ten tons of feed a week. A new bin and auger system would soon enable him to buy feeds in large quantities and handle them more efficiently. He topped his hogs out at 210 to 250 pounds. At full production in the future he hoped to produce from 1,500 to 2,000 hogs per year, or thirty to forty animals per week, with the part-time help of his son.

Asked why his pigs' tails did not curl, Stembridge explained: "They have been cut. When the pig is standing there at the feeder, his tail curls and the switch hangs. When another one wants to get to the feeder, he will just come up there and bite his tail, and they get it to bleeding, and everybody starts biting his tail. If you ever get one bleeding, he is a goner. The rest will just eat him up. When a pig is born, he has got needle teeth. You clip his teeth and then you cut his tail. I just cut the switch off my pigs' tails. A lot of folks cut it right at the ham."

Frank Nichols, near Mantachie, has a master's degree in entomology from Mississippi State University. He runs a pest-control business and is also a diversified farmer. He follows market prices closely, keeps careful records, and knows what his costs are. But Nichols, a big man with an outgoing personality, looks uncomfortable behind his desk, where he keeps two telephones and a TV set for market reports. He seems to like hard work, and he raises his own hog and cattle feed. His farrowing house has several electric fans and a roof insulated against the summer heat. The sows and little pigs are on heavy wire mesh, and there is an automatic flushing system underneath. Nichols turns out about 960 hogs a year and feeds about 30 beef cattle. Mrs. Nichols, a neat, energetic woman, joins her husband in the heavy work.

Kelly Ferguson near Blue Springs is said to be the most innovative farmer in the area. He has a master's degree in psychology and was for some years a practicing psychologist, but when his parents grew old, he returned to the family farm. He started with row crops, saw the need to diversify, and began to buy feeder pigs to top them out for market, with 400 on feed at one time. He can now market 3,000–4,000 hogs a year. Ferguson has sophisticated equipment for producing, storing, and mixing his own feed. He tops out his hogs on the ground, with well-stocked automatic feeders kept readily accessible. The system takes about a week longer to finish the hogs, but it saves on capital investment, which Ferguson has preferred to concentrate elsewhere. His brother, who works with him, gives his principal attention to the row crops.

CDF has tried to expand agricultural output by making farming more profitable. Better financial management, efficient hog production, and diversification are constituent elements in the program. Results seem slow at first, but the effects should be cumulative. The new farms require considerable capital investment but not much hired labor. Hogs, which grow quickly, do not tie up as much capital as cattle. Land requirements for feeding hogs are minimal, for it is

Top: On plastic gratings pigs thrive in temporary pens at Bob Stembridge's fire-ravaged hog farm. Stembridge (back to camera) explains a point to author Doster, while Greg Giachelli looks on. Photo: William M. Stennett.

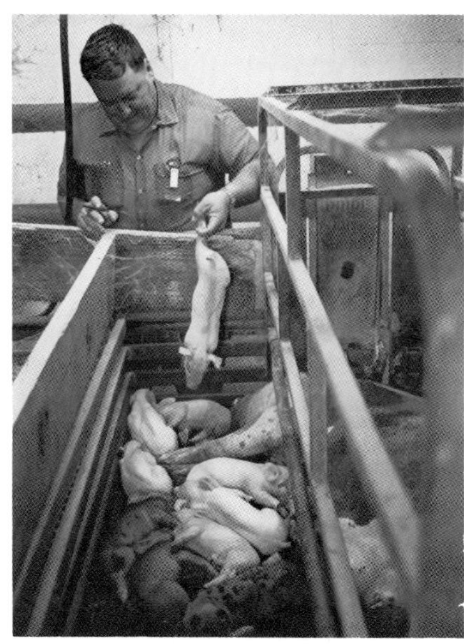

Above: Frank Nichols keeps a watchful eye on the suckling pigs in his farrowing house. With equal care he watches production costs and market trends. Photo: William M. Stennett.

Modern pigs get a carefully controlled diet. Here hog expert Greg Giachelli demonstrates Kelly Ferguson's feed mixing machine. Photo: William M. Stennett.

A Strat-O-Lounger gets final inspection as it moves on a conveyor at the Futorian plant at Okolona. The upholstered furniture industry, centered on Tupelo, has been developed by the combined talents of outside and local entrepreneurs. Photo: David C. Weaver.

possible to double-crop milo or wheat with soybeans. These crops provide the basis for excellent hog feed, so that corn, which the area does not produce as efficiently as northern competitors, is not required. Many of the farmers also have jobs in industry. Future prospects look good.

The upholstered furniture industry, which now employs thousands of people in northern Mississippi, centers in Tupelo. Its beginnings and the associated spinoffs, all developed since World War II, have laid much of the economic foundation for the new day in the Upper Tombigbee Valley. The key name is that of Morris Futorian, the Henry Ford of the upholstered furniture industry.

Futorian was born in Russia in 1907. At the age of fifteen, speaking no English, he immigrated to this country with his family. His first job was sweeping floors in a Chicago furniture factory, where his father worked. After twelve years he had risen to a foreman's position. When he lost his job in the Great Depression, he turned first to repairing furniture and then to making it. By 1941 he had a showroom at the Merchandise Mart and was operating a manufacturing plant on the fifth floor of a walk-up building. The end of World War II brought an expanding market for furniture. Futorian, an innovator, had developed techniques for the mass production of high-quality upholstered furniture, but he needed capital, factory space, and willing workers. Mississippi had plenty of unskilled people who were willing to work but who lacked jobs. It had leaders who wanted industry for their little communities but who lacked the necessary technical and entrepreneurial skill, and their capital was pitifully small. Driven by hunger for economic opportunity, they went to work. The state adopted a "balance agriculture with industry" (BAWI) program and lent its credit to industrial developers. It could issue tax-free bonds to pay for industrial plants, but to get this help, the promoters first had to raise a substantial amount of equity capital.

Futorian had a little capital, and subscribers about Tupelo bought debentures issued by his company, which were not stock but which counted as equity capital. Harry A. Martin says: "We needed a primary manufacturer, who would assemble components into a final product. Futorian had technology. Our object was not to buy stock but to put together the ingredients that would cause him to employ people. Our object has always been payrolls and people employed. We are not interested in owning and operating businesses. They bought debentures, and that allowed him to go to our state agency that handled bonds, with this much equity in his corporation."

Futorian located his plant in New Albany, brought two skilled employees with him, hired seventy or eighty local people, and started making furniture. But he needed a supply of springs and metal frames. A Jewish friend in Hoboken had the skill to make them and was willing to move. The friend had little money, but the merchants supported him with debentures, and he got a small bond issue to start a tiny company at Tupelo, named Super Sagless Spring

The birthplace and boyhood home of entertainer Elvis Presley in Tupelo is a Mecca for visitors. Photo: Jan Weaver.

Corporation. The seed thus planted grew into quite a substantial enterprise.

Futorian needed padding for his furniture, and he knew a Czechoslovakian immigrant in Chicago who had the skill to make it. The friend had no capital either, but the local people scraped out the till and provided the equity basis for his enterprise. Its technology was soon outmoded, however, and new enterprises were brought in to make padding from polyurethane foam.

With advanced production techniques and willing workers, the Futorian enterprise enjoyed a phenomenal success and established several auxiliary plants in the region. Many Mississippians trained in the business have left Futorian to organize their own enterprises, either making furniture or supplying parts. Other manufacturers came in from outside the area. Today there are some two hundred furniture manufacturers and suppliers in the region. Futorian sold out to the Mohasco Corporation of New York and has now retired, but the industry goes on, run mostly by Mississippians.

Since the Tenn-Tom country's economy just a few years ago was based almost entirely on relatively unproductive agriculture, it has been reasonable to believe that the area could not supply the skilled labor to support a large high-technology industry. Yet at Corinth there is such an industry, and it is thriving. In 1972 the W. F. Hall Printing Company of Chicago, one of the nation's largest contract printers, wanted to build a new plant away from the icy winds and labor problems of the Great Lakes. The company considered the availability of utilities, transportation, and labor. Out of the seventy possible locations the choice was reduced to two: Tupelo and Corinth. Two or three new industries already building at Tupelo might strain the labor supply, so Corinth was chosen, and a subsidiary company, Hall of Mississippi, was formed to own and operate the new plant. Then the company secured a contract to print the *National*

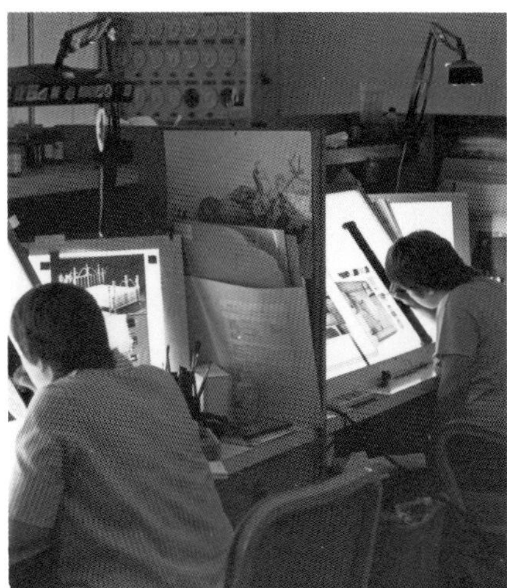

Eleven million copies of the *National Geographic Magazine* roll off the huge presses of Hall of Mississippi at Corinth each month. Locally trained skilled workers (*above*) prepare color pictures for printing. Folded sections of the *Geographic* emerge from a rotogravure press (*right*) Photos· Hall of Mississippi.

Geographic Magazine and doubled the size of its project. Hall of Mississippi now has a building covering 9.5 acres, with windowless red brick walls thirty feet high, all in a tasteful setting.

In printing the *National Geographic* at Corinth, Hall uses a highly sophisticated form of rotogravure, a process designed to provide fine-quality printing in a very large volume. It requires close control at every stage. Steel cylinders some eighty inches long, sheathed in copper and weighing nearly a ton, do the printing. Through photography, computerized scanning, and artistic retouching, the copy is separated into yellow, magenta, cyan, and black images for printing. Diamond styli engrave the image into the copper surfaces of the cylinders, leaving tiny cells, 22,500 to the square inch, to hold the ink. The deeper cells hold more ink, so the printed color will be stronger. When cylinders have been prepared for each of the four colors, proof sheets are made, tested by analysts, and marked for color corrections. The engraved cylinders are revised and corrected with chemicals and hand tools, then plated with chrome to a depth of .0002" to reduce wear when they are on the press.

The main part of the *National Geographic* is printed on two huge rotogravure presses, each 120 feet long and weighing 372 tons. Paper from rolls weighing from 2,000 to 4,500 pounds passes at twenty miles an hour through the rotary presses, which work around the clock, six days a week. A flying paster neatly attaches the end of one roll to the beginning of the next without any slackening of speed. One color at a time, the paper is printed on both sides, passed through a dryer at the top of the press, and then returned for the next color. There is a separate fifth printing for the text. As the paper comes from the final drying, it is cut into sections and folded at high speed. With the aid of a great deal of machinery the sections are later gathered and bound. Copies of the *National Geographic* are sent out each month directly from this plant to some 11 million subscribers all over the world.

Two big offset presses print the advertising pages for the *National Geographic* and pour out brochures and catalogs in color for national retailers such as Avon and Sears. Orders for less than half a million copies are not accepted. Eight or nine thousand tons of paper are consumed in the plant each month, and from 280 to 300 truck trailer loads are required to move the product out.

One of the problems faced in establishing the plant at Corinth was that of inducing technicians to move into the area. Fortunately, Corinth is well located for outdoor recreation, near Pickwick Lake on the Tennessee River, and is convenient to the city of Memphis. Of the first twenty-one technicians brought south for a look, twenty agreed to move. The state of Mississippi helped with the training of others. Eight or ten months before the plant opened, a school was set up. The local vocational-technical school worked in this enterprise, with the help of the Northeast Mississippi Junior College at Booneville and the state board of education. Hall supplied and helped pay the instructors. With specialized schooling and several months of on-the-job training, many people learned the skills required for the sophisticated processes. No one was paid for learning. Very careful attention was given to employee relations and training—and it still is.

The new plant was phased into operation early in 1978. With great numbers of inexperienced and inadequately trained people, start-up expenses must have been high and profits low in the beginning years. Today the employees seem skilled in their work and seem generally happy with their jobs, and the plant gives every appearance of efficient management.

There have been great numbers of other industrial developments in the Tenn-Tom country since 1940, and each has a story of its own. The descriptions and photographs featured here are intended only to present a varied sample and show the dynamics of change. The cities of Corinth, Tupelo, and Columbus have seen the most substantial

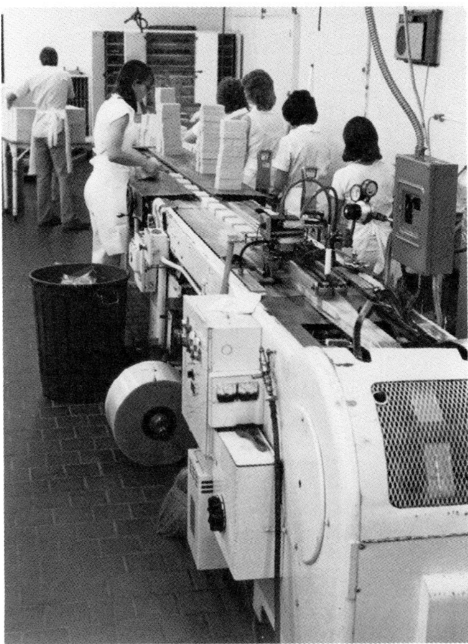

The Marathon Cheese Company gets its cheese from Wisconsin, but at Booneville its workers package seventy-five tons daily for distribution in the Southeast under "private" labels and under the nationally advertised Kraft name. Photo: Jan Weaver.

Above: Testing high-quality hydraulic pumps for Caterpillar tractors at the Tyrone Hydraulics plant in Corinth. Photo: Jan Weaver.

Left: Small refrigeration compressors move down an assembly line at the Tecumseh Products plant at Verona. Photo: William M. Stennett.

At the Mueller Brass Company's plant at Fulton, a red-hot round copper billet is readied for conversion into copper tubing in a huge extrusion press. Photo: Mueller Brass Company.

Greenwater Marina on the Yellow Creek Embayment of Pickwick Lake docks and services hundreds of pleasure craft. Immediately accessible are the Tenn-Tom Waterway and the Tennessee River. Beyond lies the whole Mississippi River system. Photo: Jan Weaver.

developments. Columbus, having the strongest base to start with, has attracted some rather large industries. Aberdeen, Amory, Fulton, Red Bay, Okolona, Iuka, Booneville, and West Point have also undergone industrial growth. Other industries have been established in rural locations, such as the new Weyerhaeuser paper mill in Lowndes County and the hazardous waste disposal facility at Emelle in Sumter County.

Federal grants for planning and technical assistance, and sometimes for construction of public facilities, have been invaluable to industrial development, and tax relief by both the states and the federal government has helped. Payrolls have been fattened, but industrial development has been heavily supported by debt, and the federal government's policies have been so biased against saving that capital accumulation in the area has been painfully slow. The expansionary economic policies, which have had the most important stimulating effects, appear to have run their course of usefulness and to promise little for the future.

Educational Development

World War II took the local people away from home in great numbers to serve in the armed forces and in war industries, and they returned with new skills and new perspectives. The G.I. Bill of Rights paid the educational expenses of veterans for four years and thus enabled many to return to school in the reconversion period. Growing needs and growing tax revenues encouraged the expansion of Livingston University, the Mississippi University for Women (which now admits men) at Columbus, and Mississippi State University at Starkville—as well as the University of Mississippi, at Oxford, which is not far from Tupelo. Black students have been admitted to all these schools and are particularly numerous at Livingston University. So far, however, the universities have given little leadership to business and industrial development.

Mississippi has an extensive network of technical schools to train skilled workers. Shown is a training class for machinists at the Vo-Tech of the Tupelo branch of Itawamba Junior College. Photo: Jan Weaver.

Every Tenn-Tom county has at least one vocational-technical school (known as "vo-tech"), and junior colleges are found in Booneville, Fulton (with a branch at Tupelo), and Columbus. All the counties have high schools which offer vocational courses. Federal and state aid and supervision by state departments of education permit flexibility in course offerings and financing to meet changing needs.

Industrial growth and education require coordination to support each other. Where the junior colleges and trade schools have been able to coordinate their work with industrial apprenticeship programs, as at Hall of Mississippi, results have been good. Yet the continuing shortage of technical skills casts clouds over the future. Converting people into labor presents difficult problems.

Better Roads

After World War II the paving of the major highways was completed. The states then turned to providing hard surfaces for secondary and farm-to-market roads. The new network promoted rapid economic developments and social changes, provided mobility for the operation of farms and industries, and revolutionized farm marketing. Many people were able to commute to jobs while continuing to live in their ancestral homes. In addition large areas became accessible for outdoor recreation. Although one highway of the new interstate system passes through Greene and Sumter counties, the main influence of the system on the Tenn-Tom country has been not local but indirect, as in facilitating the efficient nationwide delivery of the *National Geographic Magazine* by trailer trucks from Corinth.

The Geography of Change

In 1860 the prosperity of the valley was greatest in the Black Belt–Black Prairie areas and tapered off to the northward. The prosperity of the 1980s, on the other hand, is greatest in the north and tapers off rapidly below Columbus. There has been a steady outflow of population in the southern counties and little industrial development has appeared. In general, it has been the younger, better educated, and more ambitious individuals of both races who have moved away. While counties with heavy black populations were most prosperous in 1860, the counties with the heavier white populations have attained that distinction in the 1980s. Even the sewing industries have largely shunned the black counties of Noxubee, Greene, and Sumter. Although all of these are economically weak, outside help has not generally been aggressively sought, partly for the reason that it means outside interference with established social systems.

Greene County has for many years had a black government, which has been aggressive in seeking government and private grants and help from everywhere it can get it, but so far it has only a greyhound racetrack to show for its efforts to develop payrolls. An English paper company was set to build a paperboard plant on the Tenn-Tom

Greene County has a black government headed by probate judge William McKinley Branch, a former schoolteacher. Branch was running unopposed for a third six-year term in 1982 when this picture was made. Photo: Jan Weaver.

Waterway near Boligee, but skyrocketing interest rates caused cancellation of its plans. Judge Branch, the head of the county government, looks to state and federal governments and other outside sources for help, because local capital, technology, and enterprise seem entirely unequal to the task.

Greyhounds (*left*) pursue a mechanical rabbit as they strive to outdo each other at Greenetrack near Eutaw. Spectators can watch from enclosed air-conditioned stands (*below*), where they can also order dinner. Photos: Greenetrack.

Two gentlemen at Verona watch the operation of a huge metal-forming press at the Tecumseh Products plant. Author Doster (left) is instructed by plant manager Tracy Lord, while a workman in the booth supervises the operation of the heavily automated machine, which turns out 1,000 deep-drawn compressor housings per hour. Photo: William M. Stennett.

The Tenn-Tom Waterway

Construction of the Tennessee-Tombigbee Waterway was authorized by Congress in the Rivers and Harbors Act of 1946. By that time the Tennessee, Warrior, and lower Tombigbee rivers had been canalized for year-round traffic and the new canal would connect them. Advance planning and field exploration work went on until 1951, when the House Appropriations Committee decided that the project was not economically sound. Planning funds were then withdrawn, and the Tenn-Tom project was left in limbo.

The resurrection, reinvigoration, construction, and final completion of the Tennessee-Tombigbee Waterway were accomplished against aggressive and continuing opposition from many quarters. Numerous interests supported it and many individuals had an active hand in it. The most persistent leadership came from the affable but determined Glover Wilkins of Columbus. As he tells it:

"I was born in Brooksville, a little town down in Noxubee County. The nearest place we could swim was in the Tombigbee River, so we drove to the Pickensville ferry, and I learned to swim off the apron of the ferry there. I have been interested in the river all my life. After World War II, I started to work for the Columbus Chamber of Commerce, and the Tennessee-Tombigbee was our number one project. We worked through the Chamber and a few cities around here. We were not financed, so all we did was more or less keep the idea alive."

Questioned about the motives that bestirred him to great and continuing efforts, Wilkins says: "Of the people who finished high school with me in Noxubee County in 1930 I am the only one still in this area. The rest of them have left. One of the things that motivated me into wanting to do something on the Tennessee-Tombigbee was seeing my friends, everybody I grew up with, leave this area. I think that Columbus, Macon, Brooksville, and Shuqualak are so closely intertwined in interest that what helps one is going to help them all. I think that Noxubee now has a future, to be whatever its people may want it to be."

The strongest and most determined opponent of the waterway has been Prime F. Osborne, who, like Wilkins, is a native of the Black Belt. He grew up in Greensboro, Alabama, and was educated at the University of Alabama. After a long career as a lawyer for the Mobile and Ohio, Louisville and Nashville, and Atlantic Coast Line railroads, he became president of the L&N and, more recently, chairman of the CSX Corporation, its parent company. Calling Tenn-Tom "a great boondoggle," he says: "The promotion of this undertaking has been fraught with misleading statements which should affront the

Glover Wilkins (*top*) was for many years the administrator of the Tennessee-Tombigbee Waterway Development Authority, an interstate consortium charged with promotion of the waterway. Prime F. Osborne (*above*), the waterway's strongest opponent, called it "a great boondoggle." Photos: Jan Weaver; Office of University Relations, University of Alabama.

intelligence of the great people of the area concerned. My principal purpose in opposing the waterway is to avoid the wasteful use of tax dollars. Being a native of the Black Belt, I am also keenly interested in the preservation of its historical cultural values." Osborne's actions cannot be separated from the legitimate interests of the companies he has represented, but his personal feeling about the waterway and his attachment to Black Belt values are known to the authors to be deeply sincere.

Wilkins and his associates made a new start in 1956, and several friendly congressmen obtained $150,000 for a new economic study, which was carried on from 1957 to 1960. The governors of Alabama and Mississippi in 1958 formed an interstate compact, which their legislatures approved and Congress ratified, and were later joined by Tennessee, Kentucky, and Florida. Under the compact there was created the Tennessee-Tombigbee Waterway Development Authority, an interstate consortium of which Glover Wilkins was administrator for many years.

The findings of the economic study, reported in 1961, were favorable, and the Corps of Engineers recommended construction of the waterway. The Vietnam War and the death of President Kennedy caused delays. The study became outdated, and a new one had to be made. In 1967, the Corps recommended widening the Waterway to 300 feet, with lock chambers measuring 110 by 600 feet. President Lyndon B. Johnson put the project into the federal budget of 1968, and initial construction money was appropriated in May 1971. President Nixon then went to Mobile for a ceremonial groundbreaking.

A ditch 300 feet wide running across a broad expanse of country does not seem like much to contemplate until one actually sees the

President Richard M. Nixon presided over the groundbreaking for the Tenn-Tom Waterway on May 25, 1971, at Mobile. Photo: Corps of Engineers.

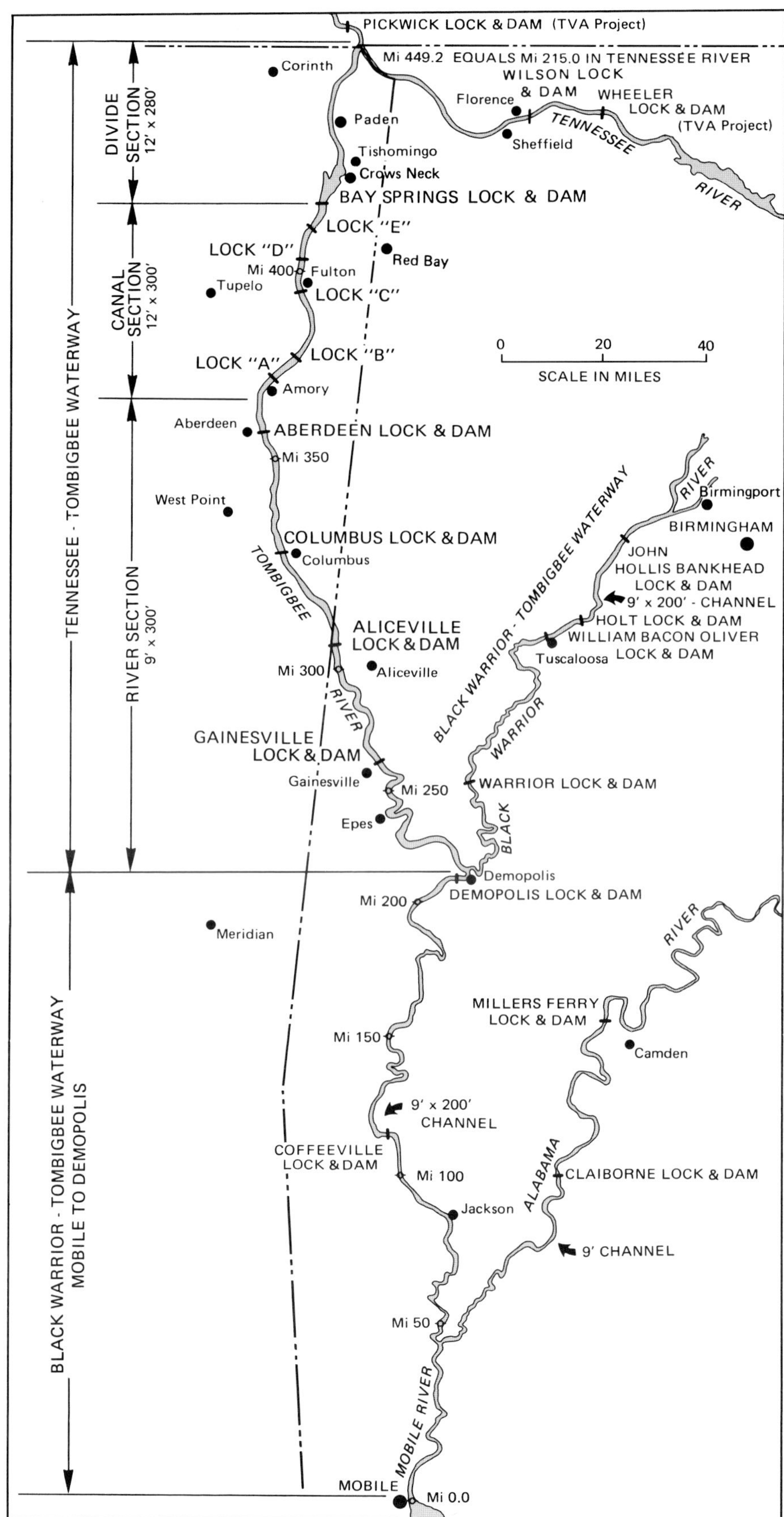

Map 15. The Tennessee-Tombigbee Waterway and navigable connections

landscape, and even then the full impact does not appear at first glance. Building the Tennessee-Tombigbee Waterway was a huge undertaking, and its influences, although hard to evaluate with precision, are far-reaching in their effects upon geography, ecology, and the lives of people. The waterway is one of the great engineering accomplishments of all time, comparable in magnitude to the Panama Canal and Egypt's Aswan Dam. The Army Corps of Engineers had the responsibility for the planning and construction, a comprehensive and arduous undertaking.

Political and economic conditions change constantly, and so does state-of-the-art engineering. Plans for the waterway, worked out over a long period of years, had frequently to be updated, and the rapid development of environmental concepts forced numerous and drastic readjustments. New concepts and new engineering technology had to be developed while the project was under way, as knowledge and experience accumulated. All this had to be done in a public, adversarial environment. Yielding too readily to criticism might produce Tower-of-Babel chaos and confusion, while an unyielding stand against critics would also lead to disaster. Continued funding by Congress could never be taken for granted. Strident critics often had nothing constructive to propose except abandonment of the project, even when their complaints had a substantial basis. It was up to the Corps to sift out the criticisms and to work out answers when they had validity. Great works are not accomplished without pain, nor are they accomplished without bold leadership. Building the Tenn-Tom Waterway was almost like conducting a war.

On July 14, 1971, the Environmental Defense Fund, a private organization, filed suit against the Corps of Engineers, and a federal district court enjoined construction until there could be a full hearing. The Louisville and Nashville Railroad Company (L&N), which could expect both direct and indirect damage to its rates and traffic from the waterway, quietly supported the move. Most of the action, however, related to environmental considerations, which might more effectively be used in the courts to block the project than the railroad's complaints. The injunction was dissolved, with prejudice, in August 1972, and the first waterway construction began on the Gainesville lock and dam the following November. Litigation and other activities in opposition continued, however, year after year. The Corps of Engineers and the Tennessee-Tombigbee Waterway Development Authority fought back, but the litigation and new congressional legislation kept the Corps under constant pressure to find means to avoid or mitigate damage to the environment and to cultural resources. Adverse and rival interests repeatedly tried to prevail upon Congress to cut off appropriations. The L&N Railroad Company, however, losing one case after another in the courts, gave up in March 1983, and the judge terminated the litigation the following May 9.

The Tennessee-Tombigbee Waterway reaches from Demopolis to the Pickwick pool of the Tennessee River. It is divided into three distinct sections, which are, from south to north, the river section,

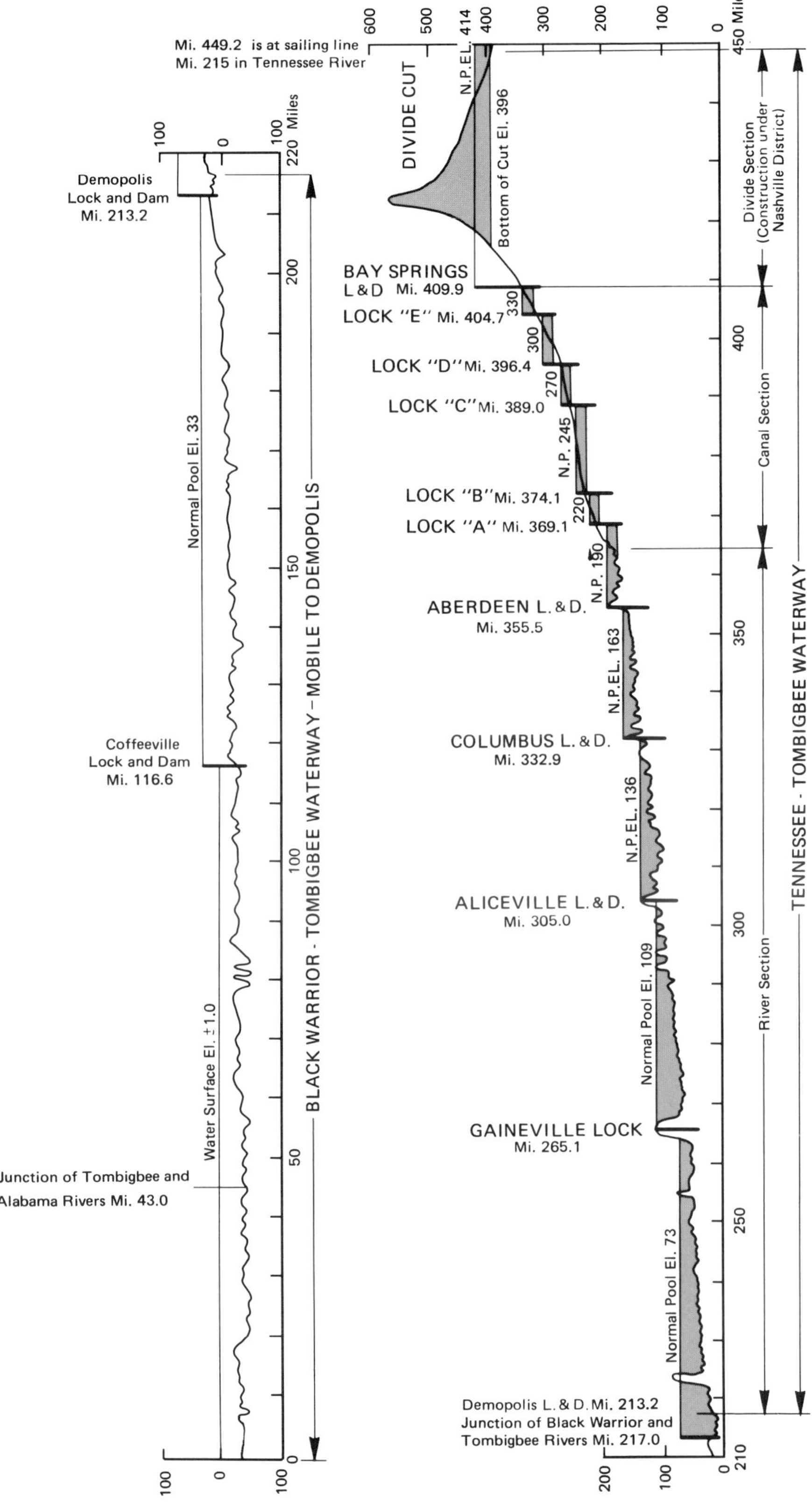

Figure 5. Waterway profiles from Mobile to Pickwick Lake.

Figure 6. Rattlesnake Bend cutoff in the river section of the Tenn-Tom Waterway. Diagram shows primary techniques of disposal for material excavated.

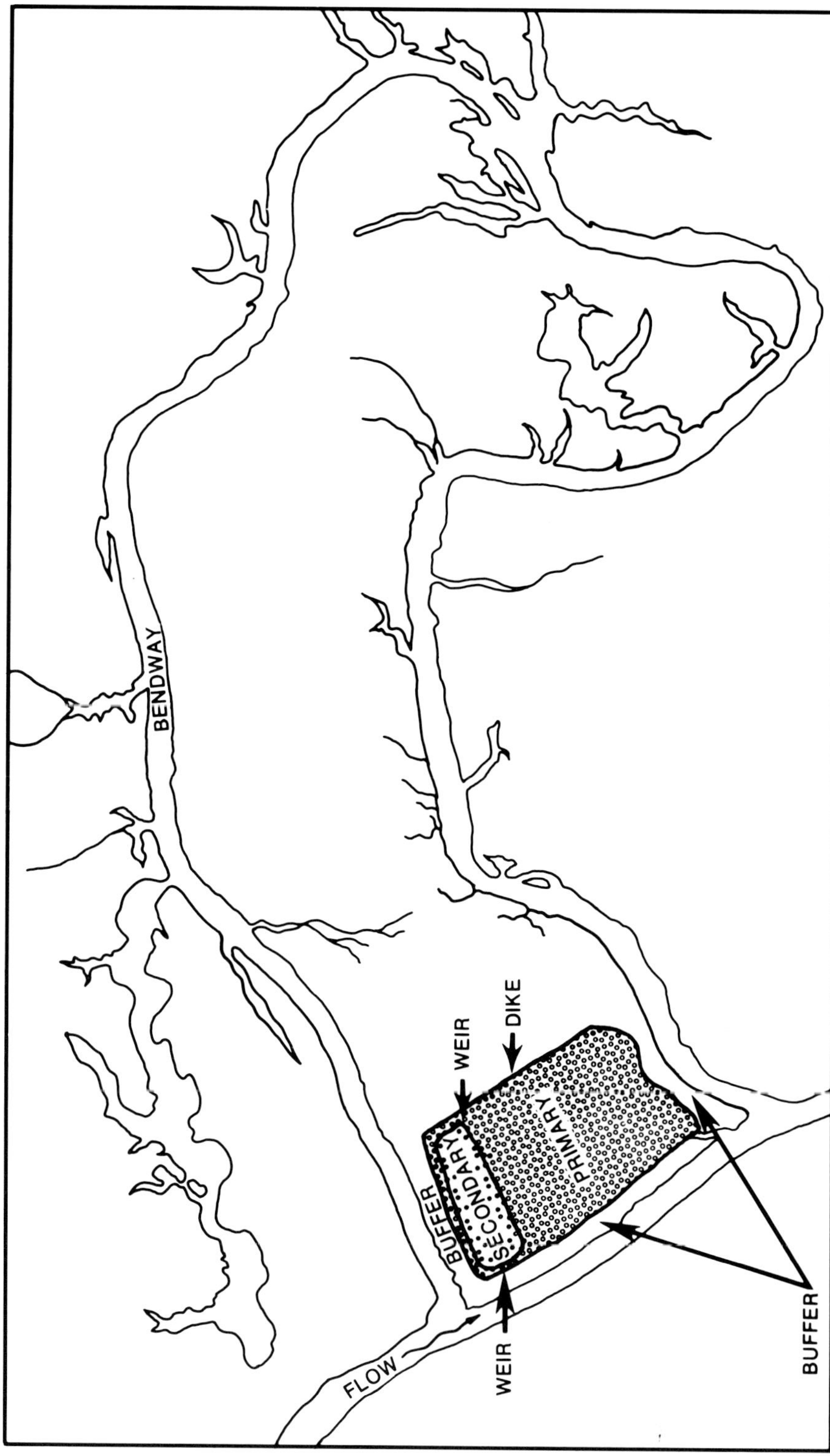

the canal section, and the divide section, with an overall length of 234 miles. The water level difference from the Demopolis pool to the Pickwick pool is 341 feet, which is navigated with the aid of ten locks.

Industry, commerce, and tourism, the promoters hope, will bring a transformation and revitalization to the region. The Tennessee-Tombigbee Waterway Development Authority coordinates activities associated with the waterway. The states of Alabama and Mississippi have their own special agencies, the Tombigbee Valley Development Authority and the Tombigbee River Valley Water Management District, respectively. The states have built bridges and water terminals, have relocated some utilities, and have also contributed about 9 percent of the construction cost.

The river section begins at Demopolis, where the Demopolis dam, a part of the Black Warrior–Tombigbee Waterway, backs up the water as far as Gainesville, a distance of fifty miles, on the Upper Tombigbee. Considerable dredging was necessary to widen the channel to 300 feet and to cut off the meandering Rattlesnake Bend. A canal guarded by dikes forms a cutoff to connect the Gainesville lock with the pool above the Gainesville dam, leaving Gainesville a short distance from the waterway but still on the river.

The Gainesville canal, lock, and highway bridge shown here are typical of similar structures in the river section. The dam, a mile or so upstream, turns the overflow through a spillway into the old river channel, not seen, on the left. Photo: Corps of Engineers.

A dredge of the Corps of Engineers is shown here cutting away the bank in the Gainesville Reservoir. Much of the work on the Tenn-Tom Waterway has been done by such dredges, which will continue to be needed for channel maintenance. Photo: Corps of Engineers.

The Aliceville lock and dam under construction, while a cofferdam keeps out the river water. Photo: Corps of Engineers.

The lake behind the Gainesville dam extends forty miles to the Aliceville dam at Pickensville. Dredging has widened the crooked river channel and has considerably straightened it, maintaining a standard 300-foot width and a 9-foot depth. The lake above Pickensville extends to Columbus, twenty-eight miles away. Several cutoffs, notably those at Pickensville, Hairston's Bend, and Columbus, have straightened the old river channel, which has also been widened as required. The cutoffs have been given an extra depth, for

Top left: The Valley Green dock in Pickens County is used for the handling of soybeans. Photo: Corps of Engineers.

Above: An engineer checks construction details on the Tenn-Tom structures at Columbus. Photo: Corps of Engineers.

Left: The Columbus lock, dam, and spillway involved massive construction and modification of the landscape. Photo: Corps of Engineers.

At Aberdeen the waterway with its spillway and the new highway and railroad bridges in the foreground has drastically altered the physical arrangements and the general appearance of things. Photo: Corps of Engineers.

reasons explained by Nathaniel D. McClure, an engineer of the Mobile District: "When your vessel moves in a confined channel, it tends to squat, and you lose some of the maneuverability of the tow. It is almost sucked toward the bottom. The extra depth is provided to facilitate navigation. That is why the cutoffs are twelve feet deep and why the canals that are in confined areas are twelve feet deep."

The Columbus dam backs the water up as far as Aberdeen, twenty-two miles away, but as the Tennessee-Tombigbee Waterway advances above Columbus it has less and less to do with the old river channel. Construction of the lock and dam at Aberdeen has cut a wide swath through the countryside and has markedly changed the appearance of the river and the areas adjacent to it. The dam creates a lake above Aberdeen that is in places some two miles wide and extends nine miles north to the beginning of the canal section, below Amory. The waterway channel, 300 feet wide and 12 feet deep, follows the general course of the river, but it is much bigger and straighter, and it crosses the river channel several times.

The canal section leaves the Tombigbee River a short distance below Amory and follows the eastern side of a valley of gradually decreasing width to Bay Springs, forty-four miles away. The original plan called for a "perched" canal, with a dike on each side, the

Lock A, near Amory, shown completed, is the southernmost lock of the canal section. Note the spillway to the left of the lock and the levee running to the left of the channel above. Photo: Corps of Engineers.

Lock B, shown here after completion, is at quite a distance from the spillway, which appears at the upper left. Levees run to the left of the waterway and its structures. Photo: Corps of Engineers.

Lock C and its spillway near Fulton were completed before the canal above was excavated. Note the levees with roads on top. Photo: Corps of Engineers.

Below: Lock D, with its spillway, shown under construction, is not near any town. The levee on the upper left appears in a partially completed state. Photo: Corps of Engineers.

Lock E and its spillway are the north-ernmost such structures of the canal section. In an isolated location, they were the last to be put under construction and were in this incomplete state when photographed in February 1984, less than a year before the opening of the waterway. Photo: Corps of Engineers.

Below: Bay Springs lock under construction. With an eighty-four-foot lift this lock holds more than twice as much water as any other in the system. Photo: David C. Weaver.

surface drainage from the creeks on the east being carried through culverts under the canal. After much study the proposed dike on the eastern side was eliminated. The navigation channel passes through five lakes impounded by dams with locks, designated A (at Amory), B (at Smithville), C (at Fulton), and D and E (not located near any town). The locks and dams, each with its spillway, were constructed on dry land before the rest of the waterway in the area was completed. The eastern margin of the lakes is determined by the level at which the water reaches the high ground sloping from the east. The channel itself runs near the dike. The water level rises somewhat at flood time. Creeks from the hill country to the east drain into the lakes, but spillways and limited flow outlets feed the creeks on the west side. Mackey's Creek on the west is joined by Brown's to form the East Fork of the Tombigbee. Then the East Fork is joined west of Amory by the West Fork, or Town Creek, to create the Tombigbee River proper, with which the canal connects just south of Amory.

The divide section, constructed by the Nashville District of the Corps of Engineers, extends from Bay Springs to the Tennessee River, forty miles away. At Bay Springs is a rock-fill earth dam 120 feet high and 2,750 feet long. The lock has an 84-foot lift, the third highest east of the Mississippi River. Mackey's Creek, a rushing stream, used to flow through the area, but most of the descending water now comes from the operation of the lock, which uses about two and a half times the amount required for the downstream locks. A conduit through the lock wall can release as much as 275 cubic feet per second to feed the streams below when the lock is not being operated. Construction of the lock and dam at Bay Springs, a work of five years, required extensive excavation in hard rock, including a cut through a rock formation below the dam.

Divide cut construction at the crest of the divide required very extensive earth removal. Huge construction machinery appears minute in this 1979 aerial photograph. Photo: Corps of Engineers.

Above: Construction traffic was heavy as the excavation of the divide cut moved north toward Burnsville. Photo: Jan Weaver.

Left: This big scraper was kept busy smoothing temporary roadways as construction advanced. Photo: Jan Weaver.

Above: A woman truck driver photographed in 1982 climbs to the cab of her fifty-ton dump truck, which is being loaded by a big backhoe at the head of the advancing cut. Photo: Jan Weaver.

Right: A woman oiler looks on as a seven-and-one-half-cubic-yard backhoe cuts away at the head end of the divide cut. Her job is to oil and clean the machine when it is not in motion. Photo: Jan Weaver.

Above: On the bottom of the cut, earth is removed by a Holland loader, which is simply a cutting blade and a conveyor with a big bulldozer at each end. The accompanying dump truck is quickly loaded. Photo: Jan Weaver.

Left: The "rock monster," a tremendous machine for spreading heavy rip-rap, or crushed rock, on the sides of the waterway, was especially designed and built for the divide cut. Photo: Corps of Engineers.

Seven miles above the high dam, at a point 417 miles from Mobile, begins the divide cut. It is twenty-seven miles long, with an average depth of excavation of about 50 feet. At the crest of the divide the depth is 175 feet. The sides rise 1 foot for every 2.5 feet of additional width. The water level in the divide cut section fluctuates with that of the lake behind Pickwick Dam on the Tennessee River. The canal channel is 12 feet deep at low water, and the bottom is 280 feet wide. At the normal pool level the full depth is 18 feet, and sloping sides give the channel a width of 302.5 feet at a depth of 9 feet. Elaborate measures have been adopted to control the effects of local streams flowing into the canal and to minimize silting and cross-currents that might interfere with the movement of barge tows. At the northern end of the divide cut the waterway, which carries the waters of Yellow Creek, enters the Yellow Creek Embayment, through which a suitable channel has been dredged six miles to the Tennessee River.

In constructing the waterway the Corps had to comply with the Reservoir Salvage Act of 1960 and the National Historic Preservation Act of 1966. The National Environmental Policy Act of 1969 introduced serious new complications. In accordance with the terms of the 1969 law, the Corps published an environmental impact statement in March 1971, which was followed by the long-lasting litigation discussed above.

A concrete inlet structure studded with baffles is designed to smooth the waters of Yellow Creek as they flow into the canal. Note the rip-rap being laid over a cloth mesh to prevent revegetation. Photo: Jan Weaver.

Above: The completed waterway at Paden, where the divide cut begins, in 1984. Photo: Corps of Engineers.

Left: At the Yellow Creek Embayment the divide cut connects with Pickwick Lake in the Tennessee River. Photo: Corps of Engineers.

Yellow Creek Port near the Tennessee
River on the Yellow Creek Embayment is connected with Corinth by a
railroad. Photo: Corps of Engineers.

The Tennessee-Tombigbee Waterway was constructed at a time
when the general realization was dawning that life and environment
on earth are essentially a part of a fragile and constantly evolving
closed system in which every action has a set of complex reactions.
Profligate use of the earth's resources and indiscriminate disposal of
wastes could leave behind a trail of destruction that could undermine
the base of future life. New ideas of considerable merit were pushed
by zealots while they were still in a raw and undigested form. The
way to avoid damage from construction of the Tenn-Tom, it was
argued, was to stop construction. The only way, it seemed, to make
an impression on the Corps of Engineers was to follow the example
of the farmer who hit his mule over the head with a two by four to
get his attention.

Gradually the Corps faced up to the fact that the problems were
real and that the critics could call attention to problems but did not
have the answers. The waterway would not be completed unless
action acceptable to the public could be taken, and only the leadership of the Corps of Engineers, backed by funds, could define and
solve the problems. The National Park Service and other federal and
state agencies and institutions were called upon for help.

The Tenn-Tom was the first waterway in the nation to be constructed under the National Environmental Policy Act of 1969. Many
different ideas were tried out, and conflicting opinions were subjected to practical tests. Much of this had to be done in an atmo-
sphere of such adversarial intensity as to obscure the fact that the
project was serving as a laboratory for defining environmental and
engineering problems and for working out practical solutions. Hundreds of studies were made. It was found that some damage could be
avoided by careful investigation, and unavoidable damage could be
partially counteracted by policies and programs of mitigation.

As far as is known, no endangered species of animal or plant has been threatened by construction of the waterway, although some habitats will be restricted. Several species of mussels which used to thrive in the clear running water on the gravel bars of the Tombigbee will lose their home and will be confined to the tributary streams. Turbidity and wave action generated by towboat and barge navigation will have some adverse effects. Fish and plant life introduced from the Tennessee River are expected to have minimal adverse effects, although unexpected problems are possible. In the Upper Tombigbee River basin 116 species of fish have been identified, and there are 51 species in the Yellow Creek and Indian Creek drainage basins. Fish dependent upon swift currents may be eliminated from the lakes and confined to the tributary streams. Mitigation of undesirable developments is generally possible, but continuing study is required to detect and analyze problems and to carry out mitigation programs.

Beavers were the first engineers in the divide cut country in the twentieth century. They constructed dams and lakes, regulated the flow of water, and destroyed many acres of woodland and farmland without regard for the environmental consequences. Human engineers dug canals in the area of the canal section to drain swamps and open up new farmland. Sediment, formerly deposited in the swamps, was brought down by swifter currents into the Tombigbee River. Farmers plowing their land encouraged erosion and made the Tombigbee a turbid stream that deposited silt in its lower valley and adversely affected the estuarine environment of Mobile Bay. Marine life suffered the consequences. Environmental change and damage did not begin with Tenn-Tom.

In the divide cut area huge amounts of earth removed in the construction of the waterway had to be put somewhere. Study and experimentation led to improved techniques of spoil disposal. Disposal areas were chosen, mostly on the eastern side of the cut, and the intervening areas, called buffer zones, were allowed to retain much of their former character. Dikes were constructed around the disposal areas to control runoff from rainfall. Acid-producing soils were placed on the bottom, and careful positioning of other spoil squeezed the water out of the beaver lakes and created a drainage system through chains of three lakes, the outflow from each being carried off from the top at a slow rate by a standpipe. The water leaving the disposal areas was thus made relatively clear, and damage from erosion was largely eliminated. The deposits were finished with rolling hills as a surface configuration and were planted in grass until more lasting vegetation could take hold. The Mississippi Fish and Game Commission, which has worked closely with the Corps of Engineers from the beginning, has stocked some of the ponds with fish. On the east side of the upper divide cut is a seventy-acre cypress swamp where the water level is controlled. The state of Mississippi is developing this area as a wildlife refuge.

The disposal areas have been given varying treatment. Quail and rabbits are now plentiful. In some places egrets and ducks are in

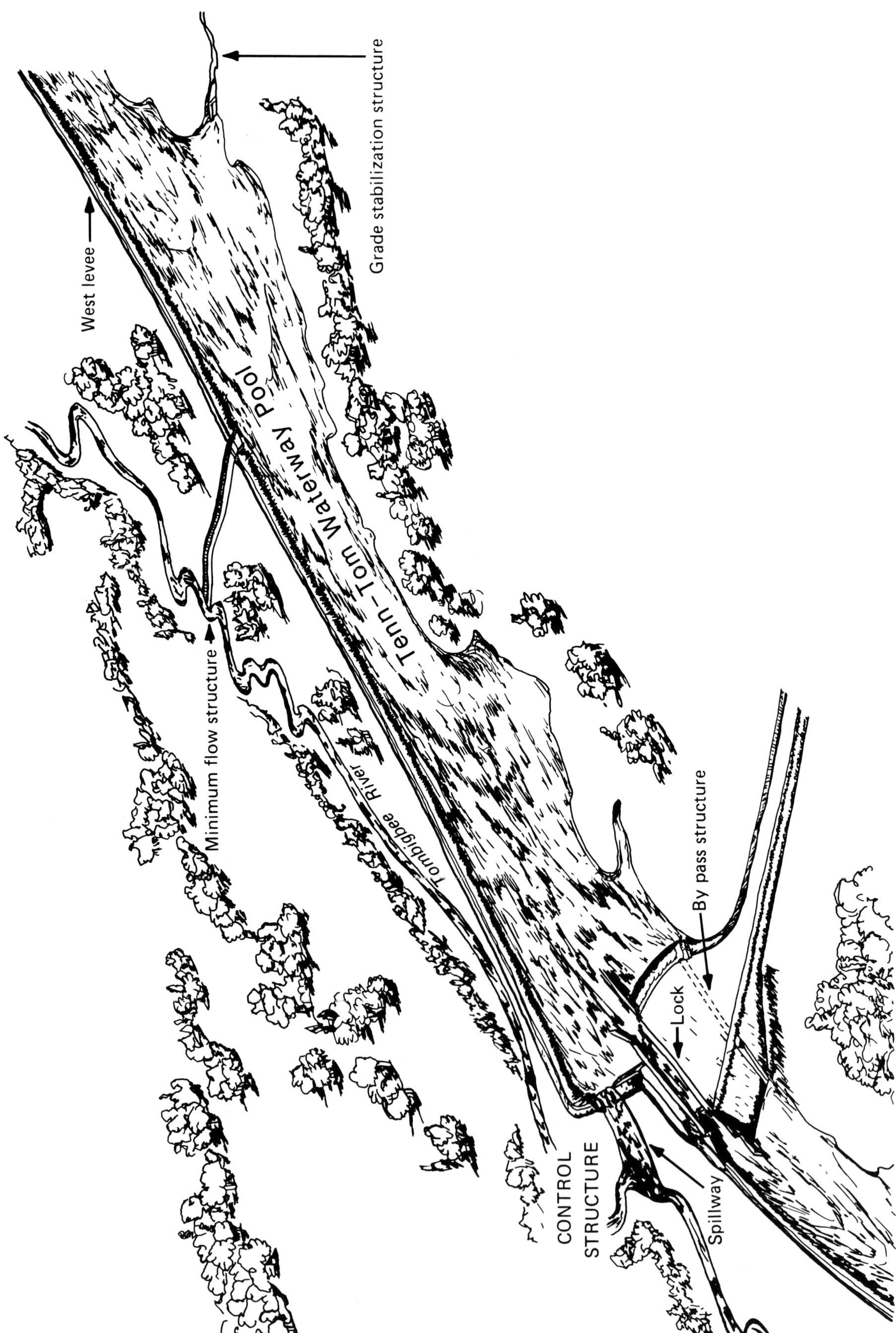

Figure 7. Chain of Lakes concept for canal section of Tenn-Tom waterway.

evidence. Mallards and whispering swans can be found. One large field, seeded in millet, is the home of great flocks of doves. Wood ducks have been attracted by nest boxes placed in disposal areas. Occasional great blue herons are seen. Hawks, too, and foxes have appeared, and coyotes have been moving in. Trees, mainly hardwoods, have been planted in some places. Willows are in evidence, and cattails have moved in on their own. Hunting is increasingly permitted in season and attracts great numbers of men from the surrounding areas. The divide cut section in the construction period displayed a great, ugly gash in the earth, but at present it looks considerably improved over its appearance in preconstruction times.

Construction of the canal section's chain of lakes destroyed several thousand acres of forest land and wildlife habitat. The lakes provide a place for the growth of aquatic plants and fish, however, and for water sports and recreation. Long-term careful study and management will be required to see that the region's potential is realized. The acquisition and intensive management of extensive new acreage is intended to mitigate the loss of forest lands and wildlife habitat. On this subject there have been a wide variety of conflicting interests and viewpoints. The chief local interest seems to be in fish and game for sport rather than in preservation of species or resources for future use. Many local landowners do not want to give up their land. As this book is being written, the plan tentatively approved by the Board of Engineers for Rivers and Harbors calls for intensive management of 72,500 acres of project lands and 20,100 acres of other Corps lands, with additional acquisitions, from willing sellers, of 46,800 acres of bottomland hardwood forest within fifty miles of the waterway.

Bull Mountain Creek, the principal tributary from the east, is a clean stream from the hills. Its waters are carried through and across the waterway with the aid of a special spillway at Smithville. The flow of water through the numerous limited flow structures and spillways, including one at each dam, will follow a preplanned distribution scheme, which may be changed or manipulated to cope with unexpected or changing circumstances. Most of the Tombigbee's pollution comes from the turbid streams to the west, which do not enter the canal section of the waterway.

The river section of the waterway presents problems created by dredged cutoffs and isolated bendways. These will need to be watched and will call for the application of corrective measures when such are indicated. The dams may provide some help in controlling flooding, and the extra water obtained from Pickwick Lake will improve the minimum flow in dry seasons.

The record of early man in North America is largely found in artifacts surviving in areas close to streams. Such remains, known as "cultural resources," were subject to destruction by the building of the waterway. Under the Reservoir Salvage Act of 1960, the National Park Service contracted with the University of Alabama Museums in 1970 to make a cultural resource survey of the Gainesville Lake area. This was the first of several such investigations undertaken in preparation for construction of the waterway. In the 1970s new laws and regulations pertaining to archaeological resources, historical preservation, and environmental protection came thick and fast, and most of these required implementation in the Tenn-Tom project. The Archeological and Historical Preservation Act of 1974 authorized the Corps to spend up to 1 percent of the appropriation for each project for the preservation of archaeological and historical data and the mitigation of damage caused by construction to "scientific, prehistorical, or archeological data."

The work was initially done by the National Park Service. In 1975 the Mobile and Nashville offices of the Corps employed archaeologists of their own. Then in 1977, to meet legislative requirements and research needs, came the creation of the Tennessee-Tombigbee Multi-Resource District, covering an area 5 miles wide centering on the Tombigbee River and extending some 130 miles from Gainesville to Paden, Mississippi, at the southern end of the divide cut. An elaborate mitigation plan was developed for concentrating on broad objectives in archaeological investigation concerned mainly with early man.

Some 900 archaeological sites had been identified along the waterway; 580 of these were within project lands, and 337 of them were expected to be damaged by construction or flooding. Dozens of investigations were put under contract, and great quantities of prehistoric artifacts were excavated. Their significance in piecing together the history of early man in North America will appear only with time, but it should be considerable.

Historic Indians did not live in significant numbers or with significant continuity along the Upper Tombigbee River, and the investigation of nineteenth-century sites has produced results that are primarily of local interest, such as at Bay Springs, Sharpley's Bottom, and Barton-Vinton. Investigation of old steamboat wrecks has been unproductive. Remains of a dugout canoe centuries old, now in a museum at Amory, were discovered incidentally in the waterway excavations.

The archaeologists have been largely confined in their efforts to mitigating construction damage to particular sites, not necessarily those likely to produce the greatest expansion of knowledge. They have had to work under time pressure and often with personnel of less comprehensive knowledge than would be desirable. Some bad mistakes have been made, but running up frequent blind alleys is an inherent part of the process of creating or discovering new knowledge. Without the research financed by the Corps in connection with Tenn-Tom, however, much of chapter 2 of this book could not have been written.

While mitigating environmental damage by supporting environmental studies and advancing capacities for future management of forest and wildlife reservations may have been effected only reluctantly and under great pressure by the Corps of Engineers, it is the Corps which has done it, and its organization is now structured to use this experience in dealing with future problems. It is not environmental damage but the advance of environmental technology and the creation of a new capacity to perform great works with a minimum disturbance to the ecology and culture of an area that is the significant development. The engineers, the environmentalists and various scientists, the historic preservationists, the archaeologists, the businessmen, the railroads, and the public officials have all made their contributions, although perhaps sometimes perversely. Many hundreds of people have had a hand in this and sometimes maybe a foot. The work is not finished.

A part of the mitigation program, shared by the Corps of Engineers and the states of Alabama and Mississippi, is the development of educational and recreational facilities along the waterway. Jutting into the Bay Springs Lake are six peninsulas, each of which has been designated for special development. Particularly notable is Crow's Neck (named for the Crow family), a 530-acre area on which an elaborate environmental and recreational center has been planned. The construction work is the responsibility of the Corps of Engineers. This enterprise was promoted by Hilda L. Hill (see also chapter 1), who induced public agencies to support it. The Crow's Neck Center is designed to carry out programs in environmental education and to provide a kind of natural laboratory, with facilities for housing about 100 schoolchildren at a time, to be brought in buses from the surrounding area. Crow's Neck Center will use the surrounding lake, forests, fields, and wetlands for interpretive experience for the general public and for students of all ages. Included in the "environment" concept are local history and historic local culture. Selected folk and vernacular homes in the area have been preserved for reconstruction on the site as funds permit. The center includes recreational facilities in a natural setting of both land and water.

At Plymouth Bluff, north of Columbus, another center comparable to Crow's Neck has long been planned on a 140-acre site under the sponsorship and management of the Mississippi University for Women at Columbus. Original plans for the waterway were drastically changed to preserve the site, which is considered of geological, paleontological, archaeological, and historical significance.

Up and down the waterway from top to bottom are recreational areas of many kinds for hunting, fishing, picnicking, boating, camping, and other activities. Some sites have been developed, while others have been reserved. The Corps of Engineers bears some of the costs, but cost sharing with local sponsors is generally demanded, with provision for the local sponsors to operate the facilities.

That the waterway can carry heavy traffic is clear enough, but where the traffic will come from is not so clear. Some of it will be taken from the L&N and other railroads. Most of it is expected to be in bulk commodities, chiefly coal, petroleum and petroleum derivatives, pulp and paper, wheat, corn, soybeans, and construction materials. Such traffic will have to move in competition with other transportation routes, other transportation modes, and other sources of supply. New traffic can develop only slowly, and much of it seems likely to be in commodities in the export trade passing through the port of Mobile. But corn will come south to Amory and Columbus, and soybeans will move from river ports to Mobile. The Tennessee Valley Authority has installed facilities at Yellow Creek Port and has built a railroad from that point to Corinth. Waterway port facilities have been built at Fulton, Amory, Aberdeen, Columbus, Cochrane, and Epes, and private barge slips and loading facilities are completed or planned at additional points. Other port facilities will certainly be developed as they are needed. At Demopolis a barge fleeting area for assembling tows has been planned but is not to be built at federal expense. The principal economic impact of Tenn-Tom on the adjacent counties so far has been in construction and maintenance employment. Construction contractors were required to employ 80 percent "local" people, 29 percent "minority," and 5.9 percent women. "Local" was interpreted to cover fifty counties. There has thus been a heavy infusion of money into an economically poor district over a considerable period of years.

New industrial growth has been expected to replace construction as a source of employment. While a generally depressed economy has obscured the picture of actual developments, several things seem clear. The buildup of waterway traffic from all sources is going to be gradual, and through barge traffic will not have much effect on the local economy. The development of local industries will require vigorous local leadership and will not come by itself. Harry A. Martin of the Community Development Foundation (Tupelo), one of the waterway's sponsors, points out that one of the world's best waterways runs the full length of Mississippi on its western side, yet there is no significant industrial development along it. Development along the waterway, he says, will not happen unless "we make it happen." The waterway is, for local purposes, just one more resource and will not be productive until it is utilized.

Only industries requiring the handling of heavy bulk commodities are likely to locate right on the waterway; others will prefer established towns and centers of business and population, and Columbus is the only considerable business center directly on the waterway. Aberdeen, Amory, Smithville, and Fulton are small but are well placed for waterway-related industry. Tupelo, Booneville, Corinth, and Iuka, all a few miles away, are well situated to benefit, but they will not automatically do so. Eutaw and Macon are short of local resources, and conspicuous local enterprise is largely absent in their vicinity. More distant places such as Tuscaloosa, Florence, Huntsville, and even Memphis and Chattanooga should benefit economically from the Tenn-Tom but this will require time.

For traffic originating on the Tennessee River, the port of Mobile is much closer than New Orleans. A comparison of costs between the two is difficult, but Mobile will certainly have a considerable share in the export business of the future, as it does in that of the present. Mobile seems in the best position to reap the benefits of the Tenn-Tom Waterway. It has a well-developed port for foreign trade, particularly in bulk commodities. New Orleans is fast becoming the

This eight-barge tow loaded with 12,000 tons of coal, photographed on the Warrior River, is of a configuration that will use the full capacity of the Tenn-Tom locks and channels. Photo: Parker Towing Company.

nation's leading port in export tonnage, but Mobile can handle the same commodities. With improved access by water to the interior, it can share considerably in the rapidly growing export business of the nation, particularly in grain and coal. Large American ports all need deeper channels to handle vessels of 150,000 tons or more, but Mobile seems to be in the front rank of those in pursuit of a fifty-five-foot depth.

From one end to the other, Tenn-Tom has been built to accommodate the efficient operation of eight-barge tows. As traffic develops, it may be expected to be primarily southbound, with barges returning empty. The lock chambers are of varying lifts, but all are 110 feet wide by 600 feet long. A standard steel barge is 35 feet wide by 195 feet long. Loaded to a draft of 9 feet, it can carry 1,500 tons. A 2,000-

The last earth plug on the Tenn-Tom Waterway, north of Amory, was opened in January 1985. The new Burlington Northern railroad bridge appears in the background. Photo: Corps of Engineers.

horsepower towboat can navigate the waterway and enter a lock with eight such barges, carrying 12,000 tons of coal. Substitution of an extra-long barge for one of those of standard length will add another thousand tons of capacity, making a maximum for the tow of 13,000 tons. Larger locks are being built on the Tennessee, which will make the use of much larger tows feasible on that connection of Tenn-Tom.

Although eight-barge tows can navigate the lower Tombigbee River, that channel must also carry the heavy traffic of the existing Black Warrior–Tombigbee Waterway. Much of it is not wide enough to permit two-way traffic for large tows. As traffic develops, inadequate locking capacity at Demopolis and Coffeeville and sharp bends and narrow channels will cause expensive delays, and a demand for additional locks and channel improvements may be expected. The meeting of tows is controlled by radio from the vessel moving downstream, and considerable time is sometimes lost even now by the ascending tow in waiting at meeting places. Some thirty miles of cutoffs have already been proposed. The problems can be solved only with heavy expenditures. The William B. Oliver lock on the Warrior, a part of the combined system, is too small to handle an eight-barge tow, but its early replacement is anticipated.

Apparently less tractable is the problem of high water. At flood time the current in many places on both the Warrior and the lower Tombigbee rivers is so swift as to render the handling of an eight- or six-barge tow unsafe. This may also prove true in the river section of the Tenn-Tom Waterway. The shortening of channels with cutoffs tends to aggravate rather than solve this problem.

On the Mississippi River there is no lock below St. Louis, and the river is sufficiently large to accommodate tows of more than forty barges under most conditions. A measure of economy is thus introduced, for large towboats do not require much larger crews than small ones. Such huge tows lack flexibility, however. They stop at terminals some miles above New Orleans, and they require local switch boats to distribute and assemble the barges, and a full-size tow is not always available.

Whether Tenn-Tom will be worth its cost remains to be seen. The answer will be long in coming and may never be clear. Projects of such a nature in the past have generally been bailed out by the rapid growth of the American economy. Where there has been excess capacity, that capacity has commonly been needed in time. Here we have a great region that is poorly developed economically, so the opportunities of the waterway cannot be quickly exploited. The opportunities created, however, may add sufficient strength to permit local enterprise to become established. The damage that the L&N Railroad may suffer will depend upon the ability of the waterway to take over the bulk traffic, particularly in coal, and on the possible mitigating effects of the future expansion of business and industry in the regions served.

Above: The Tim Parkers, senior and junior, of Tuscaloosa, are barge operators already active in the traffic of the Tenn-Tom Waterway. *Left:* A barge tow of the Parker Towing Company moves through the completed waterway. Photos: Parker Towing Company.

Appendix:
Statistics of Ten Upper Tombigbee Valley Counties, 1850-1960

Quantitative data are available from the U.S. Census for a much more detailed picture of developments through time in the Upper Tombigbee Valley than the text of this volume attempts to give. For persons who wish to see for themselves, figures are given in this appendix. The tabulations which follow show comparative values by counties for selected census years between 1850 and 1960. While there are important differences between counties, the general trends of development show broad similarities through time. Not all census years are used, but those thought to be representative have been chosen. In general there appears to have been a strong and general economic advance from 1850 to 1860, a sharp drop in 1880, and a continuing decline to 1930 but a rise of impressive dimensions in 1960. Decennial census years may not capture the timing of all trends precisely, but the general picture seems clear enough. Farms grew in size from 1850 to 1860, declined thereafter to 1930, but rose again in 1960. These trends were general throughout the counties.

There was a shocking decline in the value of farms after 1860. Particularly notable is the destruction of farm values in Greene, Sumter, Lowndes, and Noxubee counties from 1860 to 1880. These prosperous areas were essentially destroyed by the Civil War and associated developments, although they were little affected by direct military activities. They did not recover. The improvement in value per farm between 1890 and 1910 partly reflects mild inflationary trends in that period but also probably represents a genuine improvement. Even so, the figures remain astonishingly low.

The decrease in the number of hogs per person and cattle per person reflects the decline of self-sufficiency and the increasing emphasis on the market crop of cotton. The decrease in cotton production per person, despite increasing emphasis on that crop, was very general. Some of the figures suggest a modest increase in the efficiency of cotton production between 1910 and 1930. The poor counties of Itawamba and Tishomingo show resistance to the advance of the tenant system but a tendency over time to give way to it. The independent small farmers of these counties were degenerating into tenants, as were those elsewhere.

An analysis of farm ownership figures for 1910 reveals that 43 percent of the white farmers in the ten counties were owners of farms, but only 6 percent of the black farmers. Yet in Itawamba and Tishomingo counties black ownership ran to 16 percent and 25 percent, respectively. The white-black population ratio varied greatly from one county to another, from 92 percent white in Itawamba and Tishomingo counties in 1910 to 16 percent in Noxubee and Greene. Social and political differences accompanied these variations. Because of changes in counties and county boundaries, not all figures presented here are strictly comparable. The main effect of the changes, however, has been eliminated by presenting the figures on a per capita, per farm, or percentage basis. Dashes appearing in the tables indicate years when the county in question did not exist.

Table A. Average Size of Farms (acres)

County	1850	1860	1880	1890	1910	1930	1960
Greene	402	706	136	112	68	53	183
Pickens	267	394	215	149	89	77	243
Sumter	513	799	151	122	80	67	198
Clay	—	—	132	88	72	60	149
Itawamba	233	323	182	130	94	71	103
Lowndes	405	502	126	123	59	65	134
Monroe	394	463	141	92	69	60	122
Noxubee	444	574	174	105	56	53	191
Prentiss	—	—	112	135	76	58	95
Tishomingo	259	333	188	156	93	70	102
Alabama	289	347	139	126	79	68	142
Mississippi	309	370	156	122	68	55	135

Source: U.S. Census.

Table B. Average Value per Farm (dollars)

County	1850	1860	1880	1890	1910	1930	1960
Greene	3,035	11,572	634	620	1,169	1,202	9,847
Pickens	1,346	3,148	853	724	1,169	1,473	11,244
Sumter	2,870	10,650	699	583	1,360	1,524	12,381
Clay	—	—	920	906	1,542	1,616	9,852
Itawamba	647	1,404	546	424	914	1,278	7,424
Lowndes	2,839	12,053	1,089	1,229	1,507	2,179	13,351
Monroe	3,075	7,106	985	837	1,355	1,939	11,683
Noxubee	2,687	14,039	1,400	783	1,157	1,447	9,326
Prentiss	—	—	606	669	1,081	1,499	7,980
Tishomingo	734	1,428	538	426	767	1,219	6,464
Alabama	1,533	3,189	581	704	1,096	1,952	12,780
Mississippi	1,612	4,453	912	883	1,218	1,818	14,292

Source: U.S. Census.

Table C. Percentage of Farms Operated by Owners

County	1850	1860	1880	1890	1910	1930	1960
Greene	82.0	82.0	29.3	23.5	17.1	13.0	23.1
Pickens	—	—	72.5	53.5	38.9	27.7	56.1
Sumter	—	—	31.1	23.0	18.4	14.7	25.1
Clay	—	—	42.8	32.3	33.3	22.1	52.8
Itawamba	—	—	80.4	66.1	53.9	38.1	58.4
Lowndes	94.2	92.0	37.3	35.8	22.0	20.2	46.9
Monroe	—	—	46.5	30.9	32.8	24.9	46.8
Noxubee	—	—	38.2	26.9	16.9	15.6	37.5
Prentiss	—	—	60.3	67.4	39.9	29.3	47.7
Tishomingo	75.7	65.0	75.2	77.2	57.9	38.1	54.9
Alabama			53.2	51.4	39.5	35.1	72.1
Mississippi			56.2	47.2	33.6	27.5	67.9

Source: U.S. Census.

Table D. Number of Hogs per Person

County	1850	1860	1880	1890	1910	1930	1960
Greene	2.0	1.6	0.7	0.7	0.8	0.6	0.2
Pickens	2.3	2.6	1.1	1.1	0.6	0.3	0.2
Sumter	2.2	1.8	0.9	1.0	0.8	0.5	0.3
Clay	—	—	0.6	0.8	0.5	0.4	0.2
Itawamba	3.0	2.1	1.4	1.5	0.6	0.3	0.7
Lowndes	2.0	1.9	0.6	0.5	0.5	0.2	0.1
Monroe	2.2	2.2	1.1	1.0	0.5	0.3	0.4
Noxubee	3.0	2.4	0.7	0.6	0.8	0.5	0.6
Prentiss	—	—	1.2	1.0	0.5	0.3	0.5
Tishomingo	2.5	1.8	1.1	1.2	0.7	0.2	0.5
Ten counties	2.4	2.0	0.9	0.9	0.6	0.4	0.3
Alabama	2.2	2.0	1.0	0.9	0.7	0.5	0.2
Mississippi	2.5	1.6	0.9	0.9	0.6	0.3	0.4

Source: U.S. Census.

Table E. Number of Beef Cattle per Person

County	1850	1860	1880	1890	1910	1930	1960
Greene	0.5	0.4	0.2	0.5	0.4	0.5	1.8
Pickens	0.5	0.4	0.4	0.5	0.3	0.3	0.9
Sumter	0.5	0.4	0.3	0.3	0.4	0.6	2.3
Clay	—	—	0.3	0.3	0.3	0.5	0.9
Itawamba	0.7	0.5	0.4	0.5	0.4	0.2	0.4
Lowndes	0.4	0.3	0.1	0.2	0.2	0.3	0.5
Monroe	0.5	0.4	0.2	0.4	0.2	0.2	0.7
Noxubee	0.6	0.4	0.2	0.3	0.3	0.5	2.3
Prentiss	—	—	0.4	0.4	0.2	0.2	0.3
Tishomingo	0.5	0.4	0.5	0.4	0.3	0.1	0.2
Ten counties	0.5	0.4	0.3	0.4	0.3	0.3	0.9
Alabama	0.5	0.4	0.3	0.4	0.4	0.4	1.7
Mississippi	0.5	0.4	0.3	0.4	0.3	0.3	0.8

Source: U.S. Census.

Table F. Average Bales of Cotton Produced per Person

County	1850	1860	1880	1890	1910	1930	1960
Greene	0.8	1.9	0.7	0.9	0.6	0.7	0.5
Pickens	0.6	2.8	0.8	0.8	0.6	0.7	0.3
Sumter	0.6	1.5	0.8	0.9	0.7	0.6	0.3
Clay	—	—	0.8	0.6	0.7	0.7	0.2
Itawamba	0.4	0.7	0.5	0.3	0.5	0.7	0.4
Lowndes	0.8	2.2	0.8	0.6	0.5	0.6	0.4
Monroe	0.8	2.2	0.9	0.6	0.6	0.8	0.6
Noxubee	0.8	2.4	0.8	0.8	0.7	0.8	0.4
Prentiss	—	—	0.6	0.3	0.5	0.8	0.6
Tishomingo	0.3	0.5	0.3	0.2	0.3	0.6	0.4
Alabama	0.7	1.0	0.6	0.6	0.5	0.5	0.2
Mississippi	0.8	1.5	0.9	0.9	0.6	0.9	0.7

Source: U.S. Census.

Table G. Average Bushels of Corn Produced per Person

County	1850	1860	1880	1890	1910	1930	1960
Greene	42.5	42.5	18.4	22.5	11.3	16.6	21.5
Pickens	40.4	62.0	22.9	22.8	12.9	21.3	15.3
Sumter	41.7	41.5	24.4	26.6	14.9	13.1	20.7
Clay	—	—	23.1	22.8	15.8	23.6	7.1
Itawamba	39.4	35.5	28.6	24.0	28.5	32.4	33.4
Lowndes	44.6	49.0	20.6	21.7	10.5	14.3	5.2
Monroe	42.6	53.8	27.4	26.0	16.6	24.9	20.1
Noxubee	55.0	62.3	24.8	24.0	11.5	19.6	11.8
Prentiss	—	—	30.3	27.2	26.1	34.1	7.0
Tishomingo	34.0	36.6	31.9	25.6	22.3	22.4	6.8
Alabama	37.3	34.5	20.2	19.9	14.4	13.5	19.2
Mississippi	37.0	36.7	18.9	20.3	15.8	17.4	19.5

Source: U.S. Census.

Table H. Average Bales of Cotton Produced per Farm

County	1850	1860	1880	1890	1910	1930	1960
Greene	20	73	7	8	4.0	4.0	4.0
Pickens	9	49	8	7	4.0	4.0	4.0
Sumter	21	73	8	7	4.0	4.0	3.0
Clay	—	—	9	5	4.4	4.0	3.3
Itawamba	4	9	4	2	2.6	3.5	3.5
Lowndes	21	80	11	8	3.6	4.9	11.4
Monroe	21	51	9	5	3.9	4.2	7.7
Noxubee	19	84	14	8	3.8	4.4	3.1
Prentiss	—	—	4	2	2.9	4.4	5.1
Tishomingo	3	8	2	1.5	1.9	4.0	4.2
Ten counties	12.7	43.1	7.8	5.8	3.6	4.3	5.1
Alabama	13	18	5		4.3	5.1	5.9
Mississippi	14	28	10		4.1	6.0	11.3

Source: U.S. Census.

Table I. Average Bushels of Corn Produced per Farm

County	1850	1860	1880	1890	1910	1930	1960
Greene	1,020	1,654	186	198	62	92	182
Pickens	604	1,085	239	178	78	128	204
Sumter	1,387	2,001	240	217	92	80	266
Clay	—	—	266	187	103	145	102
Itawamba	356	436	217	164	141	171	284
Lowndes	1,203	1,805	300	271	78	121	139
Monroe	1,094	1,269	238	193	101	157	259
Noxubee	1,325	2,162	402	245	64	108	98
Prentiss	—	—	202	222	143	177	62
Tishomingo	422	598	260	200	138	145	74
Ten counties	816	1,153	253	197	95	132	169
Alabama	685	603	187		117	139	541
Mississippi	661	678	210		104	112	308

Source: U.S. Census.

Table J. Farm Ownership, 1910, by Race

	Number of farmers			Owners of mortgage-free farms					
County	Total	White	Black	Total	%	White	%	Black	%
Greene	4,099	563	3,536	450	11	287	51	163	5
Pickens	4,144	1,954	2,190	1,116	27	965	49	151	7
Sumter	4,624	744	3,880	532	12	349	47	183	5
Clay	3,092	851	2,241	662	21	484	57	178	8
Itawamba	2,933	2,731	202	1,155	39	1,123	41	32	16
Lowndes	4,133	836	3,297	524	13	376	45	148	5
Monroe	5,748	2,439	3,309	1,201	21	1,011	41	190	6
Noxubee	5,107	685	4,422	566	11	365	53	201	5
Prentiss	3,091	2,618	473	807	26	785	30	22	5
Tishomingo	2,114	1,983	131	881	42	848	43	33	25
Ten counties	39,085	15,404	23,681	7,894	20	6,593	43	1,301	6

Source: U.S. Census.

Table K. Farm Value and Production, 1910

	Average value per farm		Bales cotton per acre		Bushels corn per acre	
County	All farms	Black-operated farms	Black-operated farms	White-operated farms	Black-operated farms	White-operated farms
Greene	1,169	545	0.2	0.3	7.8	11.0
Pickens	1,169	591	0.2	0.3	7.4	9.1
Sumter	1,360	611	0.2	0.3	9.7	11.7
Clay	1,945	1,158	0.2	0.2	11.6	10.8
Itawamba	1,230	671	0.3	0.3	9.6	13.0
Lowndes	1,875	914	0.2	0.3	9.3	12.4
Monroe	1,707	1,102	0.2	0.3	10.8	13.6
Noxubee	1,473	873	0.2	0.2	8.2	10.2
Prentiss	1,424	898	0.2	0.3	12.6	14.2
Tishomingo	1,047	597	0.3	0.3	13.7	13.6
Ten counties	1,440	796	0.2	0.3	10.1	12.0

Source: U.S. Census.

Table L. White Percentage of Population

County	1850	1860	1880	1890	1910	1930	1960
Greene	29.4	23.5	17.2	14.7	15.9	17.6	18.7
Pickens	51.0	45.3	42.5	41.3	48.3	52.1	55.3
Sumter	33.1	24.6	22.5	20.1	18.7	21.1	23.7
Clay	—	—	30.3	30.2	30.2	38.0	48.7
Itawamba	84.2	80.0	89.6	91.6	91.8	94.2	94.2
Lowndes	32.8	29.2	19.8	22.2	29.0	42.1	61.9
Monroe	44.5	40.1	41.3	39.4	44.5	55.4	64.6
Noxubee	30.5	25.0	17.7	17.2	16.0	21.1	28.1
Prentiss	—	—	80.0	79.2	83.0	87.1	87.8
Tishomingo	87.3	79.3	86.7	89.3	91.7	93.7	95.3
Alabama	55.3	54.6	52.5		57.5	64.3	69.9
Mississippi	48.8	44.7	42.4		43.7	49.7	57.7

Source: U.S. Census.

Bibliographical
and Personal Notes

Those persons wishing to pursue further the subjects covered in this book will find useful bibliographies in two technical reports prepared by the authors for the U.S. Army Corps of Engineers. These reports, which are available in many college and university libraries of the Southeast, are: James F. Doster and David C. Weaver, *Historic Settlement in the Upper Tombigbee Valley* (1981); and David C. Weaver and James F. Doster, *Historical Geography of the Upper Tombigbee Valley* (1982).

The numerous quotations from oral statements of individuals are taken from interviews by the authors, recorded as follows:

>Roy A. Swayze at Eutaw, October 14, 1981
>Robert and Donna Snow, at Waverly, October 15, 1981
>Lucille Peacock, at Aberdeen, December 1, 1981
>Emory Jones, at Booneville, May 20, 1982
>Hilda L. Hill, at Booneville, May 20, August 10, 1982
>Jack D. Elliott, Jr., at Starkville, April 19, 1982
>Carey B. Oakley, at Moundville, August 8, 1982
>James William Furr, Jr., at Columbus, November 3, 1981
>James P. Pate, at Livingston, December 17, 1981
>William L. Jones, at Columbus, May 18, 1982
>Bob Tiffin, at Red Bay, August 16, 1982
>Thomas E. Robertson, at Corinth, August 18, 1982
>Harry A. Martin, at Tupelo, August 11, 1982
>Bob Stembridge, at Mooreville, August 23, 1982
>Frank Nichols, near Mantachie, August 23, 1982
>Glover Wilkins, at Columbus, May 19, 1982
>Prime F. Osborne, by correspondence, April 1982
>Nathaniel D. McClure, at Mobile, May 14, 1984

While this book has been in preparation, changes have occurred in the lives of many individuals. Jack D. Elliott was a graduate student in anthropology and geography at Mississippi State University when he was interviewed by the authors. With the passage of years his interests have broadened. As the book goes to press, he is residing in Israel, where he is writing a doctoral dissertation in geography for the University of Texas. Thomas E. Robertson is now president of King Manufacturing Company, Charles Wayne King having retired. Glover Wilkins and Prime F. Osborne have retired. (Osborne died on January 4, 1986.) Kelly Ferguson has moved away and left hog raising to others. Greg Giachelli no longer teaches farmers how to raise and market hogs; he is now too busy raising his own. Lucille Peacock died on March 3, 1985, at the age of eighty-four. Roy Swayze, still alive and well, has now completed the restoration of Kirkwood Mansion, and James William Furr, Jr., remains as enthusiastic and ebullient as ever.

Index

James F. Doster is Professor Emeritus at The University of Alabama, where he taught history for many years. His publications include *Alabama's First Railroad Commission, 1881–1885*; *Railroads in Alabama Politics, 1875–1914*; *The Creek Indians and Their Florida Lands*; and numerous articles in periodicals.

David C. Weaver is Professor of Geography at The University of Alabama. His recent publications include journal articles, technical reports, and maps relating to cultural resources, land use, and the environmental problems of Alabama and the other Southeastern states.

The authors observing excavation at the bottom of the divide cut. At left is James F. Doster, at center, David C. Weaver, and at right, photographer Jan Weaver. Photo: Corps of Engineers.